koren shadmi

HIGHWAYMAN

D1315419

Top Shelf Productions

HIGHWAYMAN
by Koren Shadmi

Special Thanks to Brian Merchant for Editing.

Published by Top Shelf Productions, PO Box 1282, Marietta, GA 30061-1282, USA. Top Shelf Productions is an imprint of IDW Publishing, a division of Idea and Design Works, LLC. Offices: 2765 Truxtun Road, San Diego, CA 92106. Top Shelf Productions®, the Top Shelf logo, Idea and Design Works®, and the IDW logo are registered trademarks of Idea and Design Works, LLC. All Rights Reserved. With the exception of small excerpts of artwork used for review purposes, none of the contents of this publication may be reprinted without the permission of IDW Publishing. IDW Publishing does not read or accept unsolicited submissions of ideas, stories or artwork.

Editor-in-Chief: Chris Staros.

Designed by Gilberto Lazcano.

Visit our online catalog at topshelfcomix.com.

Printed in Korea.

ISBN: 978-1-60309-441-2   22 21 20 19   4 3 2 1

I am the camera's eye.

I am the machine that shows you the world as I alone see it.

Starting from today I am forever free of human immobility.

I am in perpetual movement.

I approach and draw away from things —

I crawl under them —

I climb on them —

I am on the head of a galloping horse.

—Dziga Vertov

CHAPTER 1
MAN OF GOD

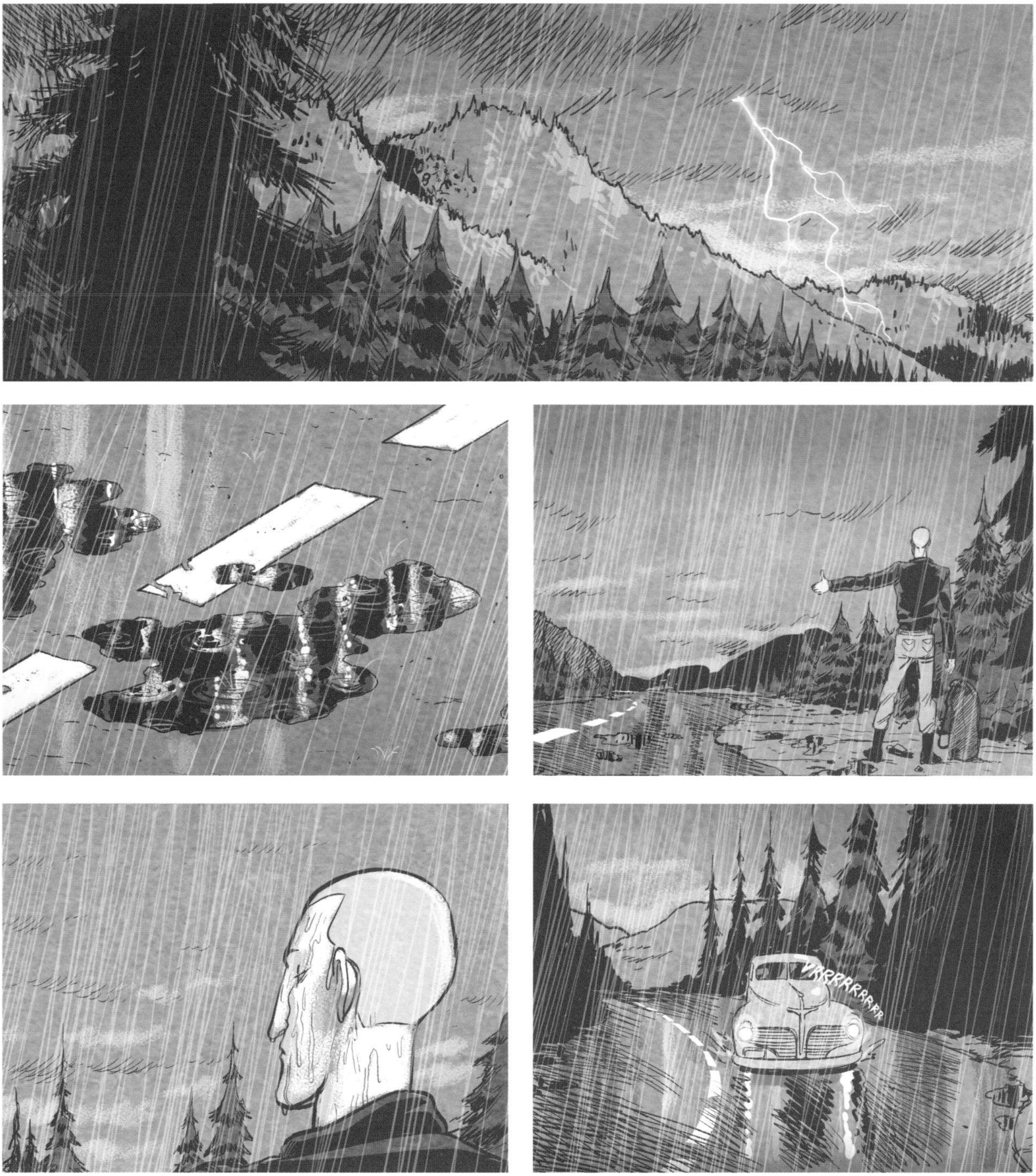
VRRRRRRRRRR

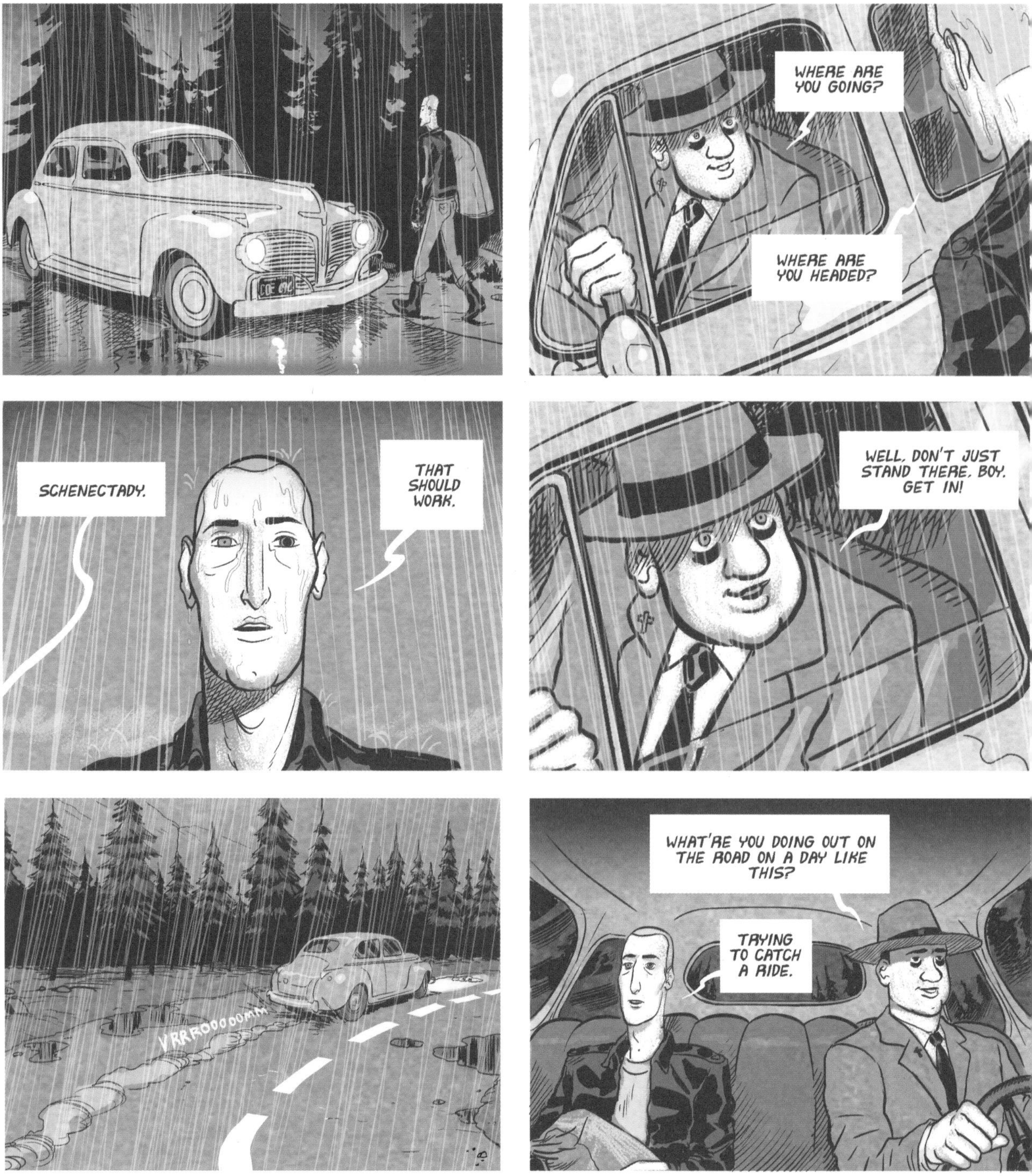
WHERE ARE YOU GOING?
WHERE ARE YOU HEADED?
SCHENECTADY.
THAT SHOULD WORK.
WELL, DON'T JUST STAND THERE, BOY. GET IN!
WHAT'RE YOU DOING OUT ON THE ROAD ON A DAY LIKE THIS?
TRYING TO CATCH A RIDE.

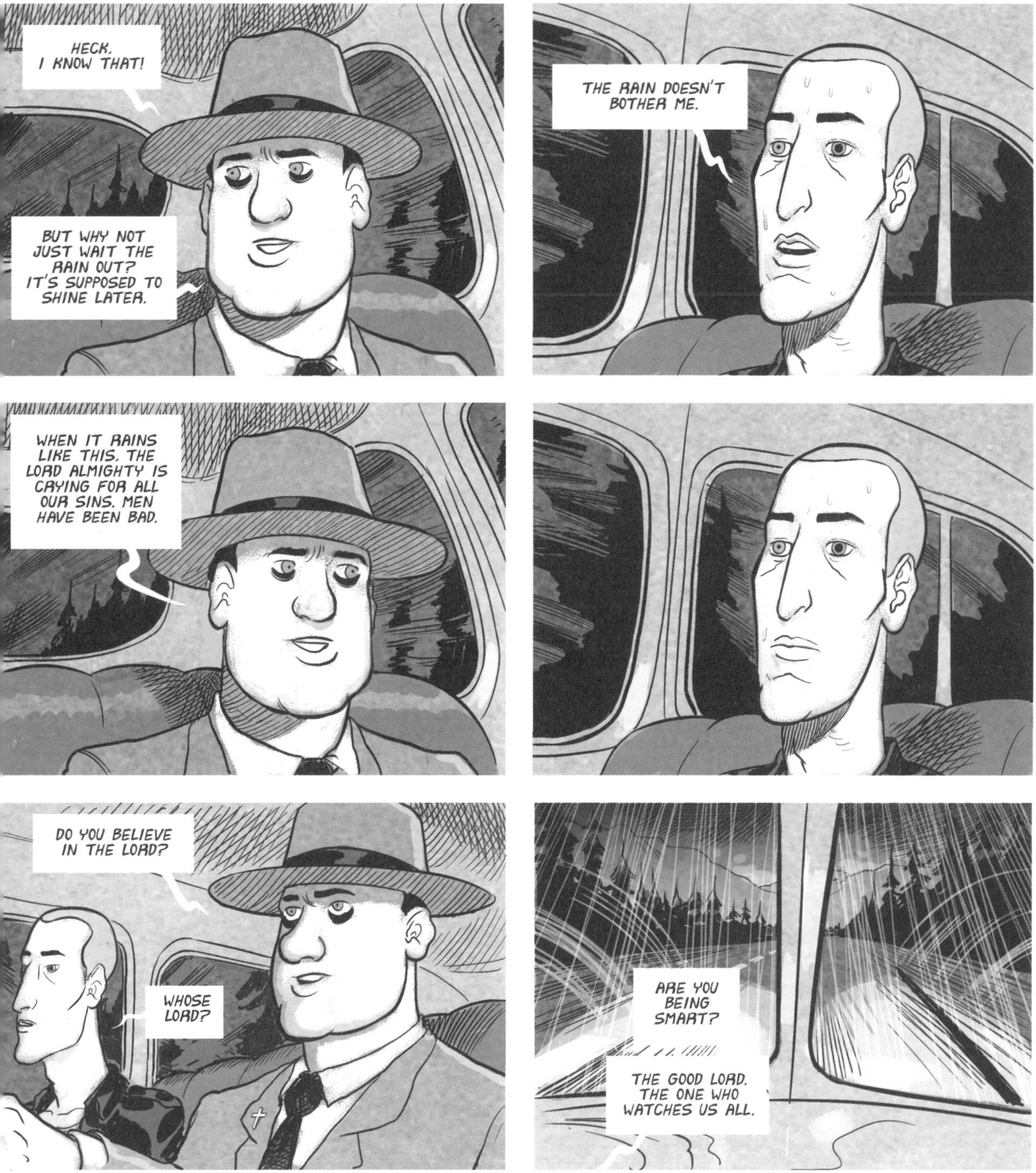
HECK. I KNOW THAT!
BUT WHY NOT JUST WAIT THE RAIN OUT? IT'S SUPPOSED TO SHINE LATER.
THE RAIN DOESN'T BOTHER ME.
WHEN IT RAINS LIKE THIS, THE LORD ALMIGHTY IS CRYING FOR ALL OUR SINS. MEN HAVE BEEN BAD.
DO YOU BELIEVE IN THE LORD?
WHOSE LORD?
ARE YOU BEING SMART?
THE GOOD LORD. THE ONE WHO WATCHES US ALL.

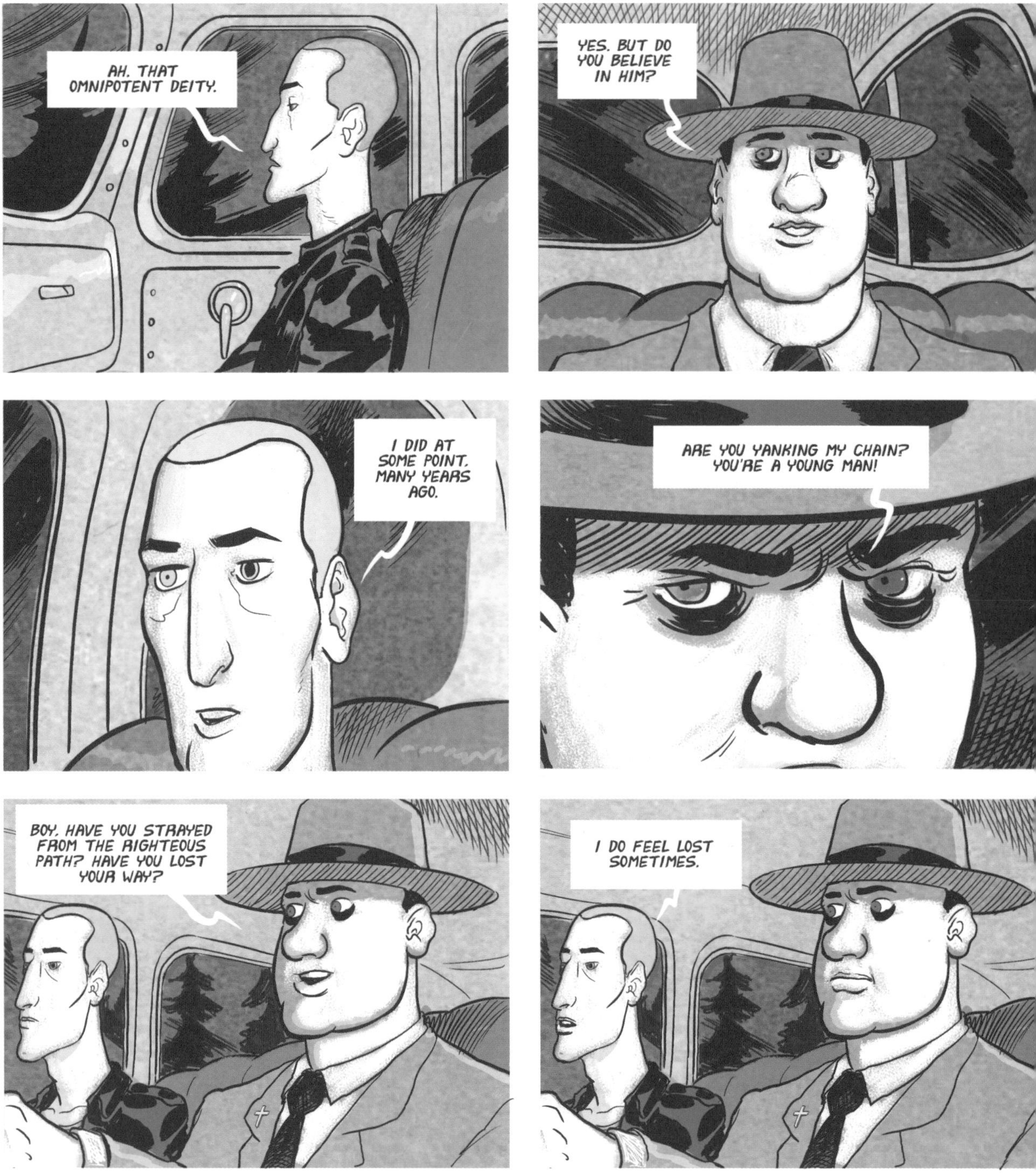
AH. THAT OMNIPOTENT DEITY.
YES. BUT DO YOU BELIEVE IN HIM?
I DID AT SOME POINT. MANY YEARS AGO.
ARE YOU YANKING MY CHAIN? YOU'RE A YOUNG MAN!
BOY, HAVE YOU STRAYED FROM THE RIGHTEOUS PATH? HAVE YOU LOST YOUR WAY?
I DO FEEL LOST SOMETIMES.

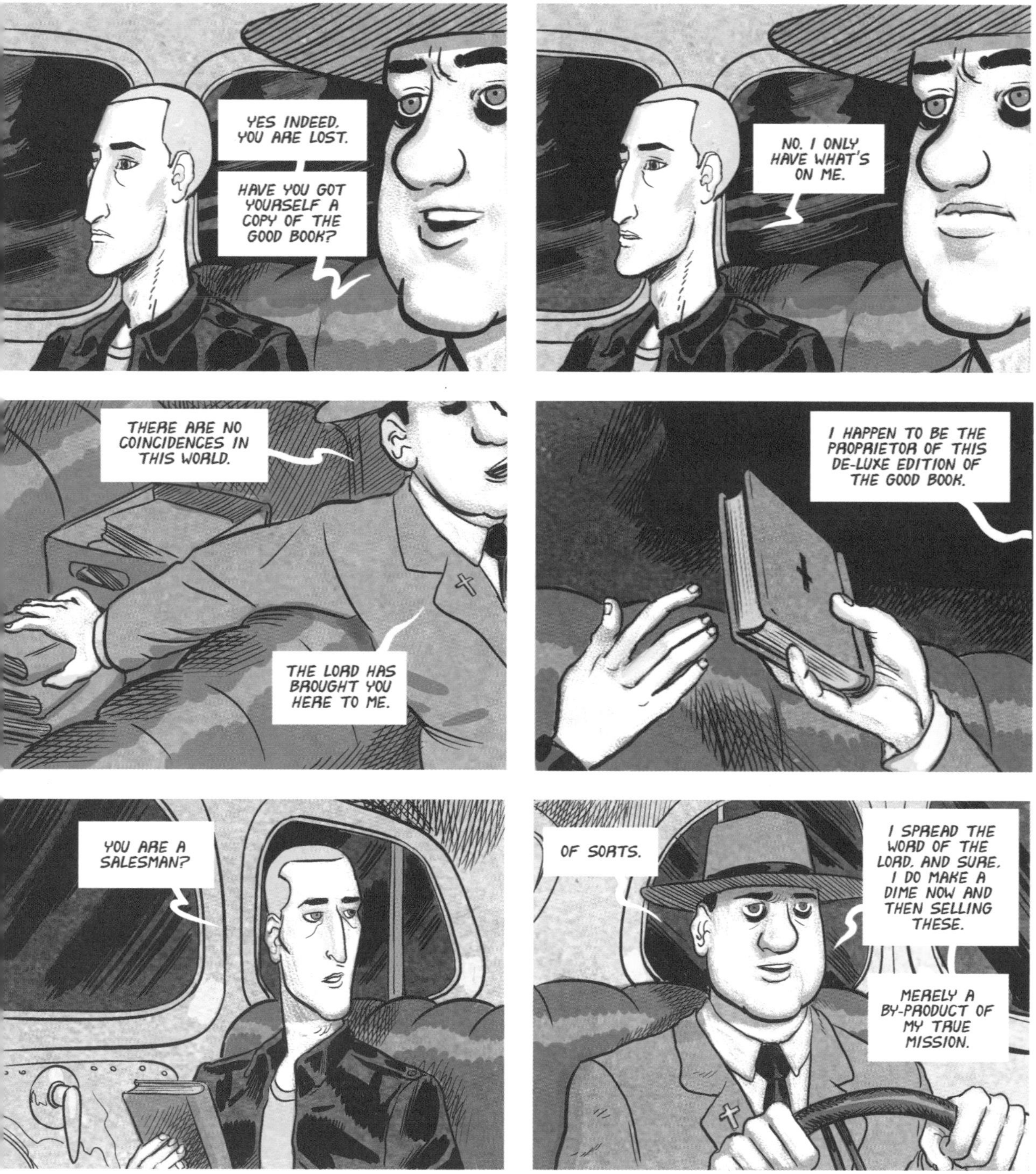
YES INDEED. YOU ARE LOST.
HAVE YOU GOT YOURSELF A COPY OF THE GOOD BOOK?
NO. I ONLY HAVE WHAT'S ON ME.
THERE ARE NO COINCIDENCES IN THIS WORLD.
THE LORD HAS BROUGHT YOU HERE TO ME.
I HAPPEN TO BE THE PROPRIETOR OF THIS DE-LUXE EDITION OF THE GOOD BOOK.
YOU ARE A SALESMAN?
OF SORTS.
I SPREAD THE WORD OF THE LORD. AND SURE, I DO MAKE A DIME NOW AND THEN SELLING THESE.
MERELY A BY-PRODUCT OF MY TRUE MISSION.

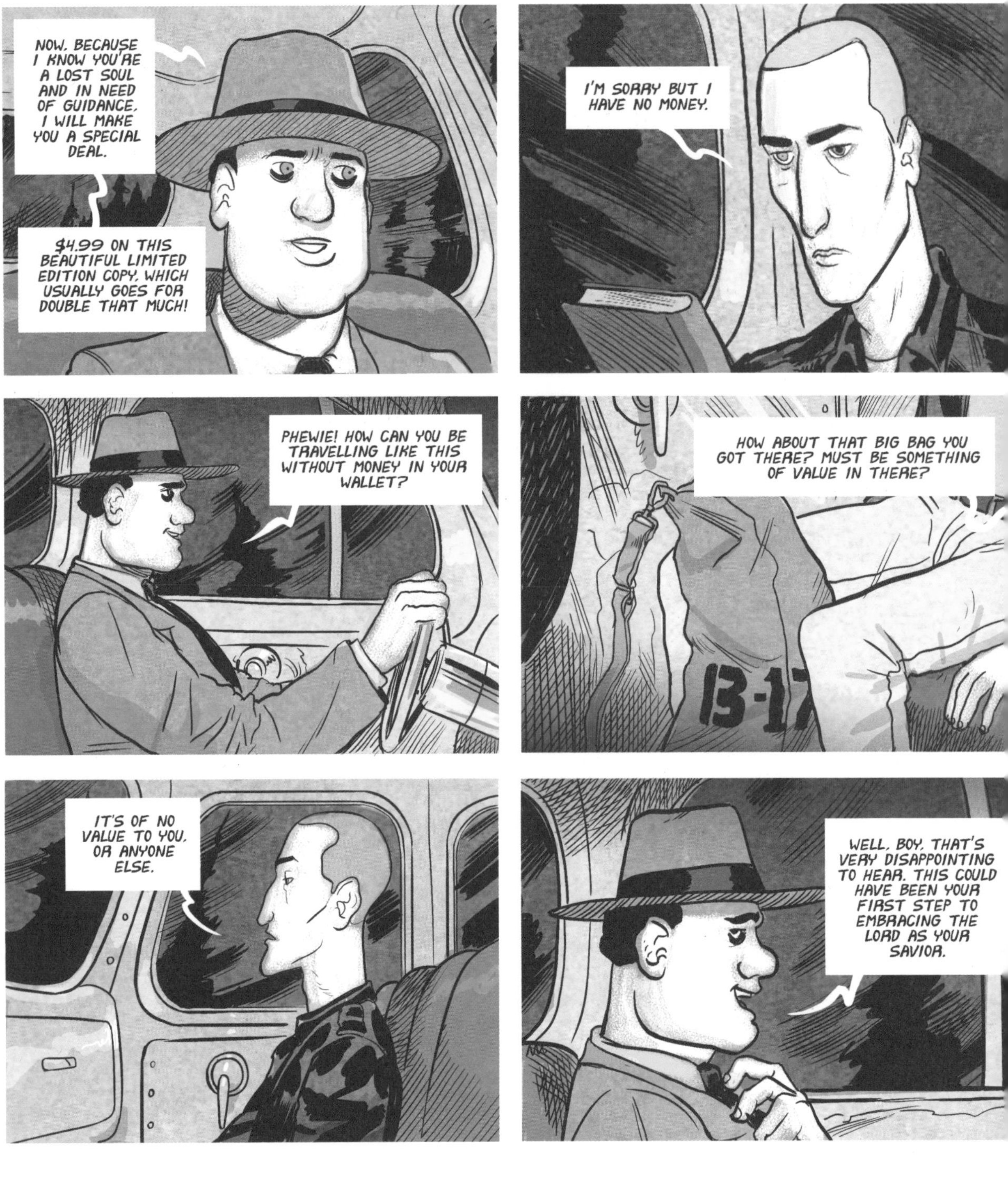
NOW, BECAUSE I KNOW YOU'RE A LOST SOUL AND IN NEED OF GUIDANCE, I WILL MAKE YOU A SPECIAL DEAL.
$4.99 ON THIS BEAUTIFUL LIMITED EDITION COPY, WHICH USUALLY GOES FOR DOUBLE THAT MUCH!
I'M SORRY BUT I HAVE NO MONEY.
PHEWIE! HOW CAN YOU BE TRAVELLING LIKE THIS WITHOUT MONEY IN YOUR WALLET?
HOW ABOUT THAT BIG BAG YOU GOT THERE? MUST BE SOMETHING OF VALUE IN THERE?
13-17
IT'S OF NO VALUE TO YOU, OR ANYONE ELSE.
WELL, BOY, THAT'S VERY DISAPPOINTING TO HEAR. THIS COULD HAVE BEEN YOUR FIRST STEP TO EMBRACING THE LORD AS YOUR SAVIOR.

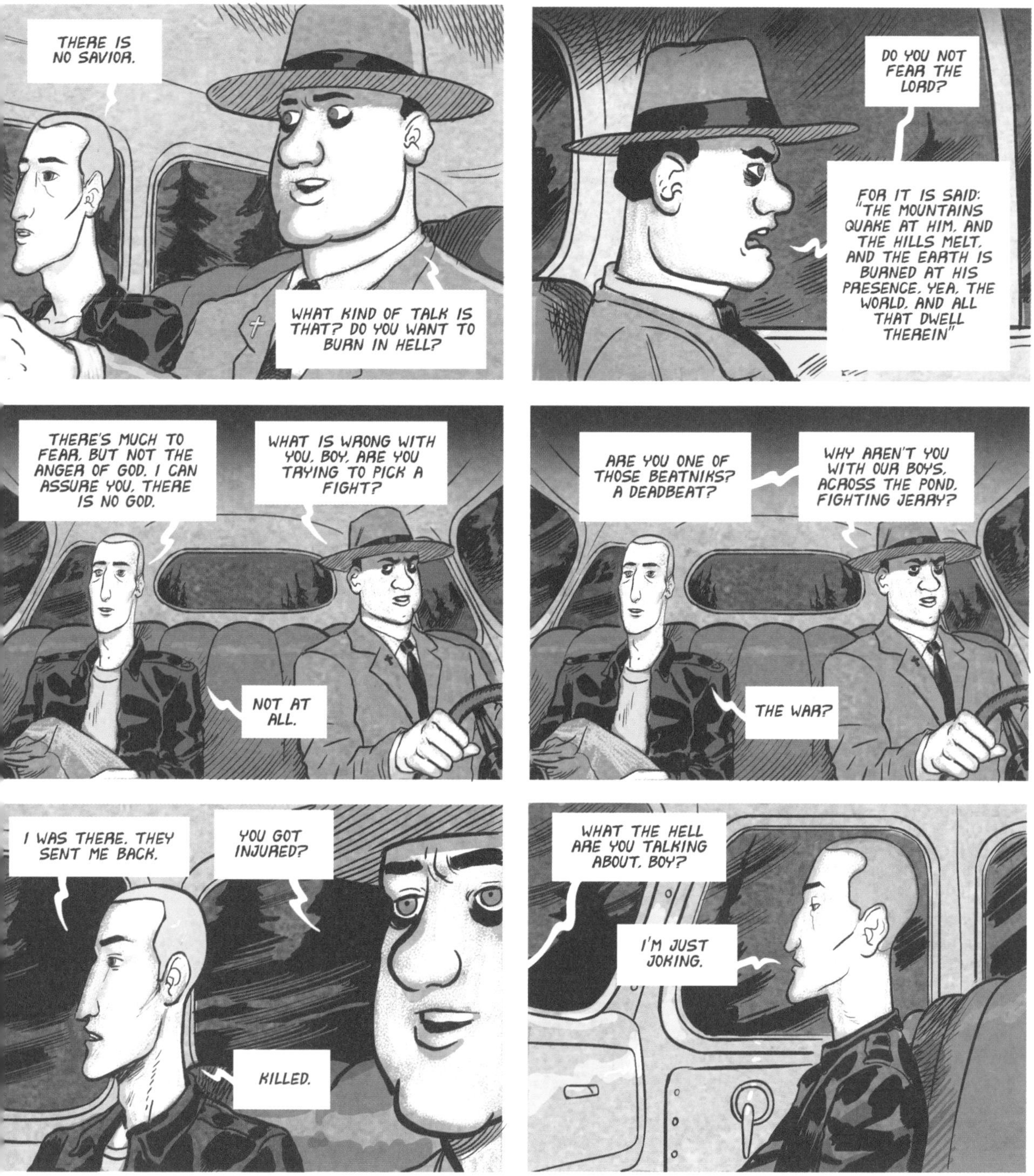
THERE IS NO SAVIOR.
WHAT KIND OF TALK IS THAT? DO YOU WANT TO BURN IN HELL?
DO YOU NOT FEAR THE LORD?
FOR IT IS SAID: "THE MOUNTAINS QUAKE AT HIM, AND THE HILLS MELT, AND THE EARTH IS BURNED AT HIS PRESENCE, YEA, THE WORLD, AND ALL THAT DWELL THEREIN"
THERE'S MUCH TO FEAR, BUT NOT THE ANGER OF GOD. I CAN ASSURE YOU, THERE IS NO GOD.
WHAT IS WRONG WITH YOU, BOY, ARE YOU TRYING TO PICK A FIGHT?
NOT AT ALL.
ARE YOU ONE OF THOSE BEATNIKS? A DEADBEAT?
WHY AREN'T YOU WITH OUR BOYS, ACROSS THE POND, FIGHTING JERRY?
THE WAR?
I WAS THERE. THEY SENT ME BACK.
YOU GOT INJURED?
KILLED.
WHAT THE HELL ARE YOU TALKING ABOUT, BOY?
I'M JUST JOKING.

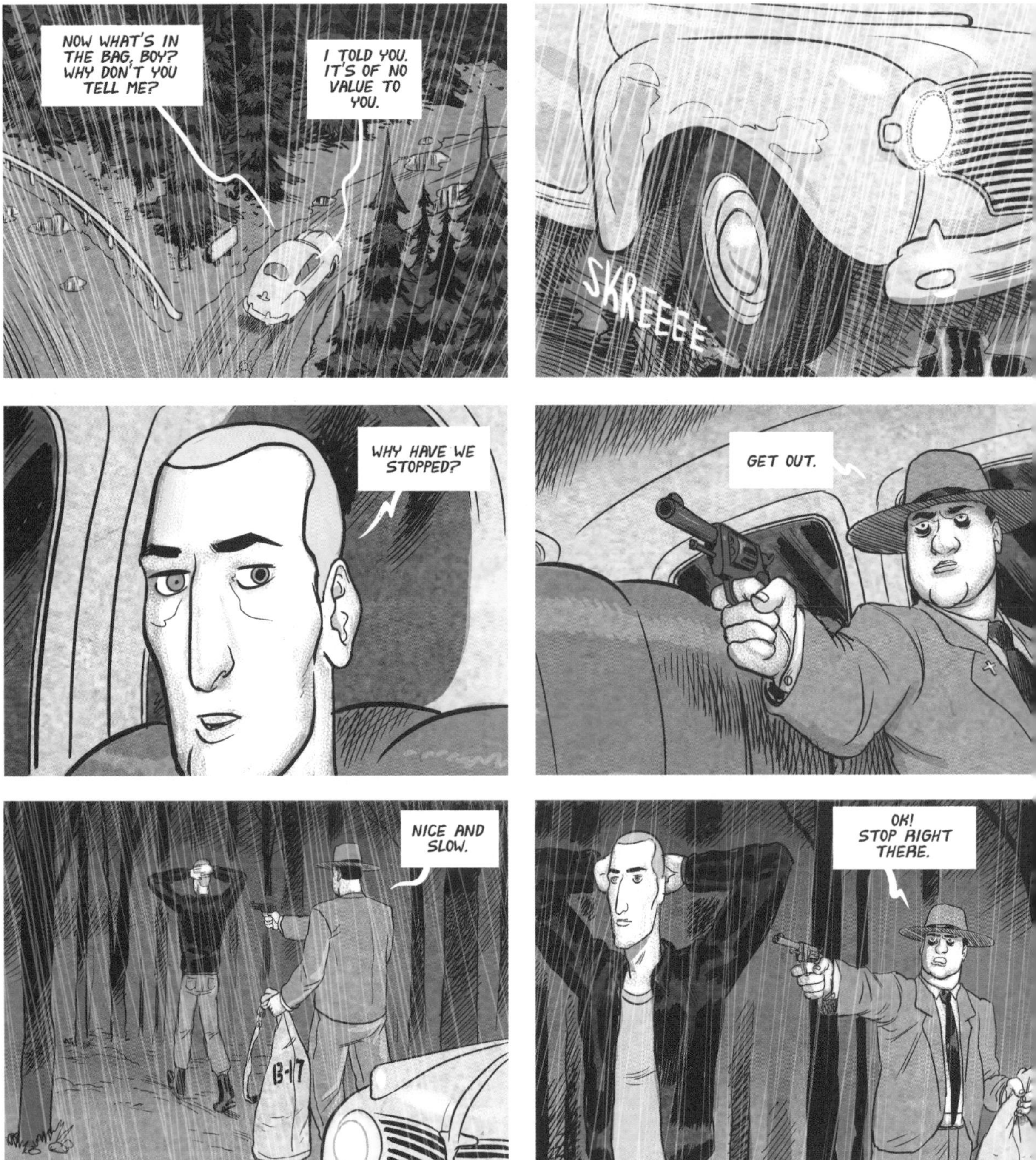
NOW WHAT'S IN THE BAG, BOY? WHY DON'T YOU TELL ME?
I TOLD YOU. IT'S OF NO VALUE TO YOU.
SKREEEGE
WHY HAVE WE STOPPED?
GET OUT.
NICE AND SLOW.
B-17
OK! STOP RIGHT THERE.

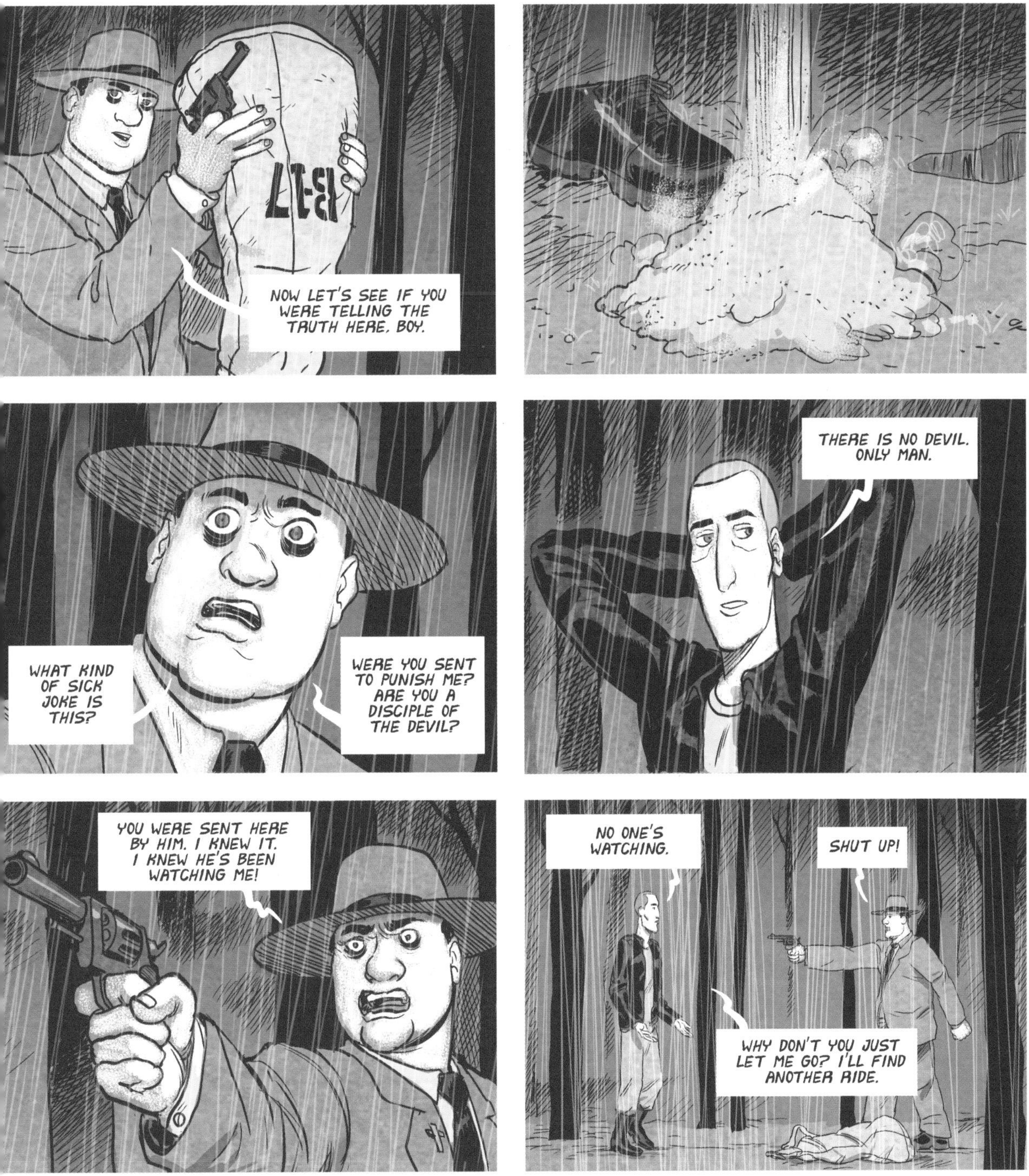
NOW LET'S SEE IF YOU WERE TELLING THE TRUTH HERE, BOY.
WHAT KIND OF SICK JOKE IS THIS?
WERE YOU SENT TO PUNISH ME? ARE YOU A DISCIPLE OF THE DEVIL?
THERE IS NO DEVIL. ONLY MAN.
YOU WERE SENT HERE BY HIM. I KNEW IT. I KNEW HE'S BEEN WATCHING ME!
NO ONE'S WATCHING.
SHUT UP!
WHY DON'T YOU JUST LET ME GO? I'LL FIND ANOTHER RIDE.

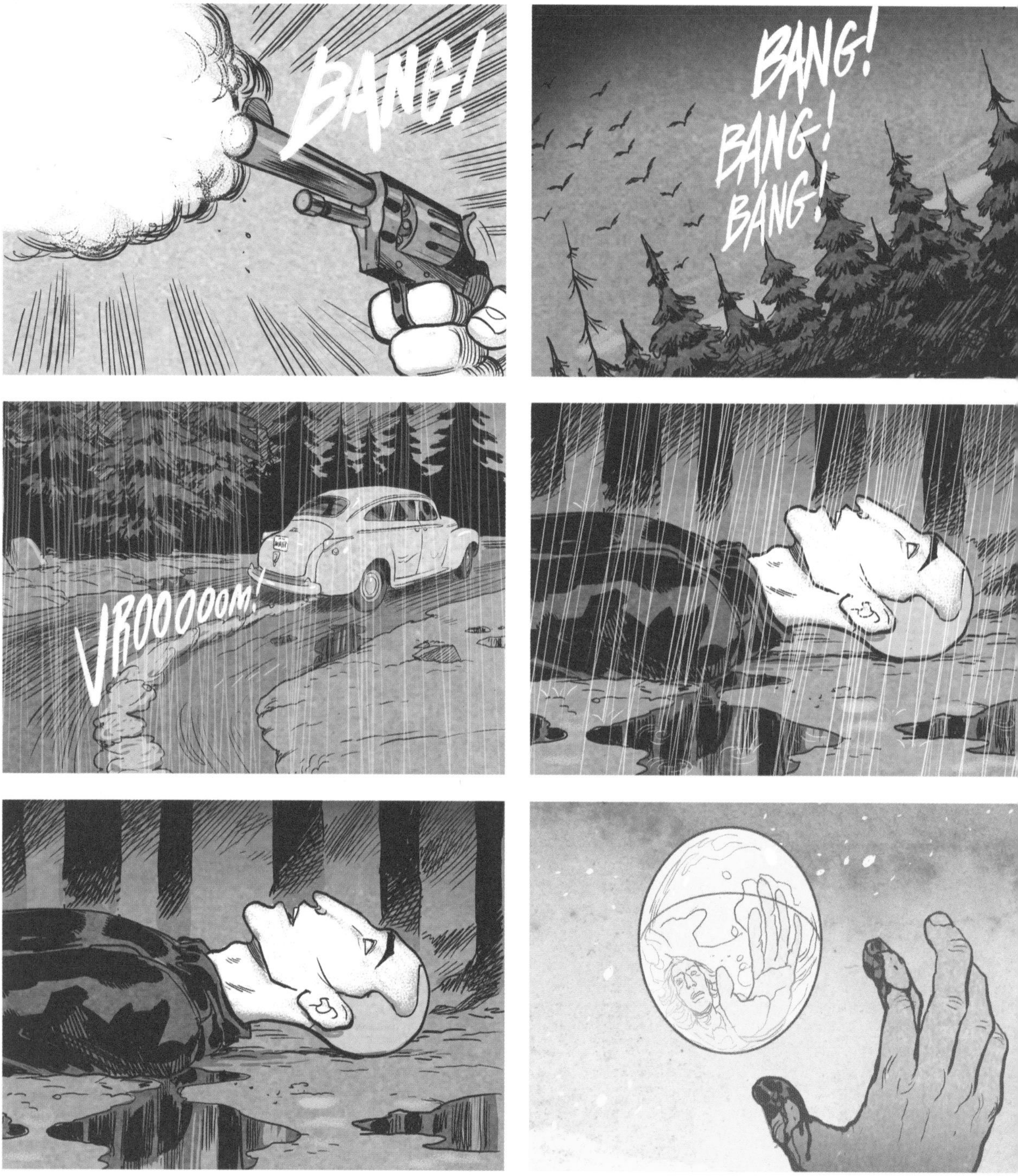
BANG!
BANG!
BANG!
BANG!
VROOOOOM!

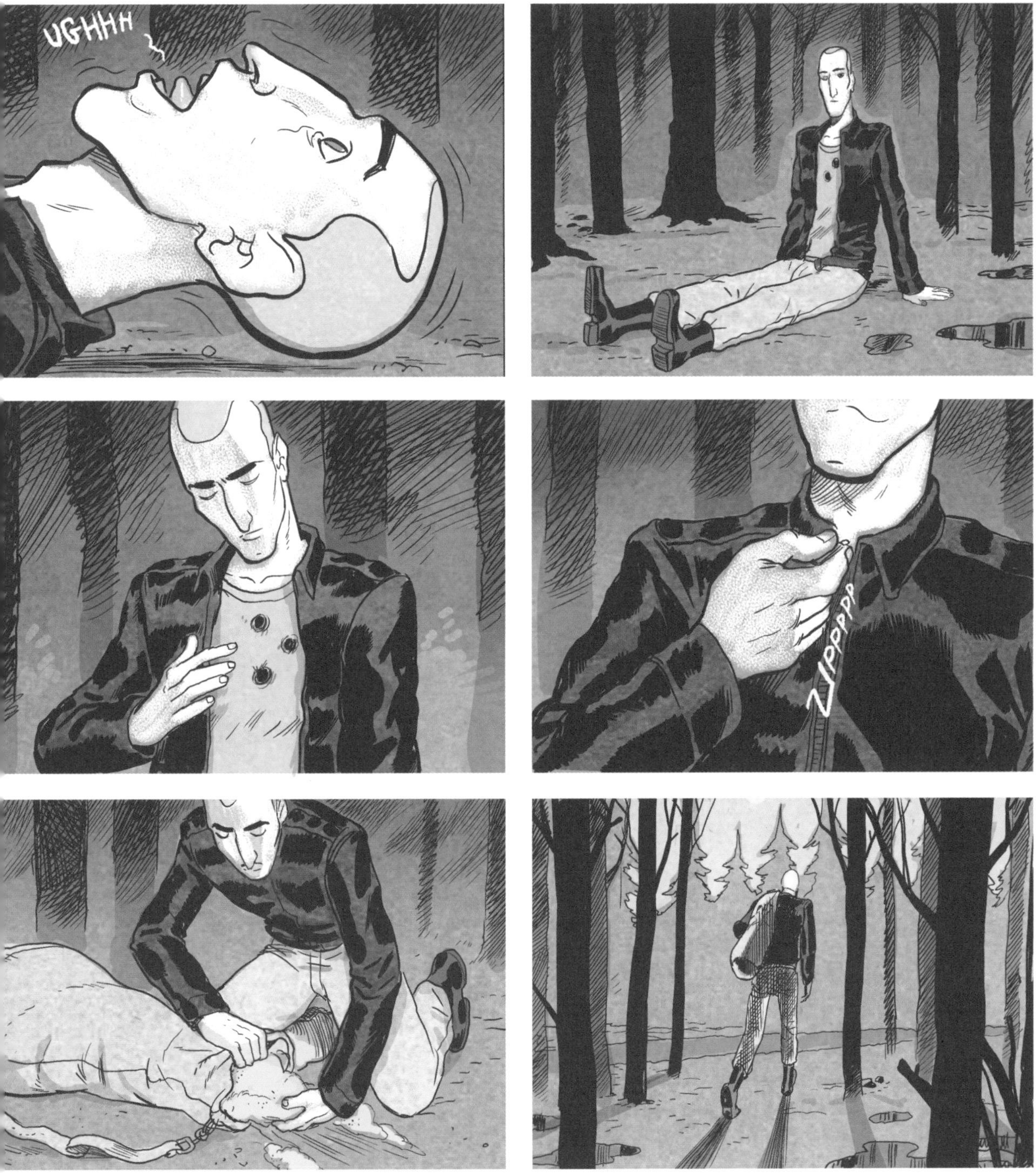
UGHHH
ZIPPPPP

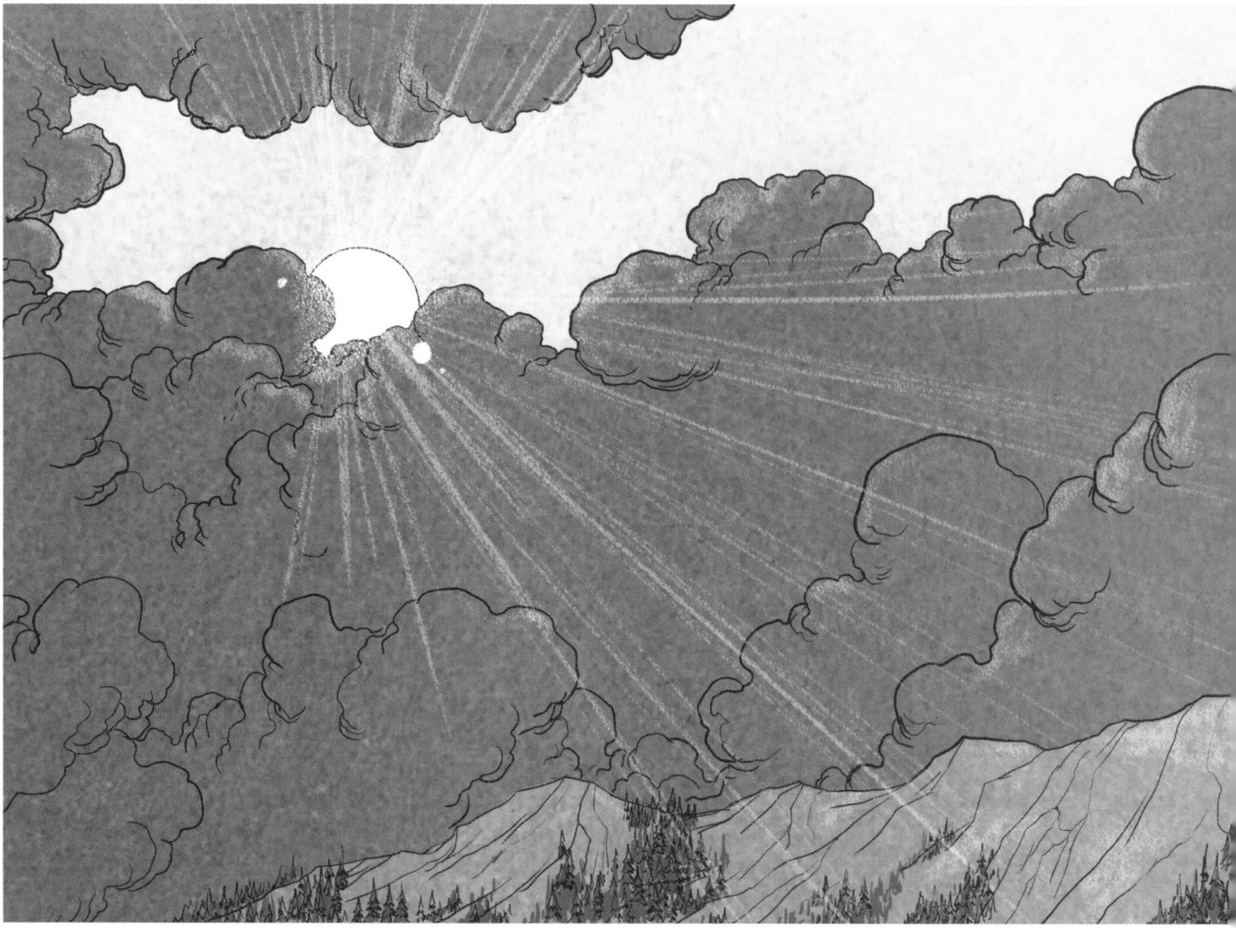

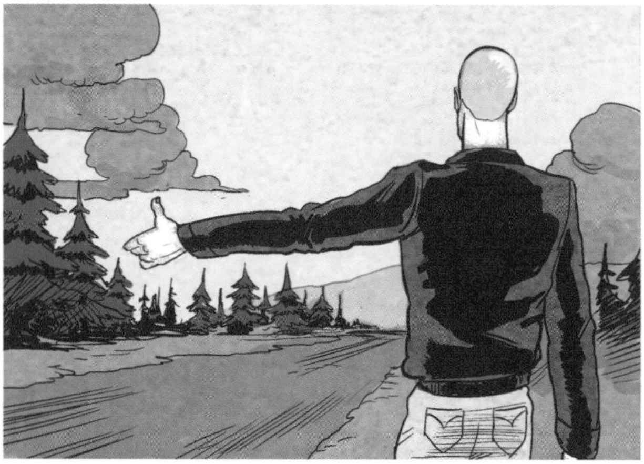

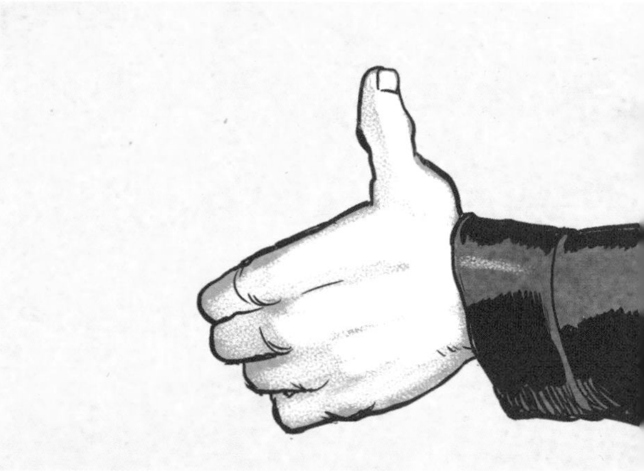

CHAPTER 2
AFTERGLOW

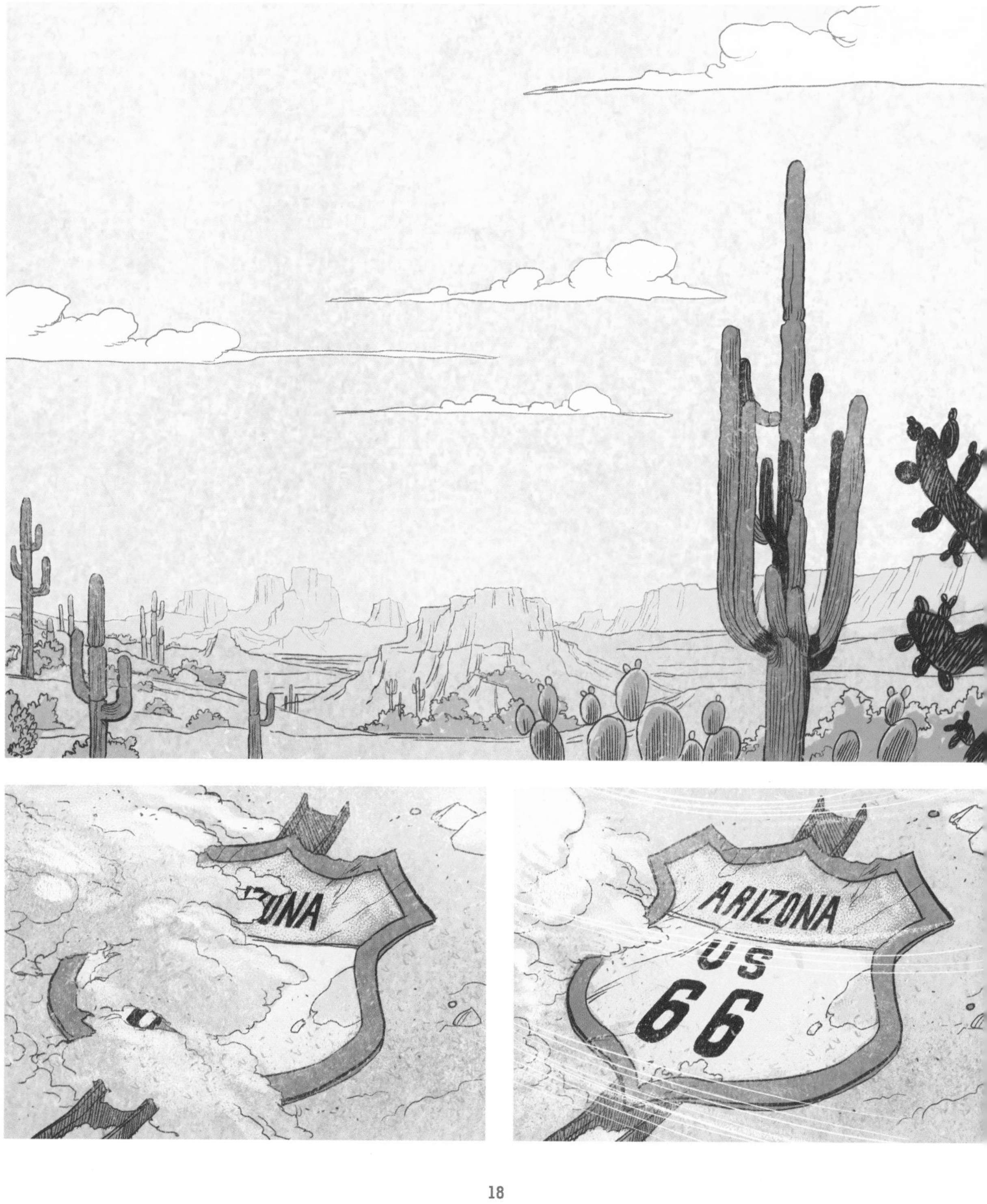
ARIZONA
US
66

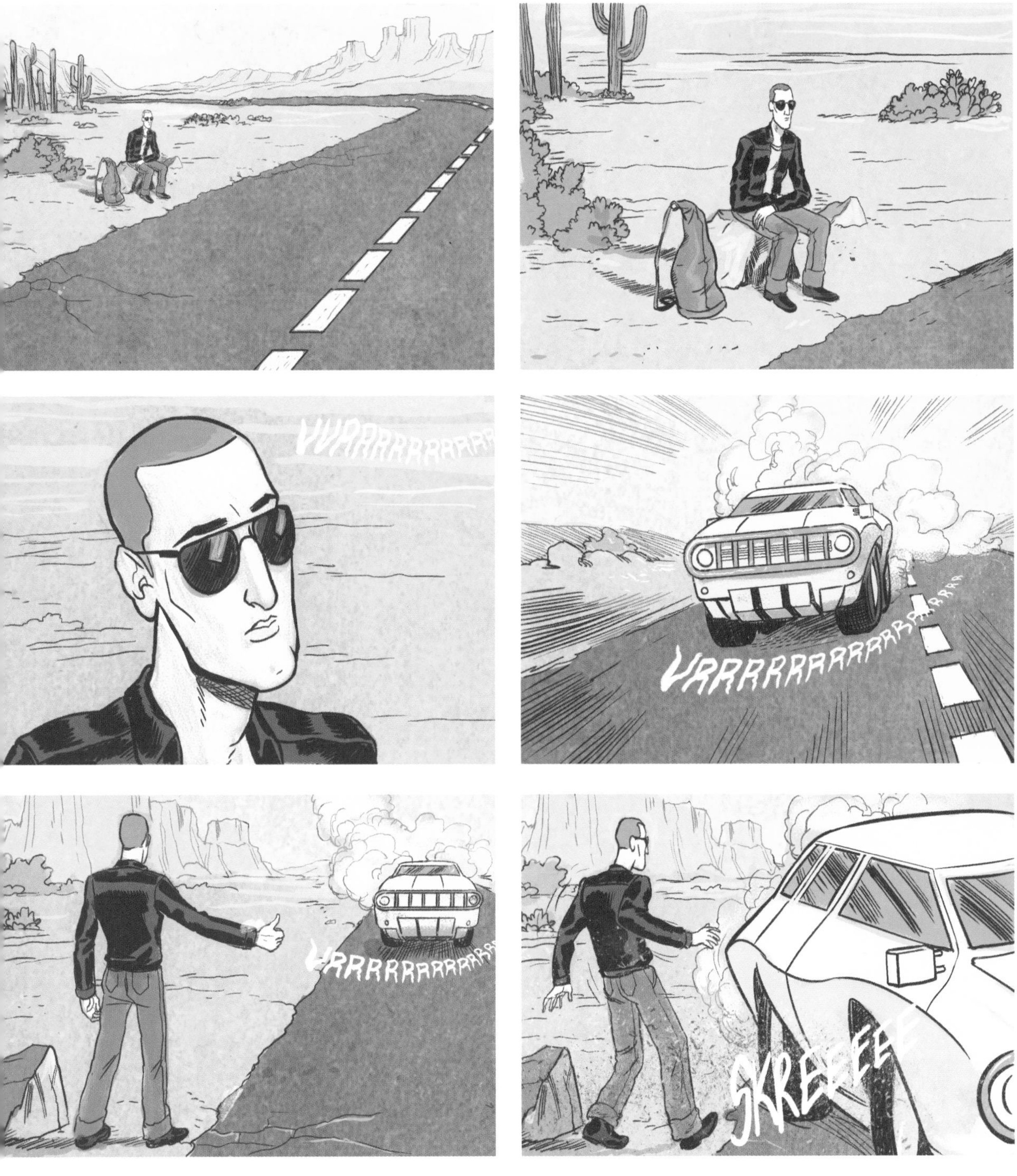
VVRRRRRRRRRRR
URRRRRRRRRRRRRRRRRR
URRRRRRRRRRRR
SKREEEEE

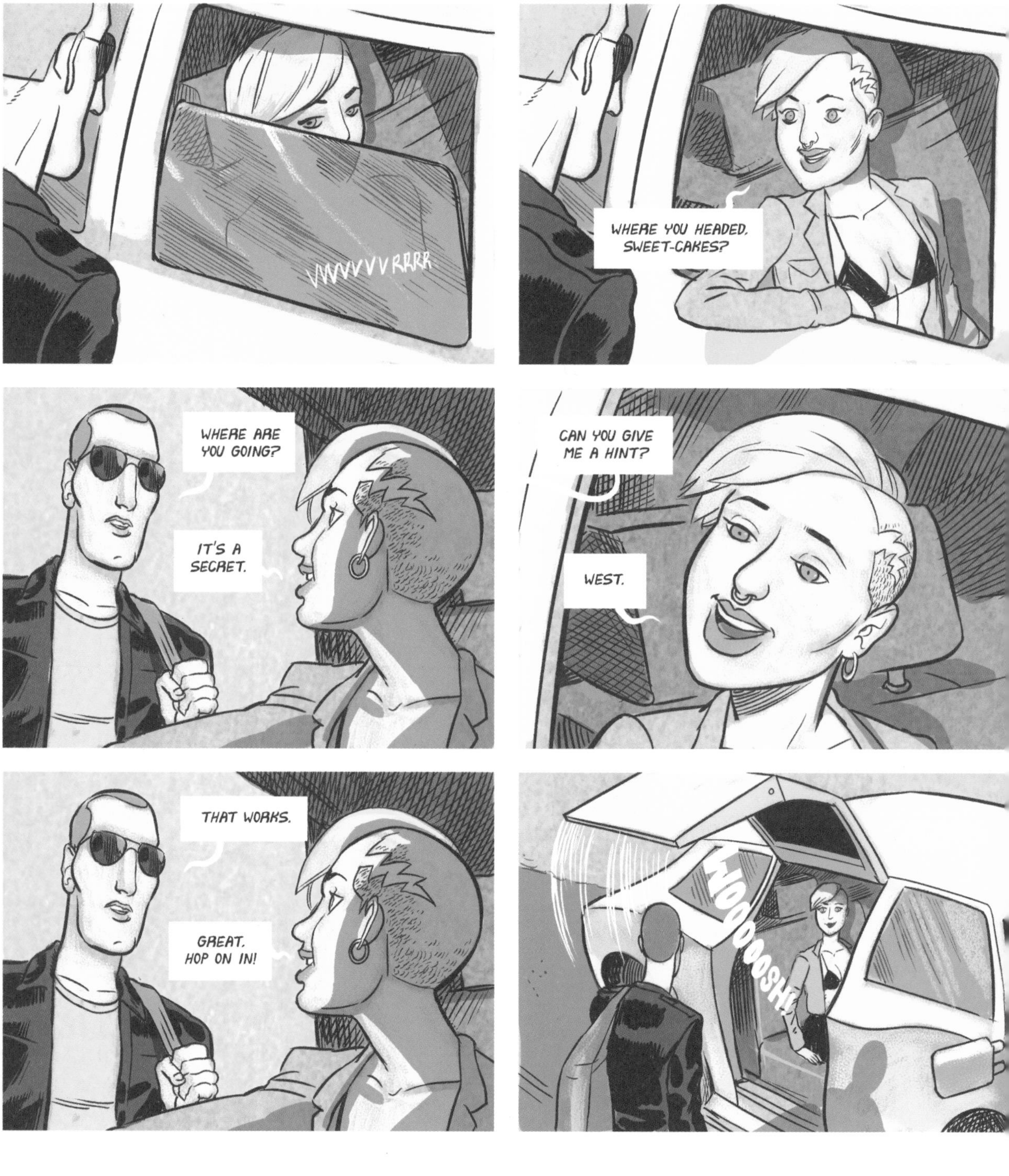
VVVVVVVRRRR
WHERE YOU HEADED, SWEET-CAKES?
WHERE ARE YOU GOING?
IT'S A SECRET.
CAN YOU GIVE ME A HINT?
WEST.
THAT WORKS.
GREAT. HOP ON IN!
WOOOOOSH!

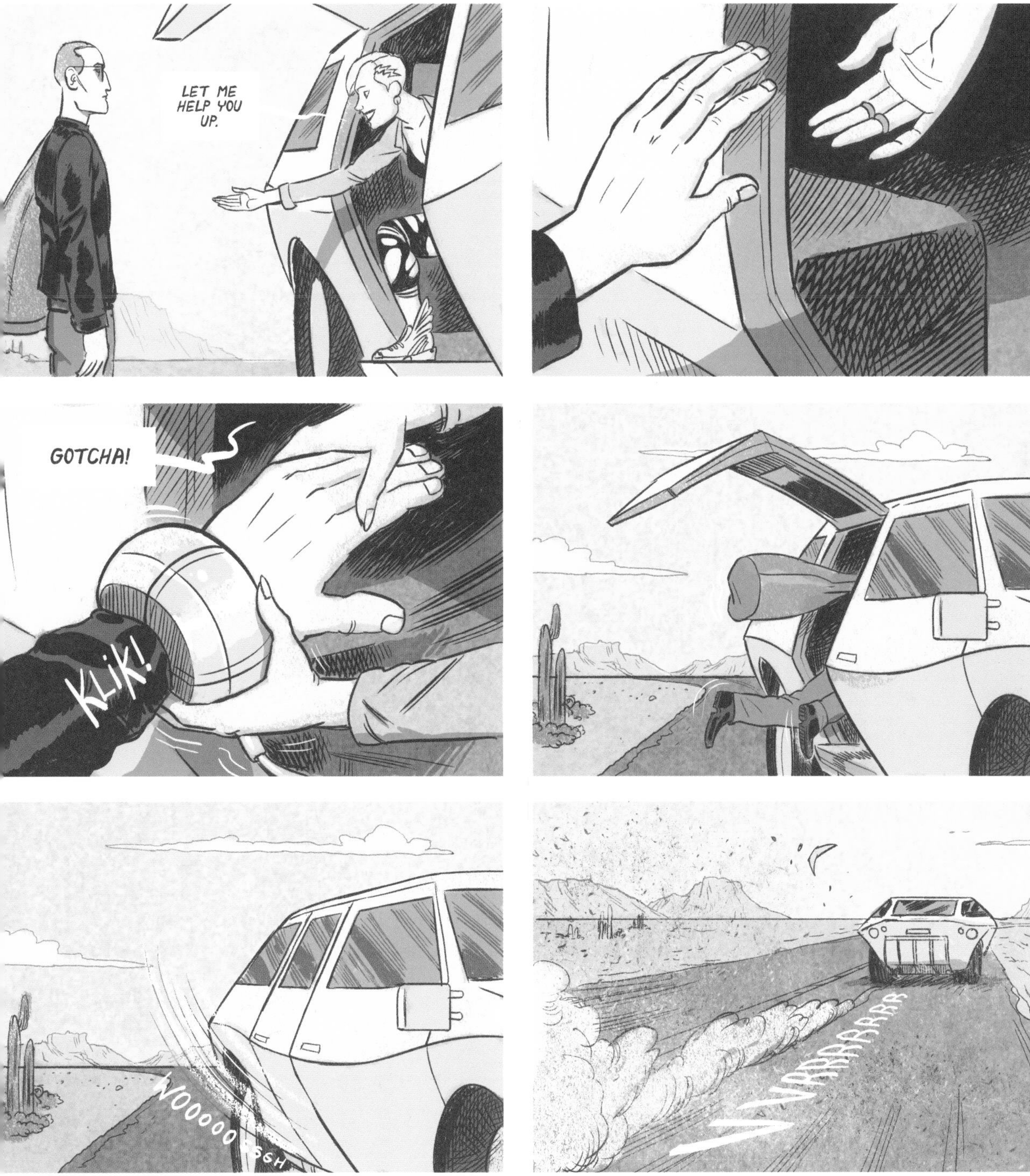
LET ME HELP YOU UP.
GOTCHA!
KLIK!
WOOOOOSSGH
VVARRRRRRRR

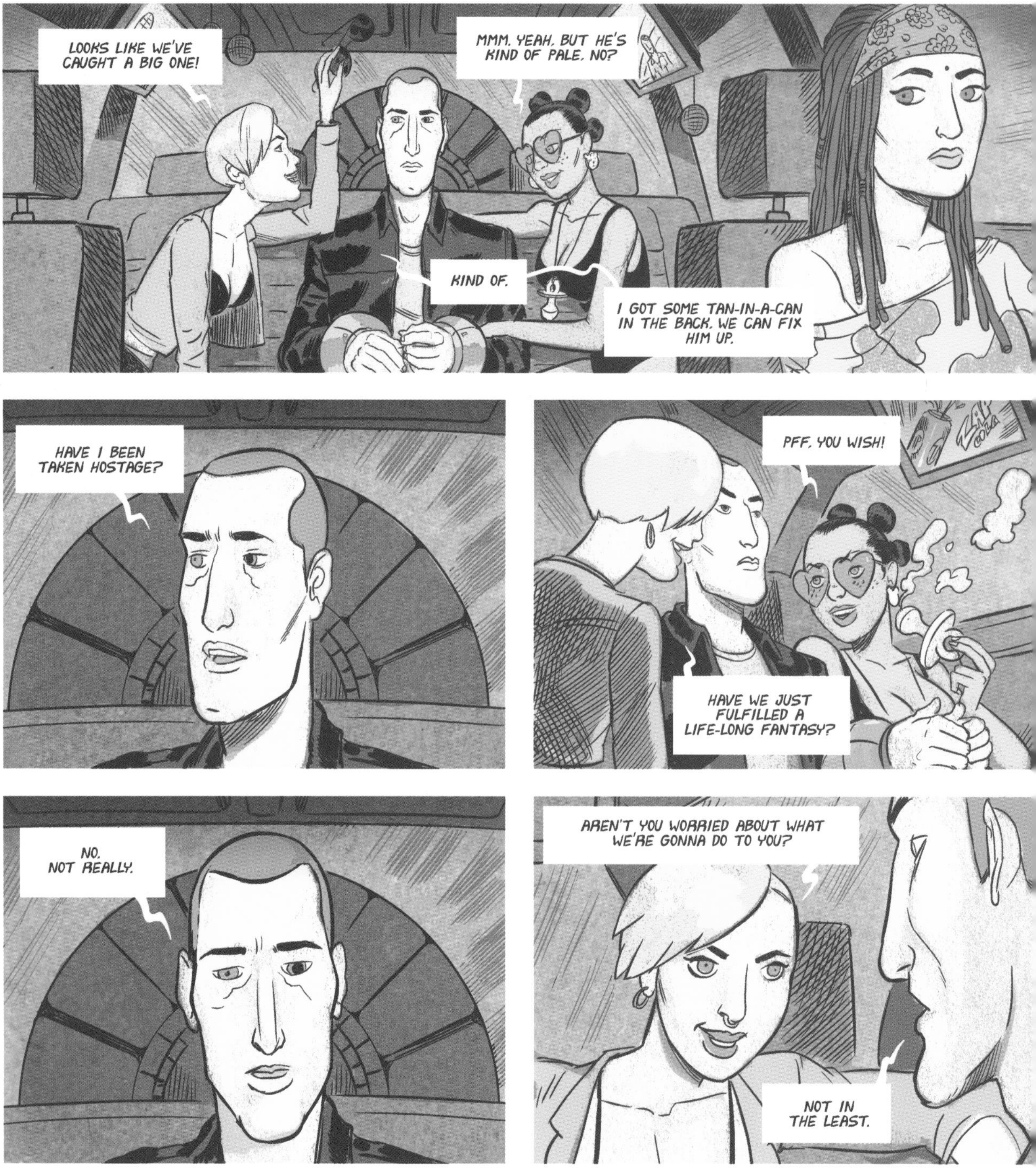
LOOKS LIKE WE'VE CAUGHT A BIG ONE!
MMM. YEAH. BUT HE'S KIND OF PALE, NO?
KIND OF.
I GOT SOME TAN-IN-A-CAN IN THE BACK. WE CAN FIX HIM UP.
HAVE I BEEN TAKEN HOSTAGE?
PFF, YOU WISH!
HAVE WE JUST FULFILLED A LIFE-LONG FANTASY?
NO. NOT REALLY.
AREN'T YOU WORRIED ABOUT WHAT WE'RE GONNA DO TO YOU?
NOT IN THE LEAST.

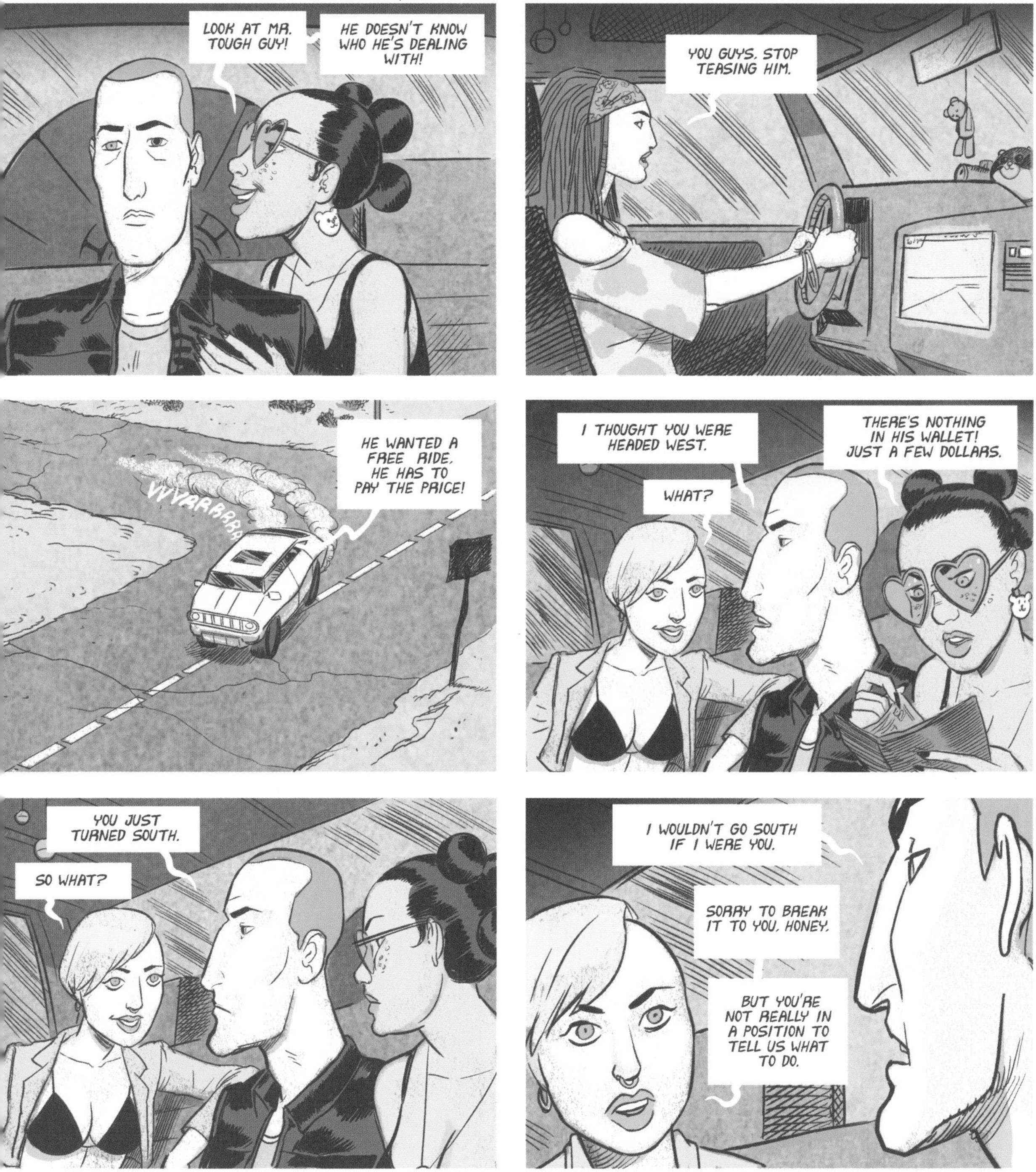
LOOK AT MR. TOUGH GUY!
HE DOESN'T KNOW WHO HE'S DEALING WITH!
YOU GUYS, STOP TEASING HIM.
HE WANTED A FREE RIDE, HE HAS TO PAY THE PRICE!
VVVARRRRR
I THOUGHT YOU WERE HEADED WEST.
WHAT?
THERE'S NOTHING IN HIS WALLET! JUST A FEW DOLLARS.
YOU JUST TURNED SOUTH.
SO WHAT?
I WOULDN'T GO SOUTH IF I WERE YOU.
SORRY TO BREAK IT TO YOU, HONEY,
BUT YOU'RE NOT REALLY IN A POSITION TO TELL US WHAT TO DO.

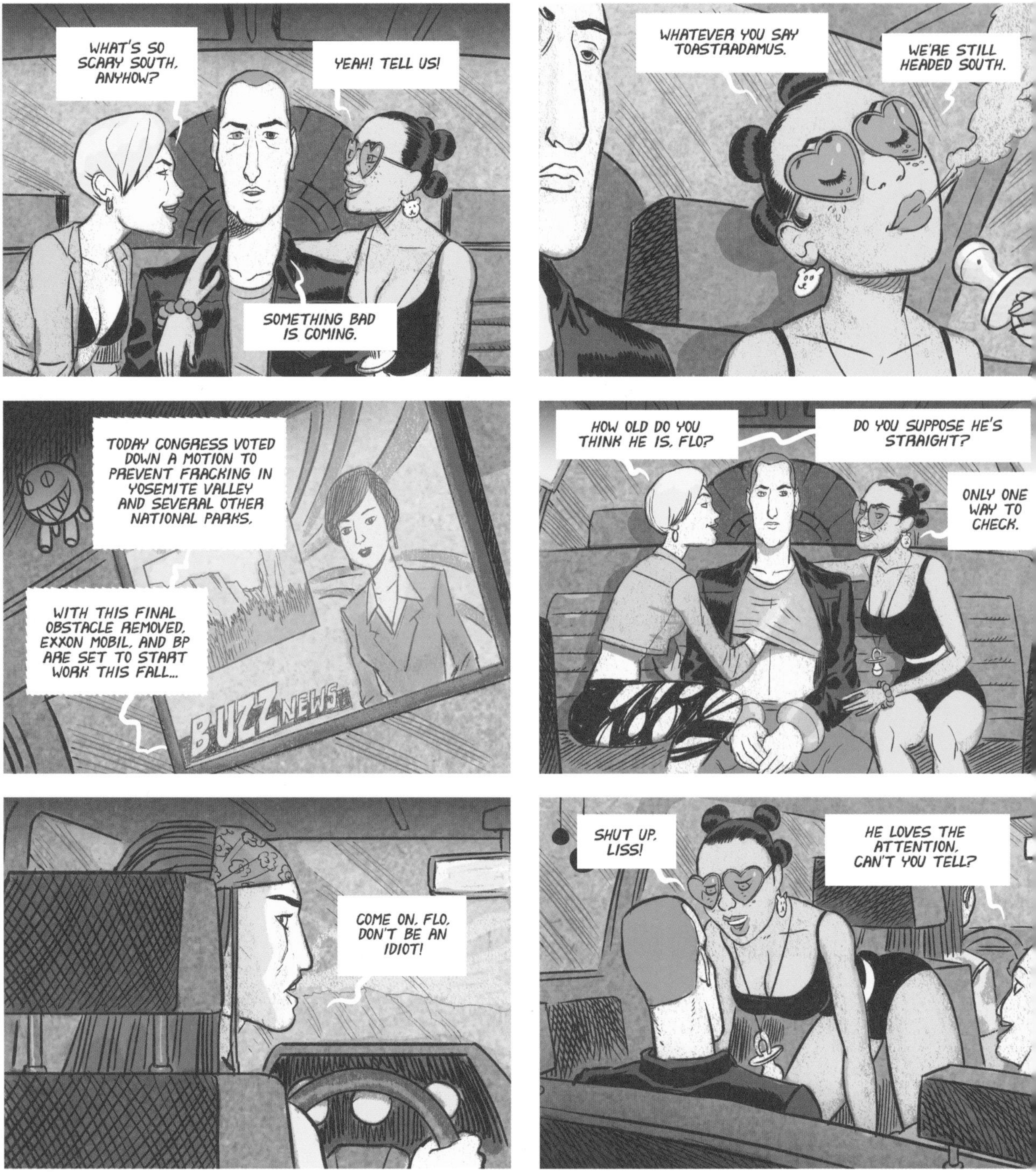
WHAT'S SO SCARY SOUTH, ANYHOW?
YEAH! TELL US!
SOMETHING BAD IS COMING.
WHATEVER YOU SAY TOASTRADAMUS.
WE'RE STILL HEADED SOUTH.
TODAY CONGRESS VOTED DOWN A MOTION TO PREVENT FRACKING IN YOSEMITE VALLEY AND SEVERAL OTHER NATIONAL PARKS.
WITH THIS FINAL OBSTACLE REMOVED, EXXON MOBIL, AND BP ARE SET TO START WORK THIS FALL...
BUZZ NEWS
HOW OLD DO YOU THINK HE IS, FLO?
DO YOU SUPPOSE HE'S STRAIGHT?
ONLY ONE WAY TO CHECK.
COME ON, FLO, DON'T BE AN IDIOT!
SHUT UP, LISS!
HE LOVES THE ATTENTION, CAN'T YOU TELL?

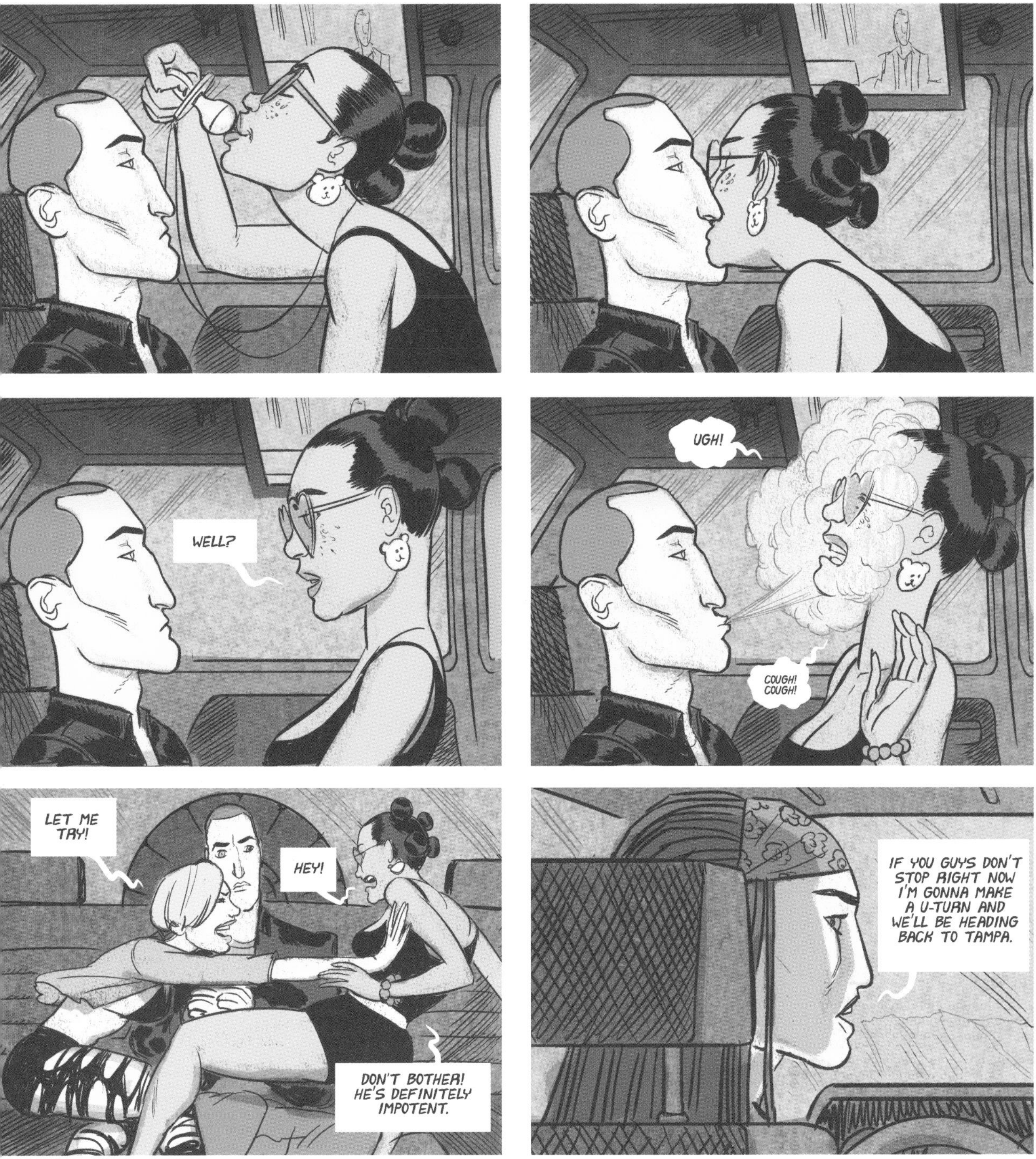
WELL?
UGH!
COUGH! COUGH!
LET ME TRY!
HEY!
DON'T BOTHER! HE'S DEFINITELY IMPOTENT.
IF YOU GUYS DON'T STOP RIGHT NOW I'M GONNA MAKE A U-TURN AND WE'LL BE HEADING BACK TO TAMPA.

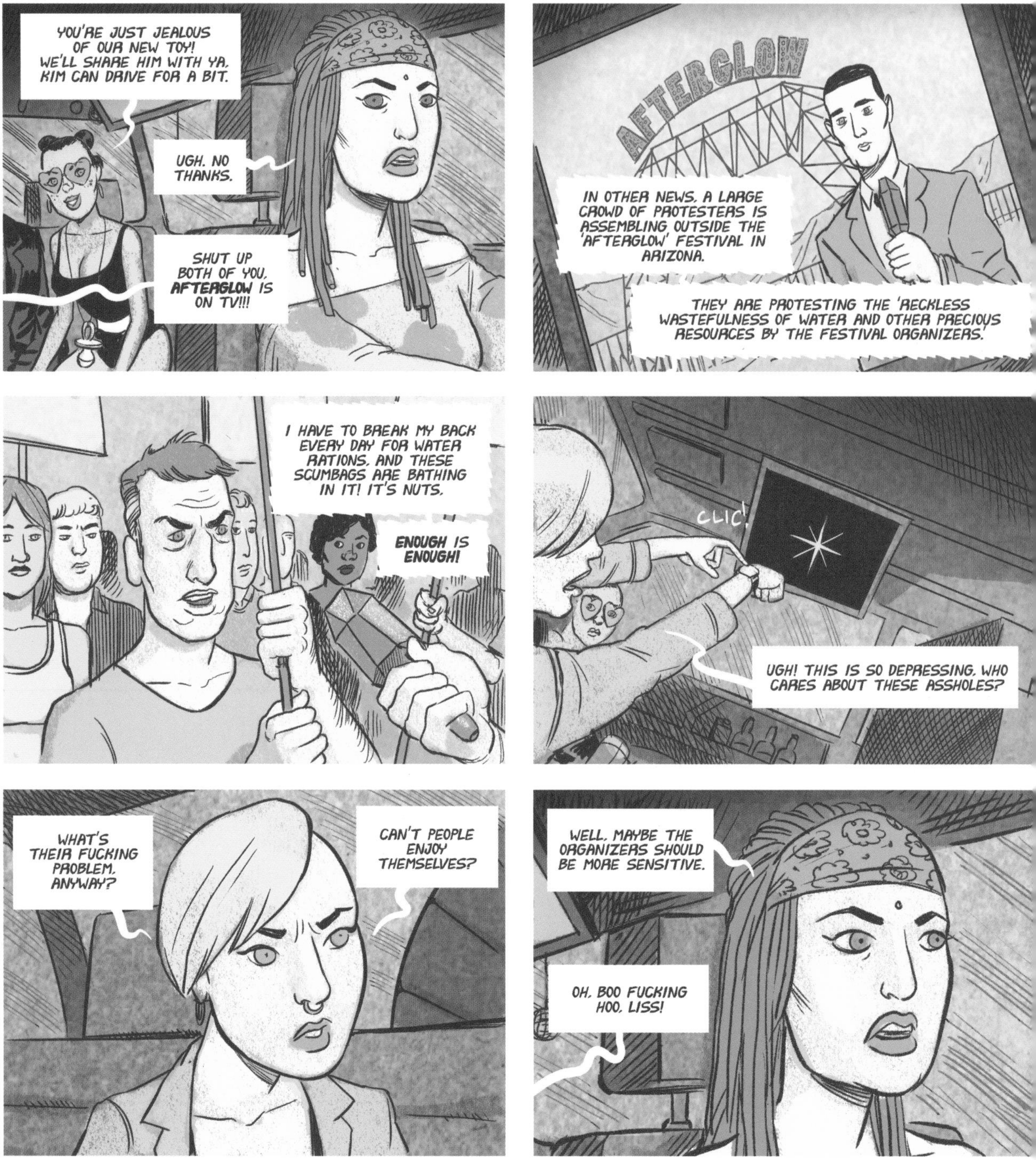

YOU'RE JUST JEALOUS OF OUR NEW TOY! WE'LL SHARE HIM WITH YA. KIM CAN DRIVE FOR A BIT.
UGH. NO THANKS.
SHUT UP BOTH OF YOU. AFTERGLOW IS ON TV!!!
AFTERGLOW
IN OTHER NEWS, A LARGE CROWD OF PROTESTERS IS ASSEMBLING OUTSIDE THE 'AFTERGLOW' FESTIVAL IN ARIZONA.
THEY ARE PROTESTING THE 'RECKLESS WASTEFULNESS OF WATER AND OTHER PRECIOUS RESOURCES BY THE FESTIVAL ORGANIZERS.'
I HAVE TO BREAK MY BACK EVERY DAY FOR WATER RATIONS, AND THESE SCUMBAGS ARE BATHING IN IT! IT'S NUTS.
ENOUGH IS ENOUGH!
CLIC!
UGH! THIS IS SO DEPRESSING. WHO CARES ABOUT THESE ASSHOLES?
WHAT'S THEIR FUCKING PROBLEM, ANYWAY?
CAN'T PEOPLE ENJOY THEMSELVES?
WELL, MAYBE THE ORGANIZERS SHOULD BE MORE SENSITIVE.
OH, BOO FUCKING HOO, LISS!

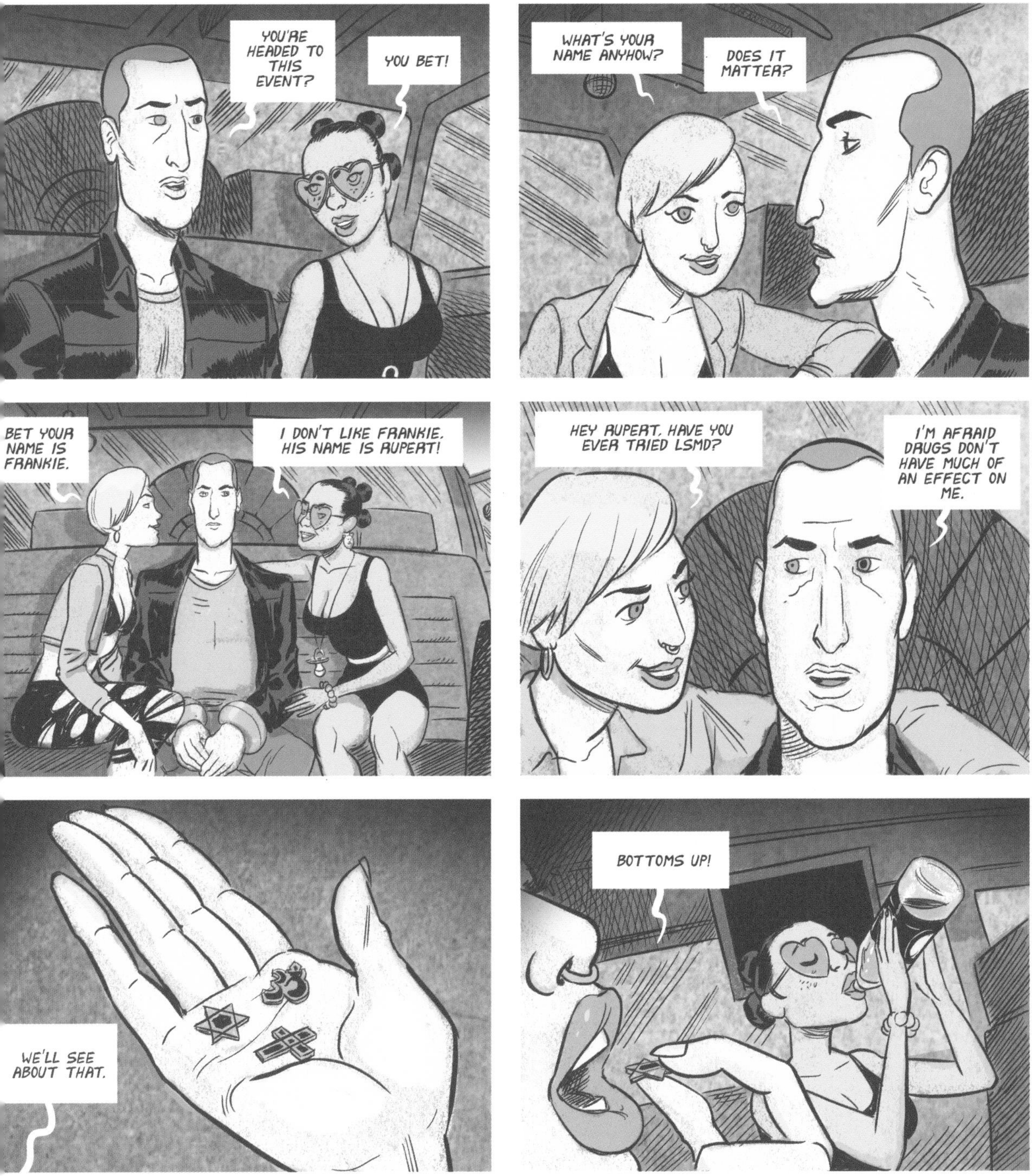
YOU'RE HEADED TO THIS EVENT?
YOU BET!
WHAT'S YOUR NAME ANYHOW?
DOES IT MATTER?
BET YOUR NAME IS FRANKIE.
I DON'T LIKE FRANKIE. HIS NAME IS RUPERT!
HEY RUPERT, HAVE YOU EVER TRIED LSMD?
I'M AFRAID DRUGS DON'T HAVE MUCH OF AN EFFECT ON ME.
WE'LL SEE ABOUT THAT.
BOTTOMS UP!

C'MON. THAT'S A GOOD BOY.
HAHA!
NOW SWALLOW...
HEY. WE'RE SLOWING DOWN.
WHY THE FUCK ARE WE SLOWING DOWN?
WE'LL MISS THE FIREWORKS!
IT'S ONE OF THOSE CLEAN WATER DISTRIBUTION THINGIES.
LISS. SWITCH LANES AND GET AROUND THIS BUTTPLUG TRAFFIC JAM.
THAT'S DANGEROUS.
GODDAMN IT. JUST DO IT!!

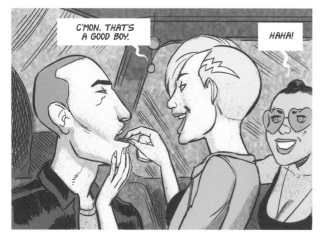

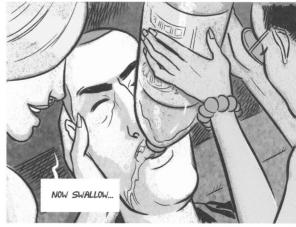

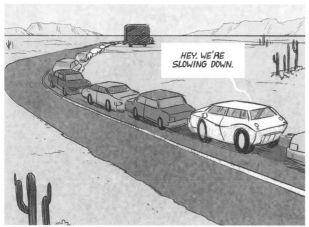

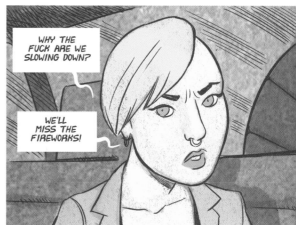

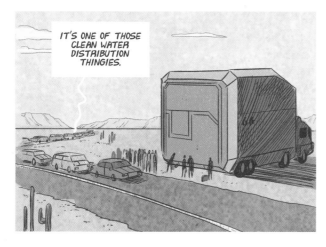

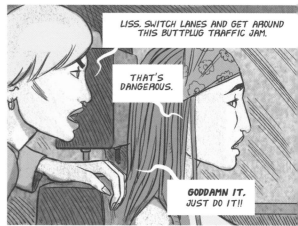

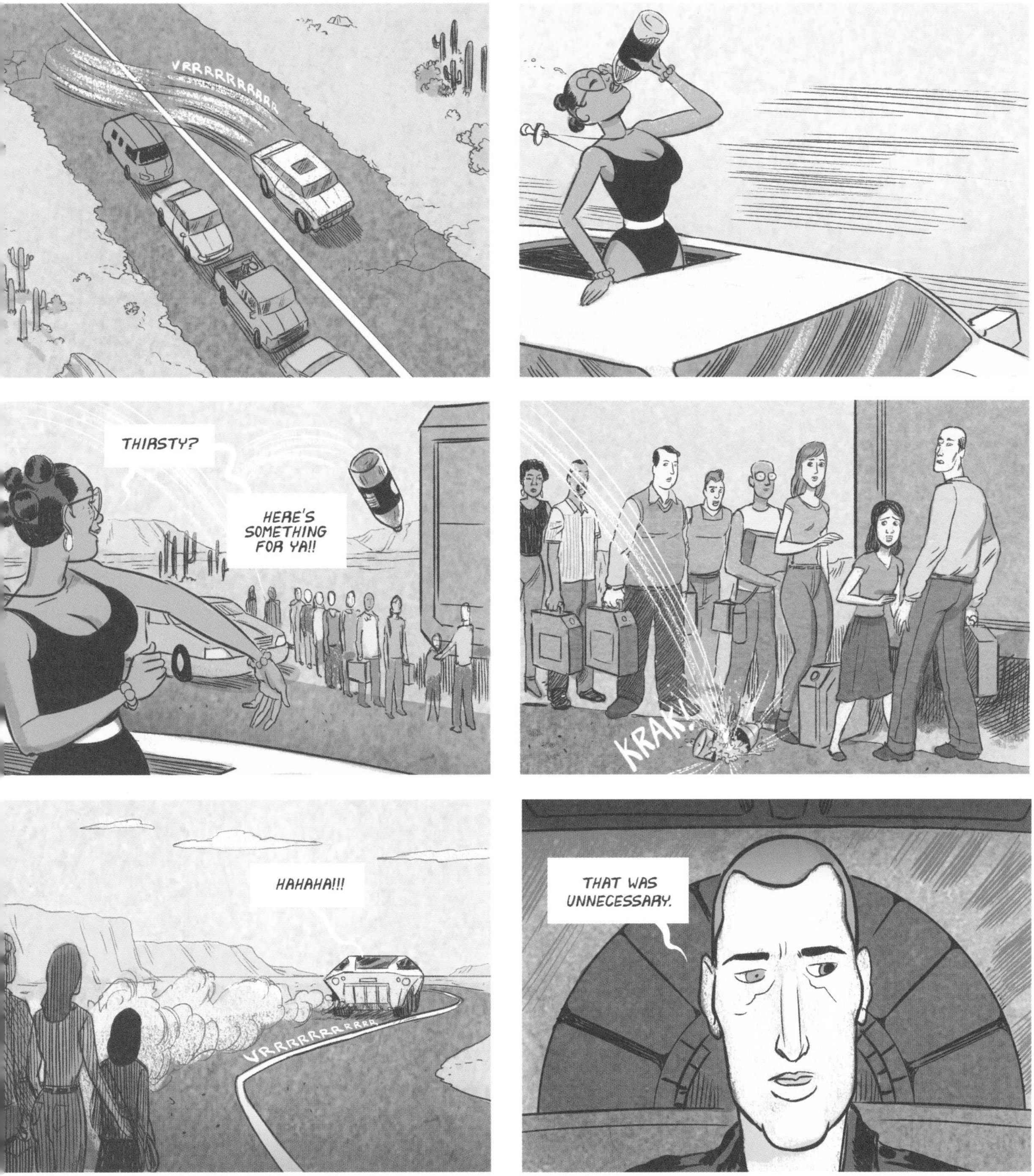
VRRRRRRRRRRRR
THIRSTY?
HERE'S SOMETHING FOR YA!!
KRAK!
HAHAHA!!!
VRRRRRRRRRRRR
THAT WAS UNNECESSARY.

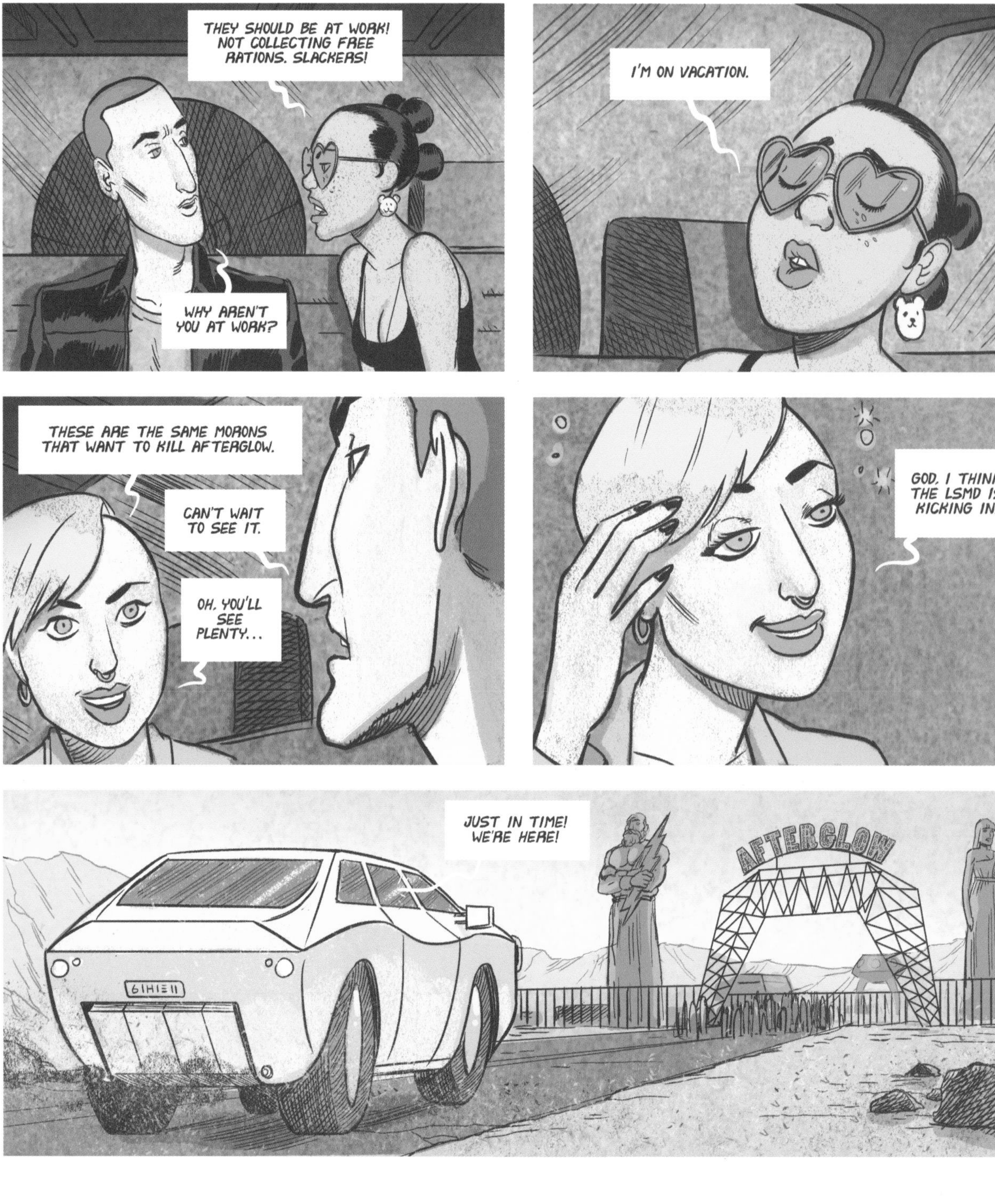
THEY SHOULD BE AT WORK! NOT COLLECTING FREE RATIONS. SLACKERS!
WHY AREN'T YOU AT WORK?
I'M ON VACATION.
THESE ARE THE SAME MORONS THAT WANT TO KILL AFTERGLOW.
CAN'T WAIT TO SEE IT.
OH, YOU'LL SEE PLENTY...
GOD, I THINK THE LSMD IS KICKING IN.
JUST IN TIME! WE'RE HERE!
AFTERGLOW

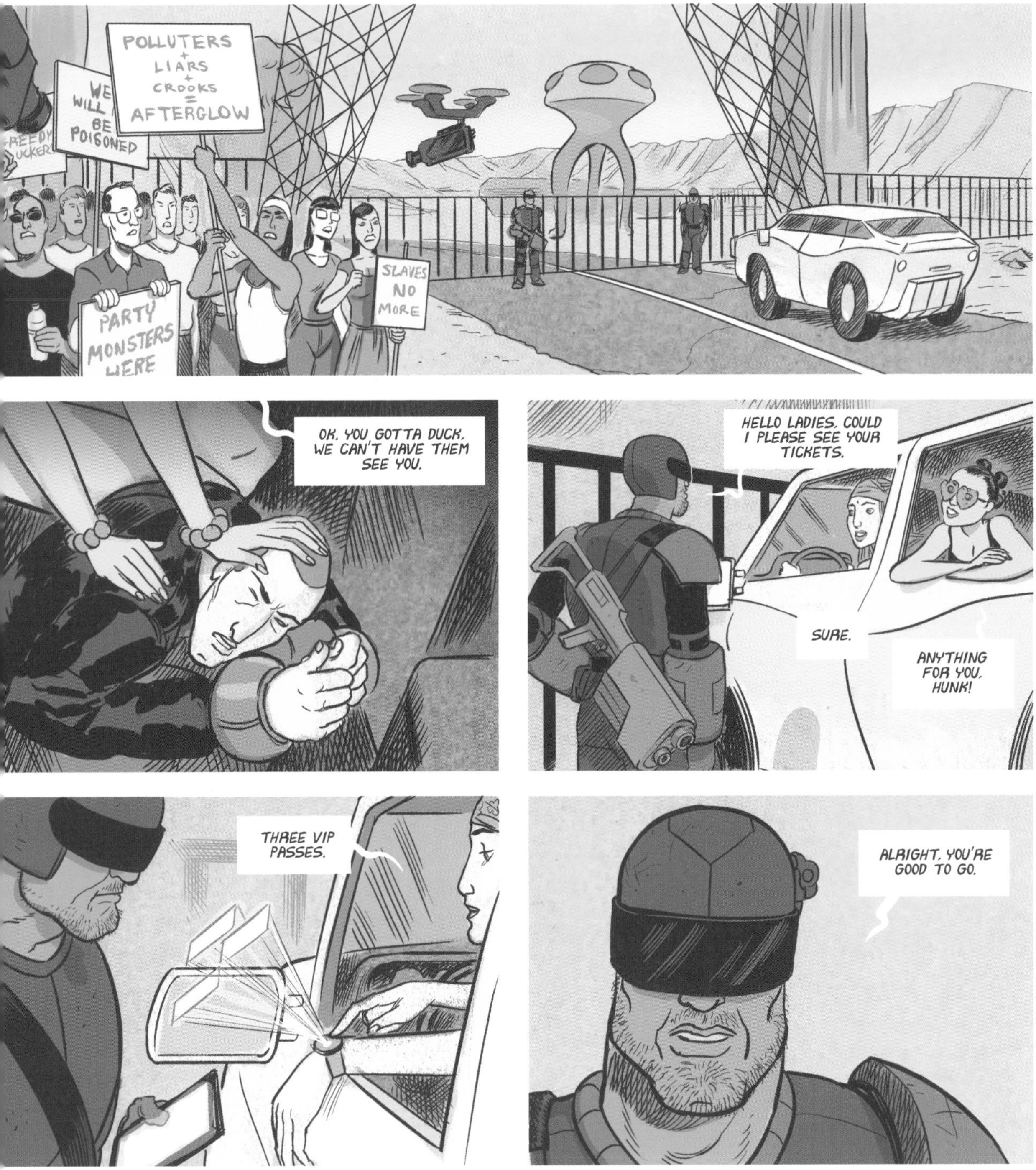
POLLUTERS + LIARS + CROOKS = AFTERGLOW
WE WILL BE POISONED
PARTY MONSTERS HERE
SLAVES NO MORE
OK. YOU GOTTA DUCK. WE CAN'T HAVE THEM SEE YOU.
HELLO LADIES. COULD I PLEASE SEE YOUR TICKETS.
SURE.
ANYTHING FOR YOU, HUNK!
THREE VIP PASSES.
ALRIGHT. YOU'RE GOOD TO GO.

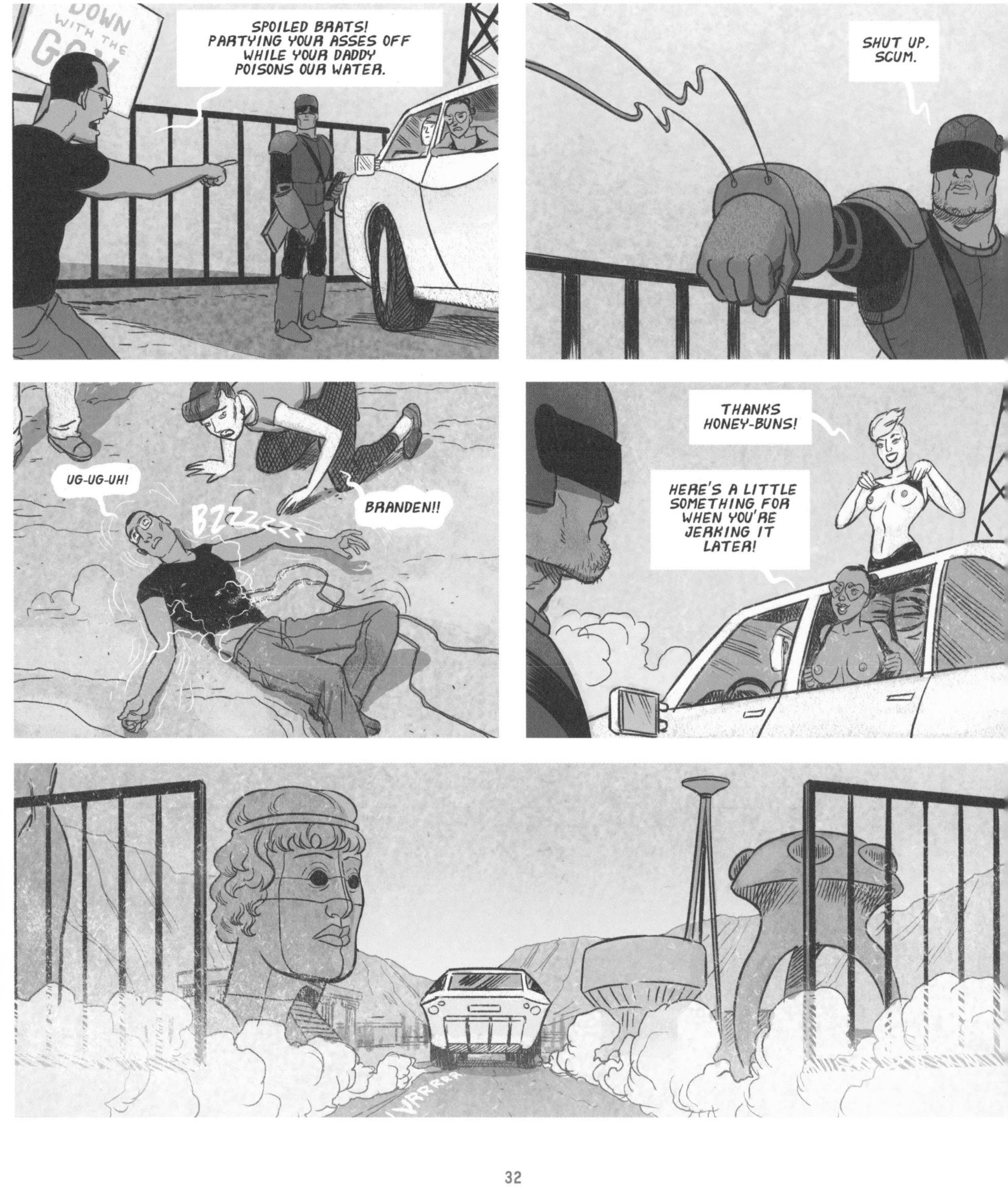
DOWN WITH THE GOV
SPOILED BRATS! PARTYING YOUR ASSES OFF WHILE YOUR DADDY POISONS OUR WATER.
SHUT UP, SCUM.
UG-UG-UH!
BZZZZZZZ
BRANDEN!!
THANKS HONEY-BUNS!
HERE'S A LITTLE SOMETHING FOR WHEN YOU'RE JERKING IT LATER!
VRRRRR

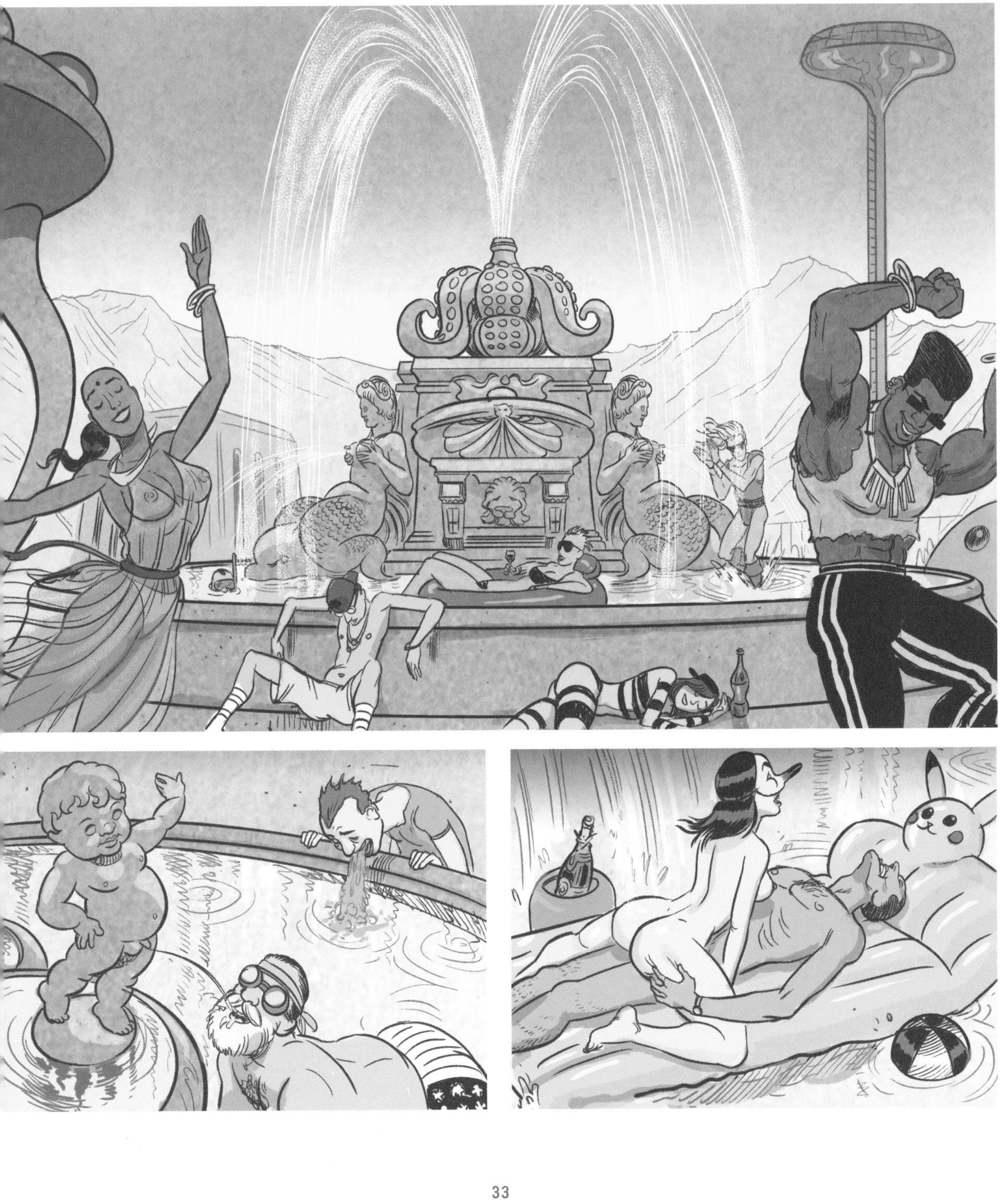

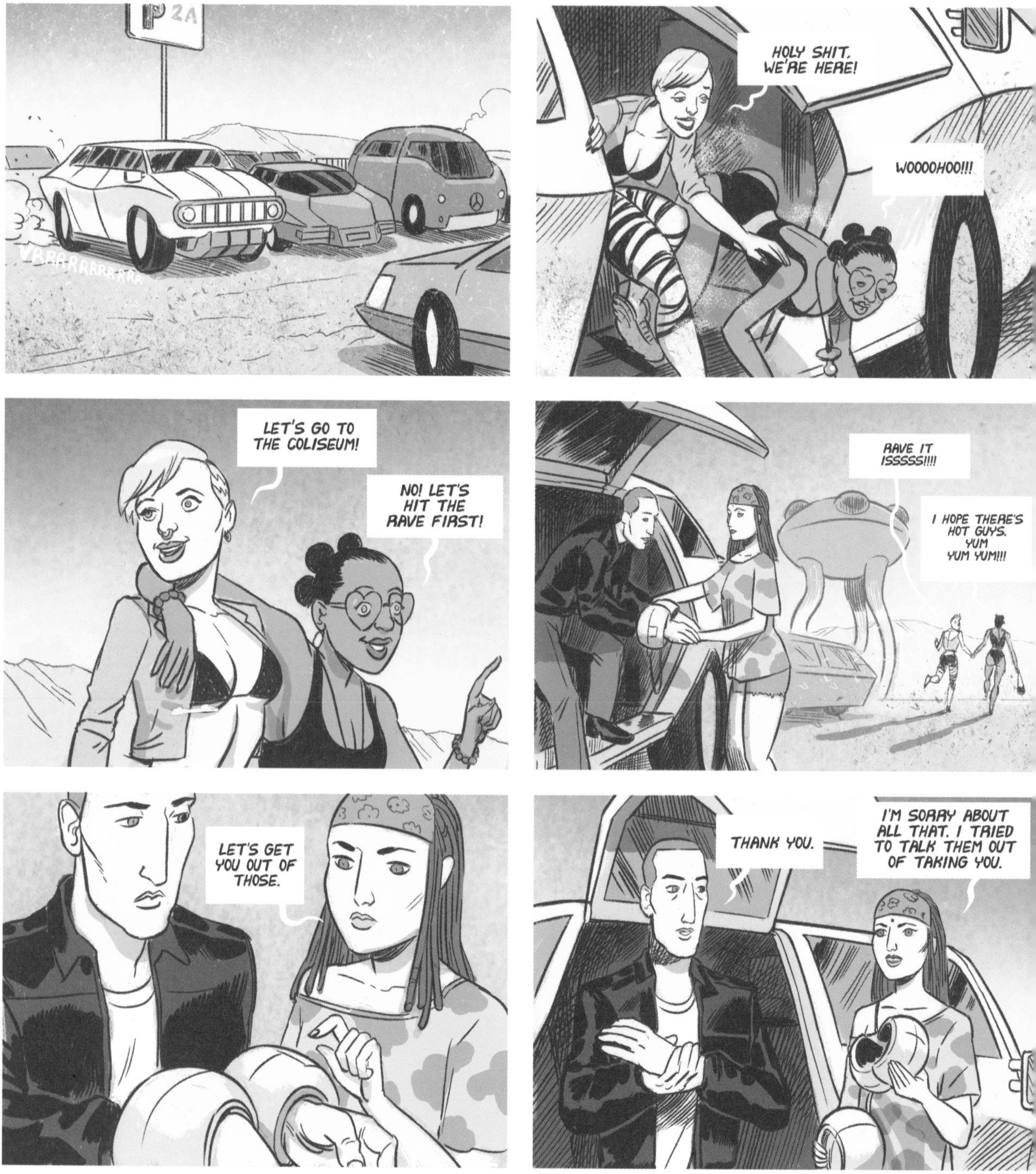
P 2A
VRRRRRRRRRRA
HOLY SHIT. WE'RE HERE!
WOOOOHOO!!!
LET'S GO TO THE COLISEUM!
NO! LET'S HIT THE RAVE FIRST!
RAVE IT ISSSSS!!!!
I HOPE THERE'S HOT GUYS. YUM YUM YUM!!!
LET'S GET YOU OUT OF THOSE.
THANK YOU.
I'M SORRY ABOUT ALL THAT. I TRIED TO TALK THEM OUT OF TAKING YOU.

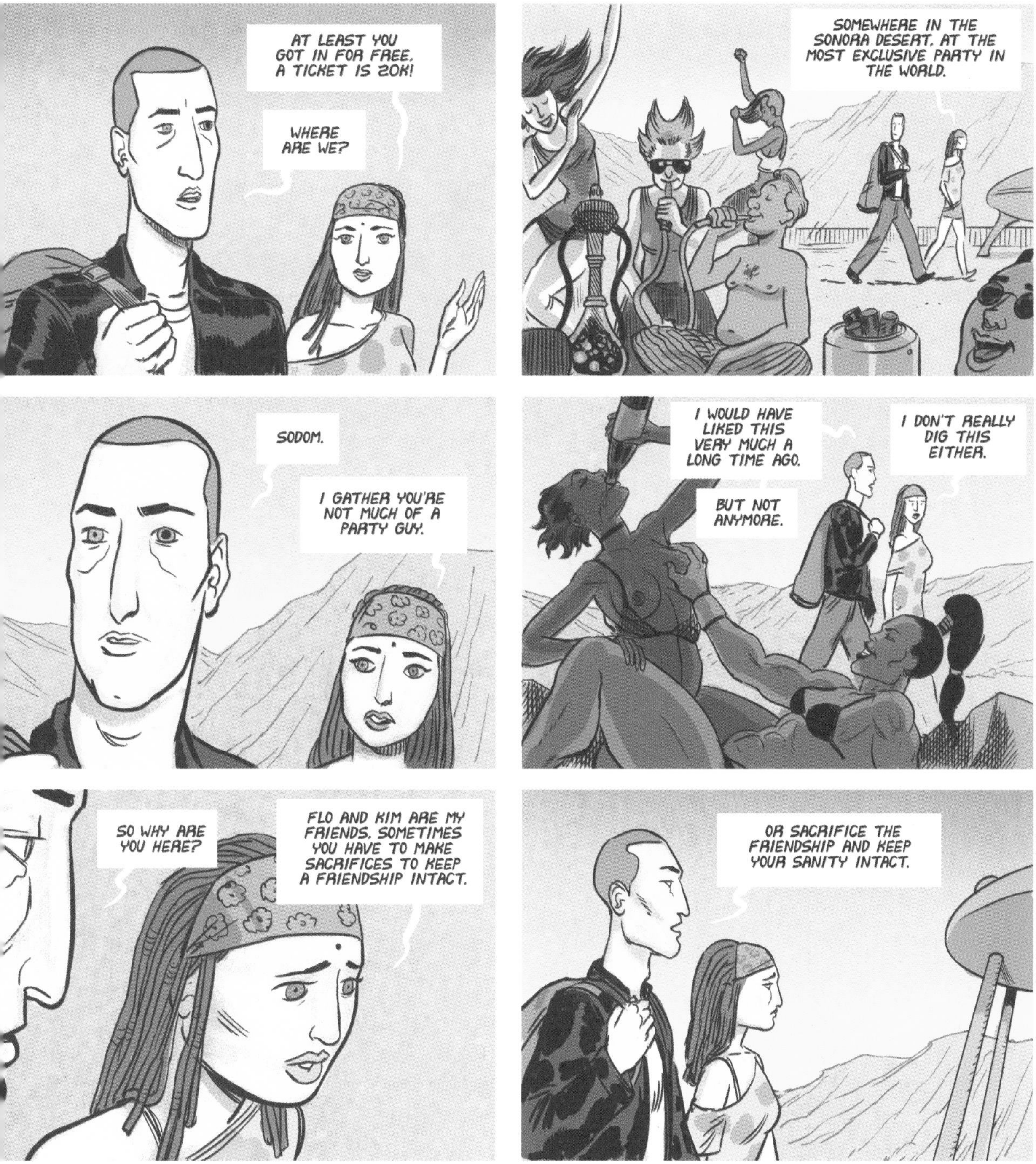
AT LEAST YOU GOT IN FOR FREE. A TICKET IS 20K!
WHERE ARE WE?
SOMEWHERE IN THE SONORA DESERT, AT THE MOST EXCLUSIVE PARTY IN THE WORLD.
SODOM.
I GATHER YOU'RE NOT MUCH OF A PARTY GUY.
I WOULD HAVE LIKED THIS VERY MUCH A LONG TIME AGO.
BUT NOT ANYMORE.
I DON'T REALLY DIG THIS EITHER.
SO WHY ARE YOU HERE?
FLO AND KIM ARE MY FRIENDS. SOMETIMES YOU HAVE TO MAKE SACRIFICES TO KEEP A FRIENDSHIP INTACT.
OR SACRIFICE THE FRIENDSHIP AND KEEP YOUR SANITY INTACT.

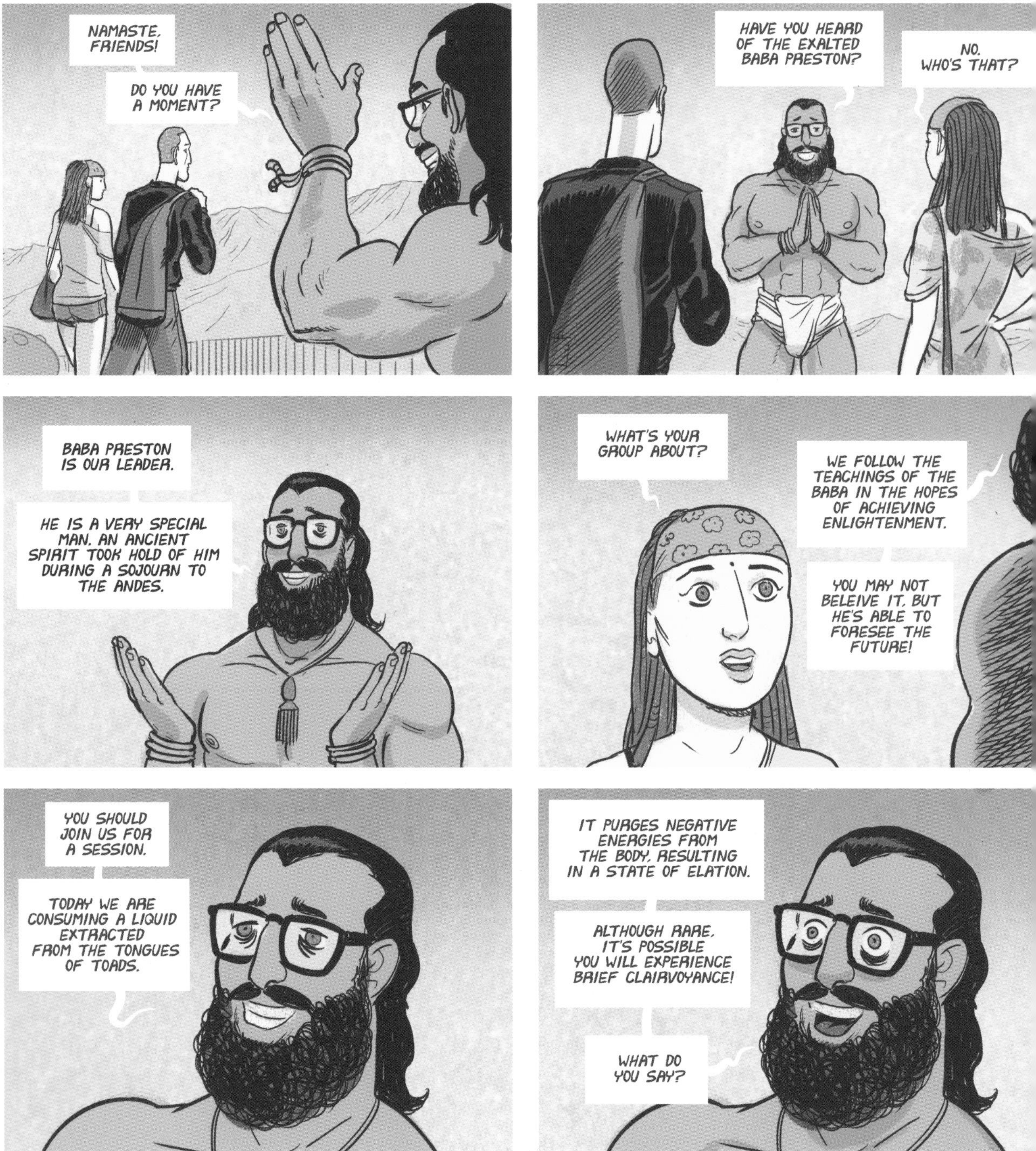
NAMASTE, FRIENDS!
DO YOU HAVE A MOMENT?
HAVE YOU HEARD OF THE EXALTED BABA PRESTON?
NO. WHO'S THAT?
BABA PRESTON IS OUR LEADER.
HE IS A VERY SPECIAL MAN. AN ANCIENT SPIRIT TOOK HOLD OF HIM DURING A SOJOURN TO THE ANDES.
WHAT'S YOUR GROUP ABOUT?
WE FOLLOW THE TEACHINGS OF THE BABA IN THE HOPES OF ACHIEVING ENLIGHTENMENT.
YOU MAY NOT BELEIVE IT, BUT HE'S ABLE TO FORESEE THE FUTURE!
YOU SHOULD JOIN US FOR A SESSION.
TODAY WE ARE CONSUMING A LIQUID EXTRACTED FROM THE TONGUES OF TOADS.
IT PURGES NEGATIVE ENERGIES FROM THE BODY, RESULTING IN A STATE OF ELATION.
ALTHOUGH RARE, IT'S POSSIBLE YOU WILL EXPERIENCE BRIEF CLAIRVOYANCE!
WHAT DO YOU SAY?

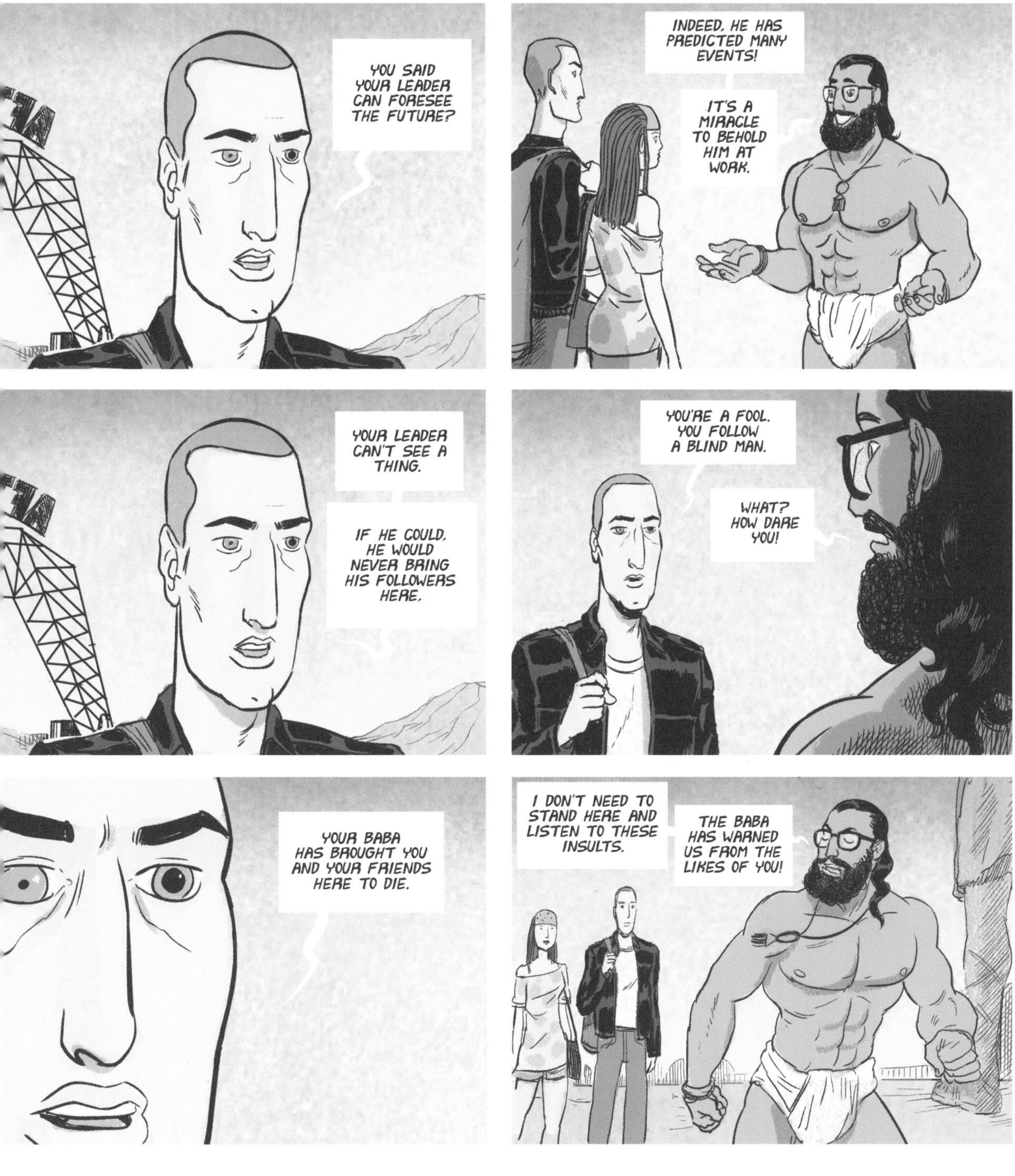
YOU SAID YOUR LEADER CAN FORESEE THE FUTURE?
INDEED, HE HAS PREDICTED MANY EVENTS!
IT'S A MIRACLE TO BEHOLD HIM AT WORK.
YOUR LEADER CAN'T SEE A THING.
IF HE COULD, HE WOULD NEVER BRING HIS FOLLOWERS HERE.
YOU'RE A FOOL. YOU FOLLOW A BLIND MAN.
WHAT? HOW DARE YOU!
YOUR BABA HAS BROUGHT YOU AND YOUR FRIENDS HERE TO DIE.
I DON'T NEED TO STAND HERE AND LISTEN TO THESE INSULTS.
THE BABA HAS WARNED US FROM THE LIKES OF YOU!

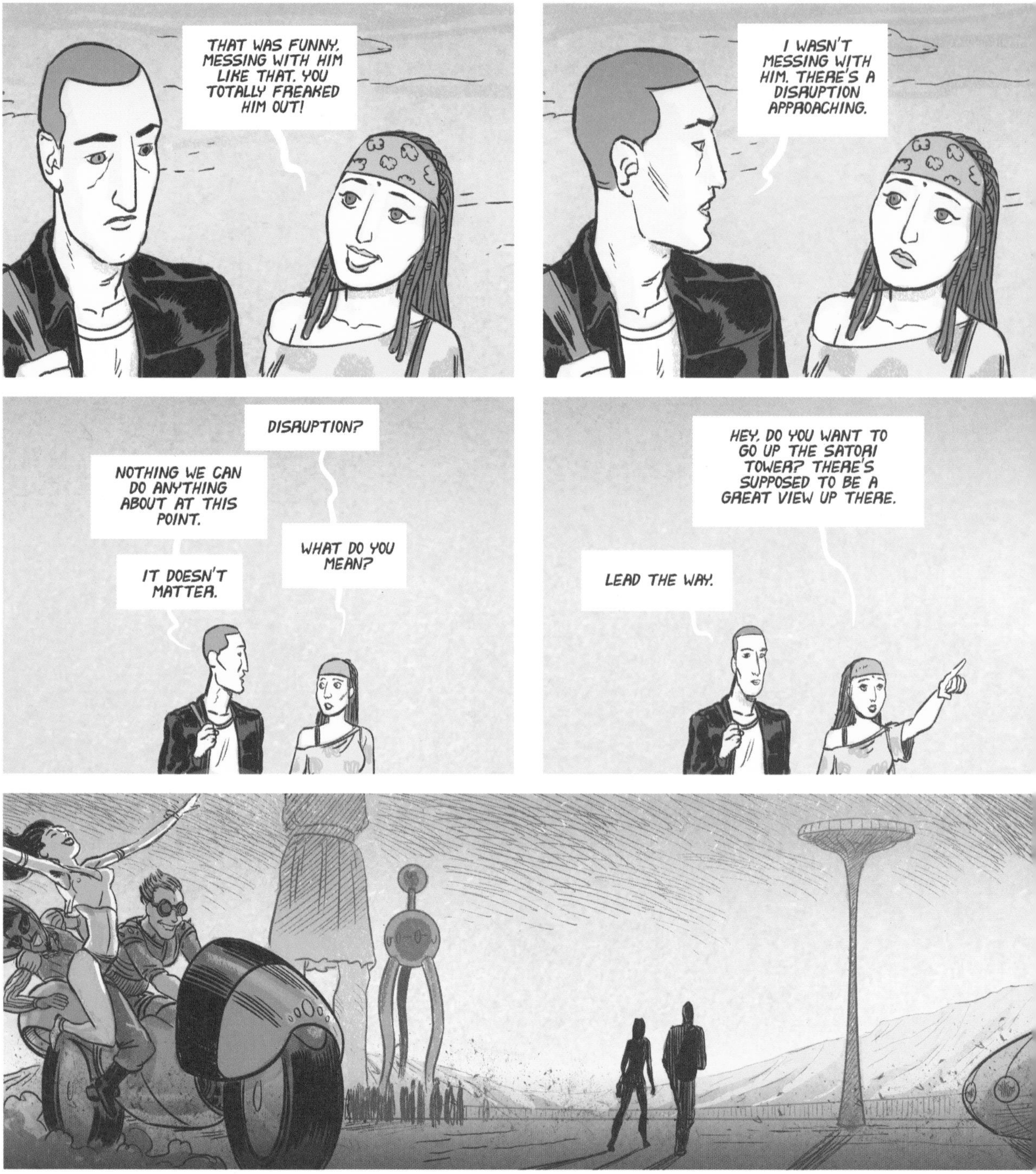
THAT WAS FUNNY, MESSING WITH HIM LIKE THAT. YOU TOTALLY FREAKED HIM OUT!
I WASN'T MESSING WITH HIM. THERE'S A DISRUPTION APPROACHING.
DISRUPTION?
NOTHING WE CAN DO ANYTHING ABOUT AT THIS POINT.
WHAT DO YOU MEAN?
IT DOESN'T MATTER.
HEY, DO YOU WANT TO GO UP THE SATORI TOWER? THERE'S SUPPOSED TO BE A GREAT VIEW UP THERE.
LEAD THE WAY.

WHERE WERE YOU HEADED WHEN WE PICKED YOU UP?

NOWHERE SPECIFIC.

YOU'RE JUST TRAVELING FOR THE SAKE OF IT?

NOT EXACTLY.

HOW LONG HAVE YOU BEEN HITCHHIKING LIKE THIS?

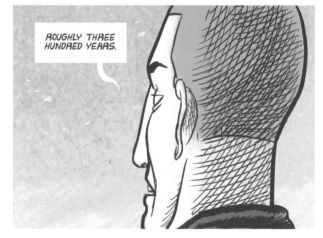

ROUGHLY THREE HUNDRED YEARS.

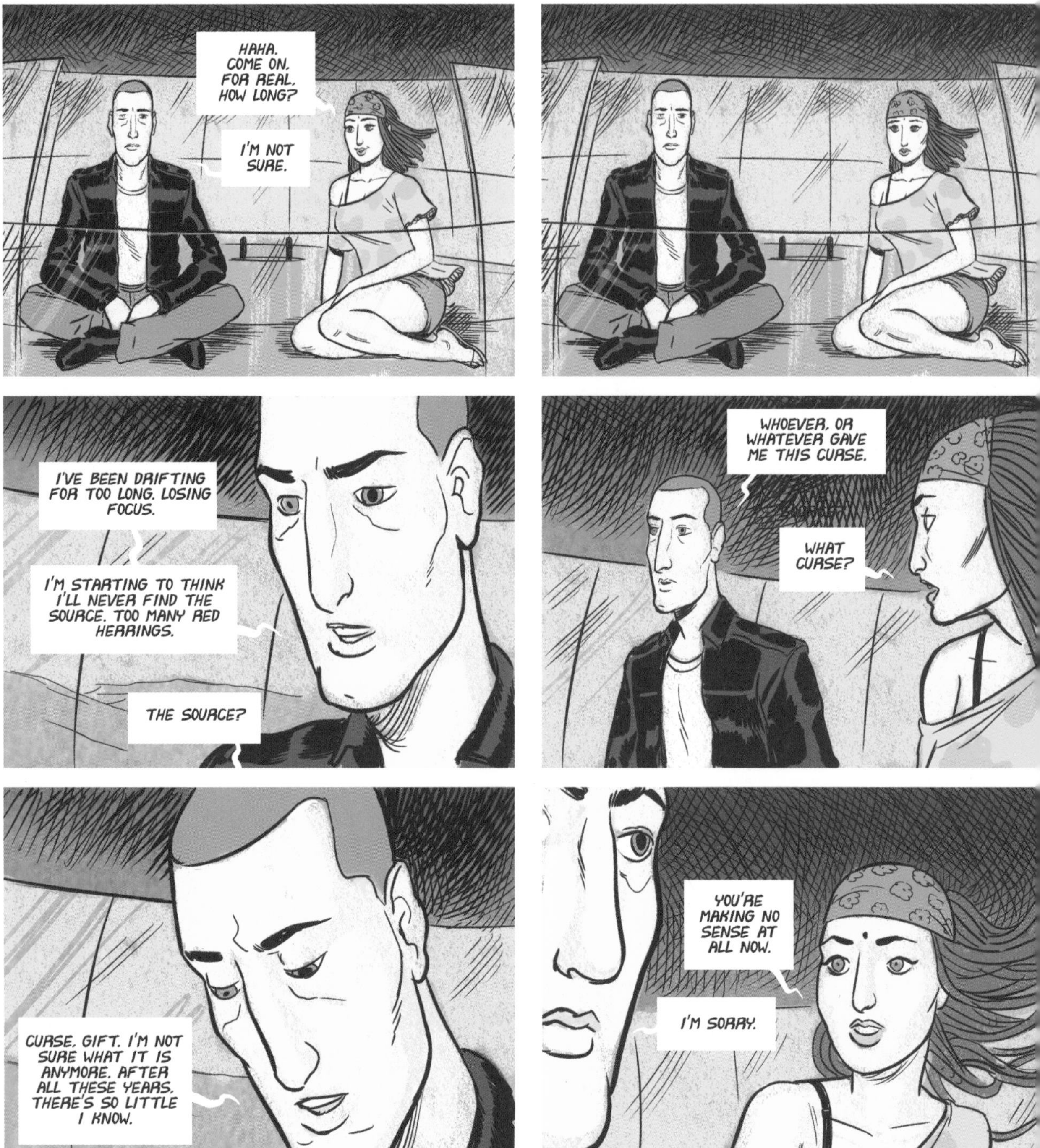
HAHA. COME ON. FOR REAL. HOW LONG?
I'M NOT SURE.
I'VE BEEN DRIFTING FOR TOO LONG. LOSING FOCUS.
I'M STARTING TO THINK I'LL NEVER FIND THE SOURCE. TOO MANY RED HERRINGS.
THE SOURCE?
WHOEVER, OR WHATEVER GAVE ME THIS CURSE.
WHAT CURSE?
CURSE, GIFT. I'M NOT SURE WHAT IT IS ANYMORE. AFTER ALL THESE YEARS, THERE'S SO LITTLE I KNOW.
YOU'RE MAKING NO SENSE AT ALL NOW.
I'M SORRY.

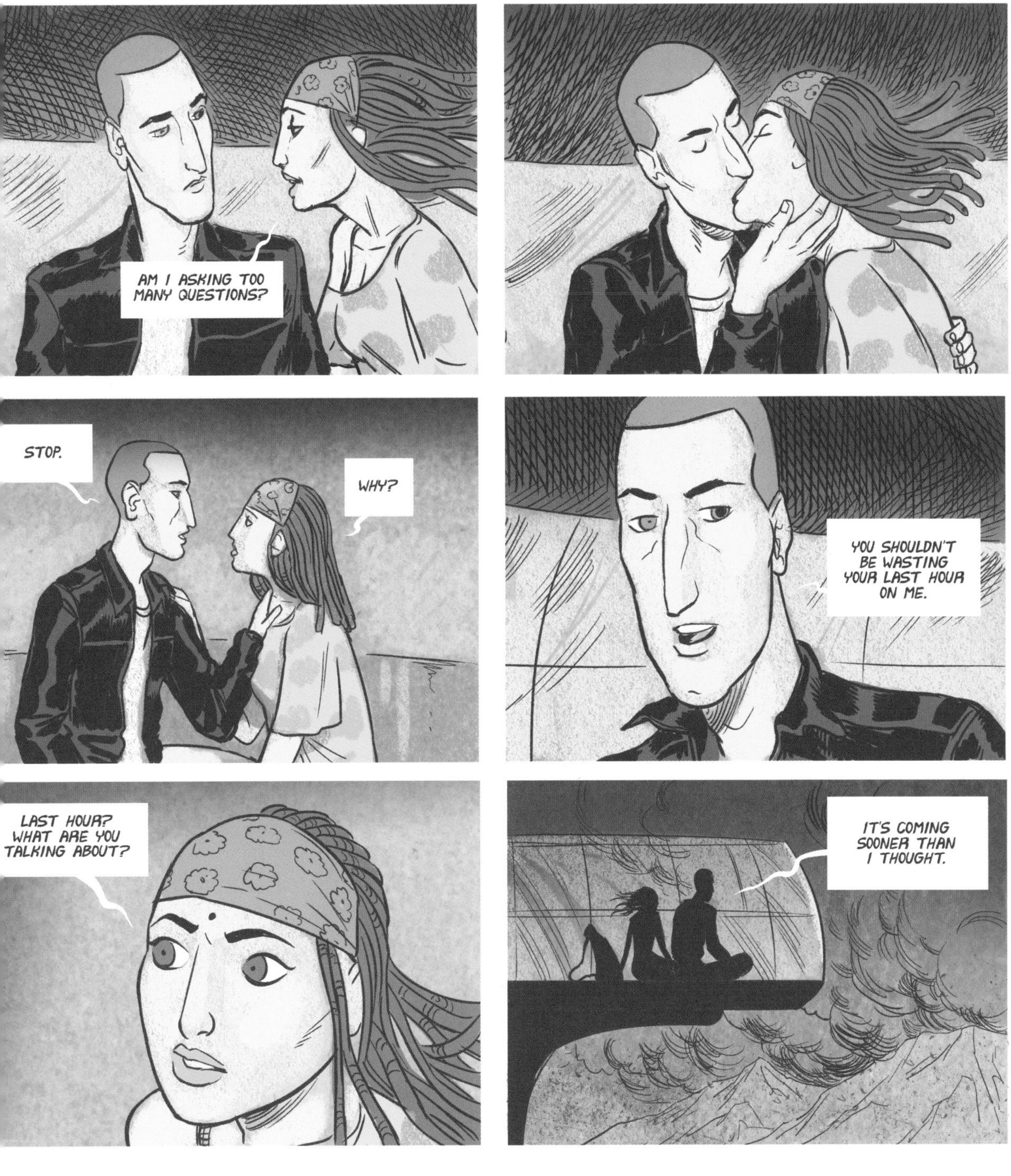

AM I ASKING TOO MANY QUESTIONS?
STOP.
WHY?
YOU SHOULDN'T BE WASTING YOUR LAST HOUR ON ME.
LAST HOUR? WHAT ARE YOU TALKING ABOUT?
IT'S COMING SOONER THAN I THOUGHT.

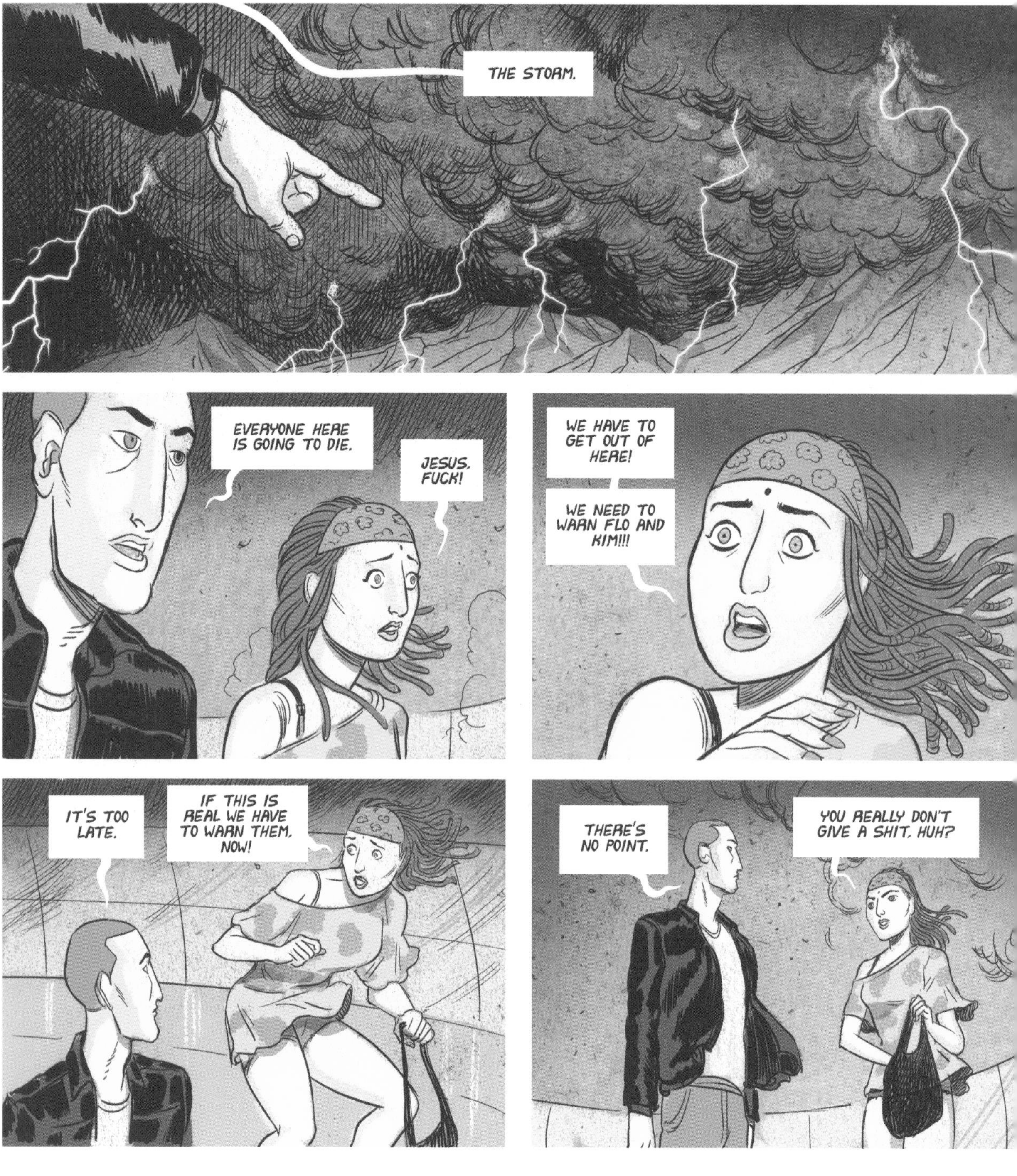
THE STORM.
EVERYONE HERE IS GOING TO DIE.
JESUS. FUCK!
WE HAVE TO GET OUT OF HERE!
WE NEED TO WARN FLO AND KIM!!!
IT'S TOO LATE.
IF THIS IS REAL WE HAVE TO WARN THEM. NOW!
THERE'S NO POINT.
YOU REALLY DON'T GIVE A SHIT, HUH?

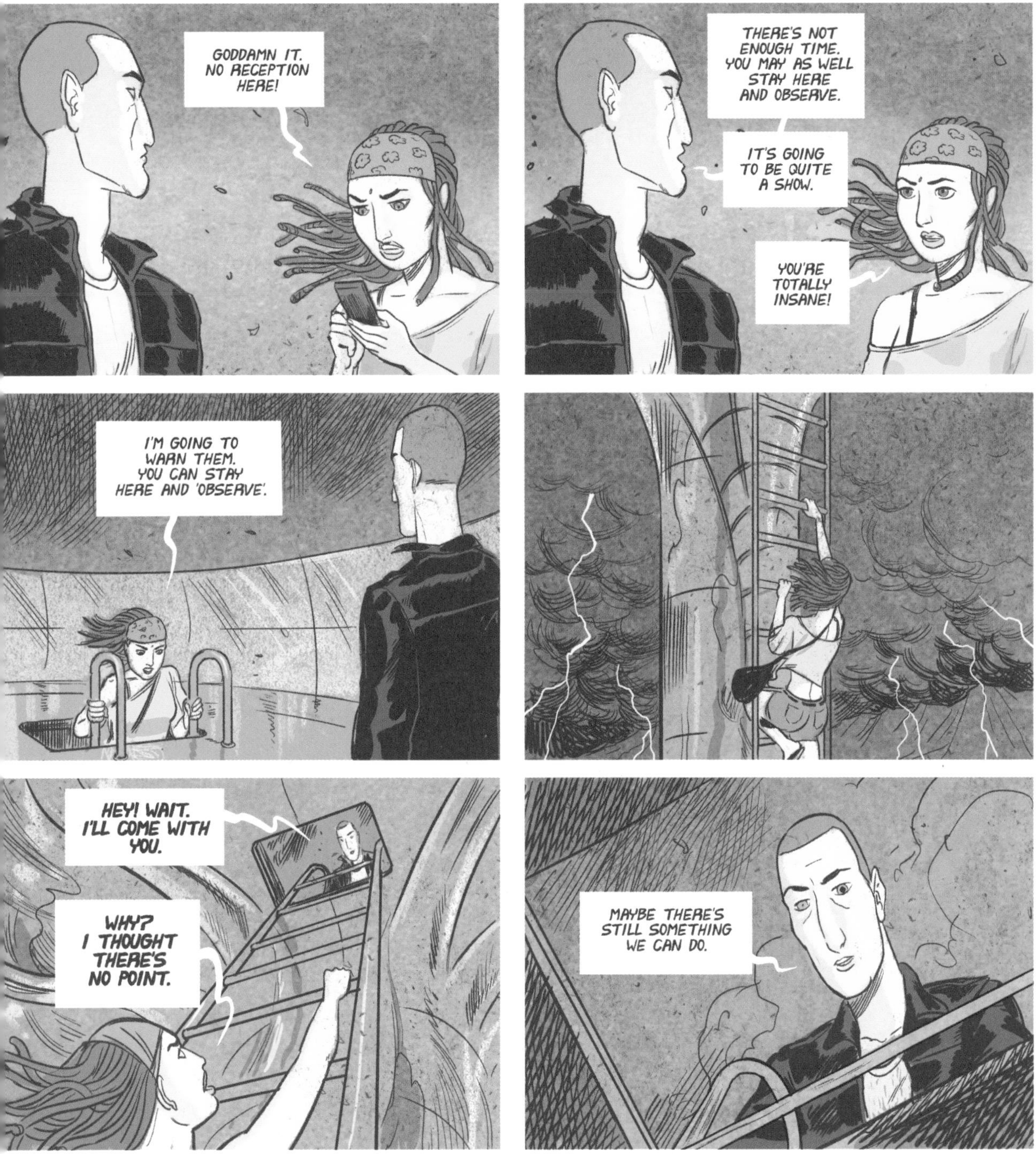
GODDAMN IT. NO RECEPTION HERE!
THERE'S NOT ENOUGH TIME. YOU MAY AS WELL STAY HERE AND OBSERVE.
IT'S GOING TO BE QUITE A SHOW.
YOU'RE TOTALLY INSANE!
I'M GOING TO WARN THEM. YOU CAN STAY HERE AND 'OBSERVE'.
HEY! WAIT. I'LL COME WITH YOU.
WHY? I THOUGHT THERE'S NO POINT.
MAYBE THERE'S STILL SOMETHING WE CAN DO.

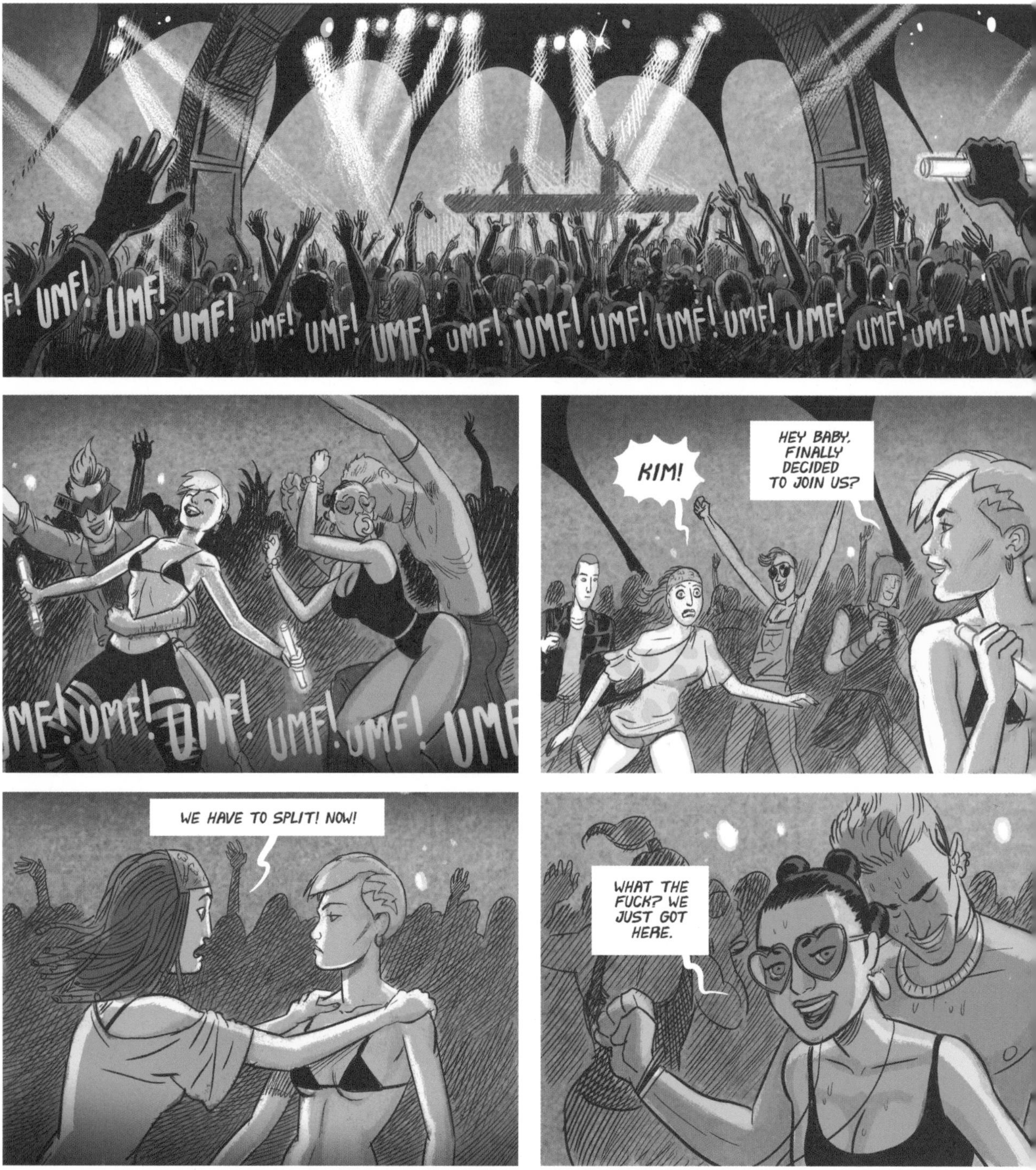

F! UMF! UMF! UMF! UMF! UMF! UMF! UMF! UMF! UMF! UMF! UMF! UMF! UMF! UMF! UMF
MF! UMF! UMF! UMF! UMF! UMF
KIM!
HEY BABY, FINALLY DECIDED TO JOIN US?
WE HAVE TO SPLIT! NOW!
WHAT THE FUCK? WE JUST GOT HERE.

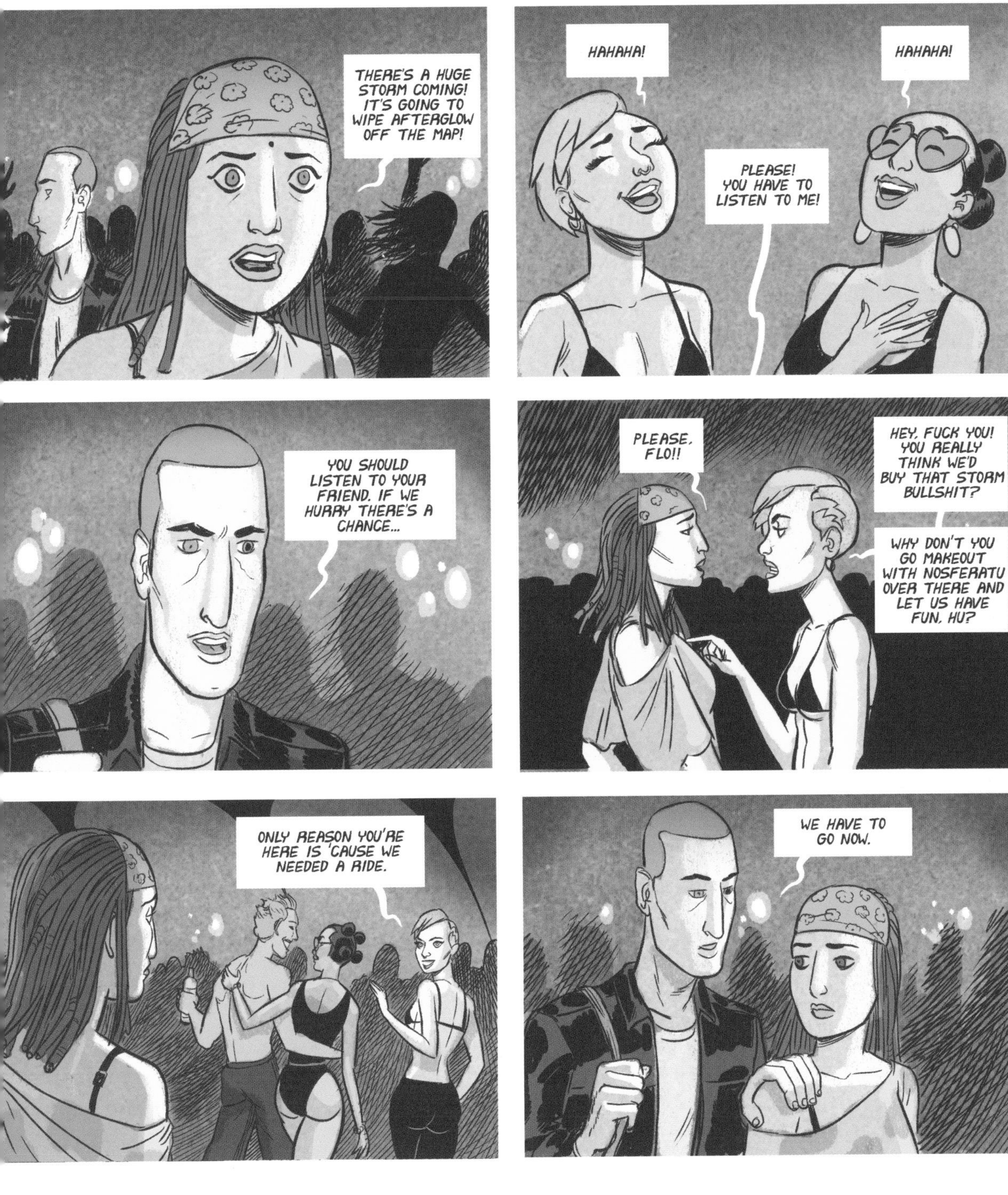
THERE'S A HUGE STORM COMING! IT'S GOING TO WIPE AFTERGLOW OFF THE MAP!
HAHAHA!
HAHAHA!
PLEASE! YOU HAVE TO LISTEN TO ME!
YOU SHOULD LISTEN TO YOUR FRIEND. IF WE HURRY THERE'S A CHANCE...
PLEASE, FLO!!
HEY, FUCK YOU! YOU REALLY THINK WE'D BUY THAT STORM BULLSHIT?
WHY DON'T YOU GO MAKEOUT WITH NOSFERATU OVER THERE AND LET US HAVE FUN, HU?
ONLY REASON YOU'RE HERE IS 'CAUSE WE NEEDED A RIDE.
WE HAVE TO GO NOW.

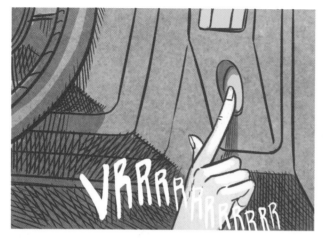

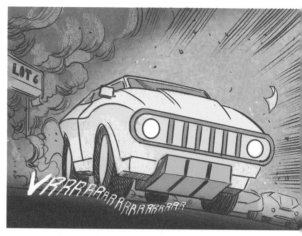

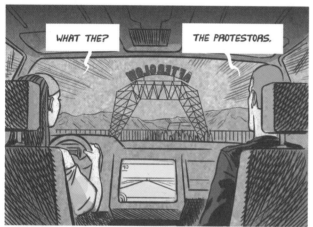

VRRRRRRRRRRRR
LOT 6
VRRRRRRRRRRRRRRRRRRR
WHAT THE?
THE PROTESTORS.
NO ONE'S GETTING OUT!
YOU'RE STUCK WITH US NOW, ASSHOLES!
YOU NEED TO BACK UP, THEN DRIVE THROUGH THE FENCE.
WHAT?
DO IT.
THIS TANK SHOULD MAKE IT THROUGH.

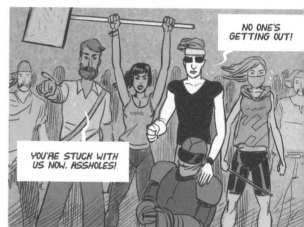

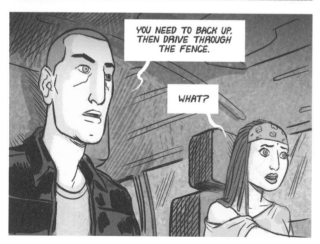

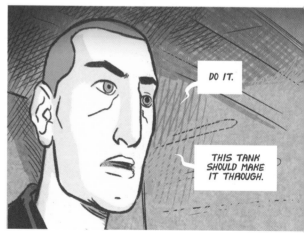

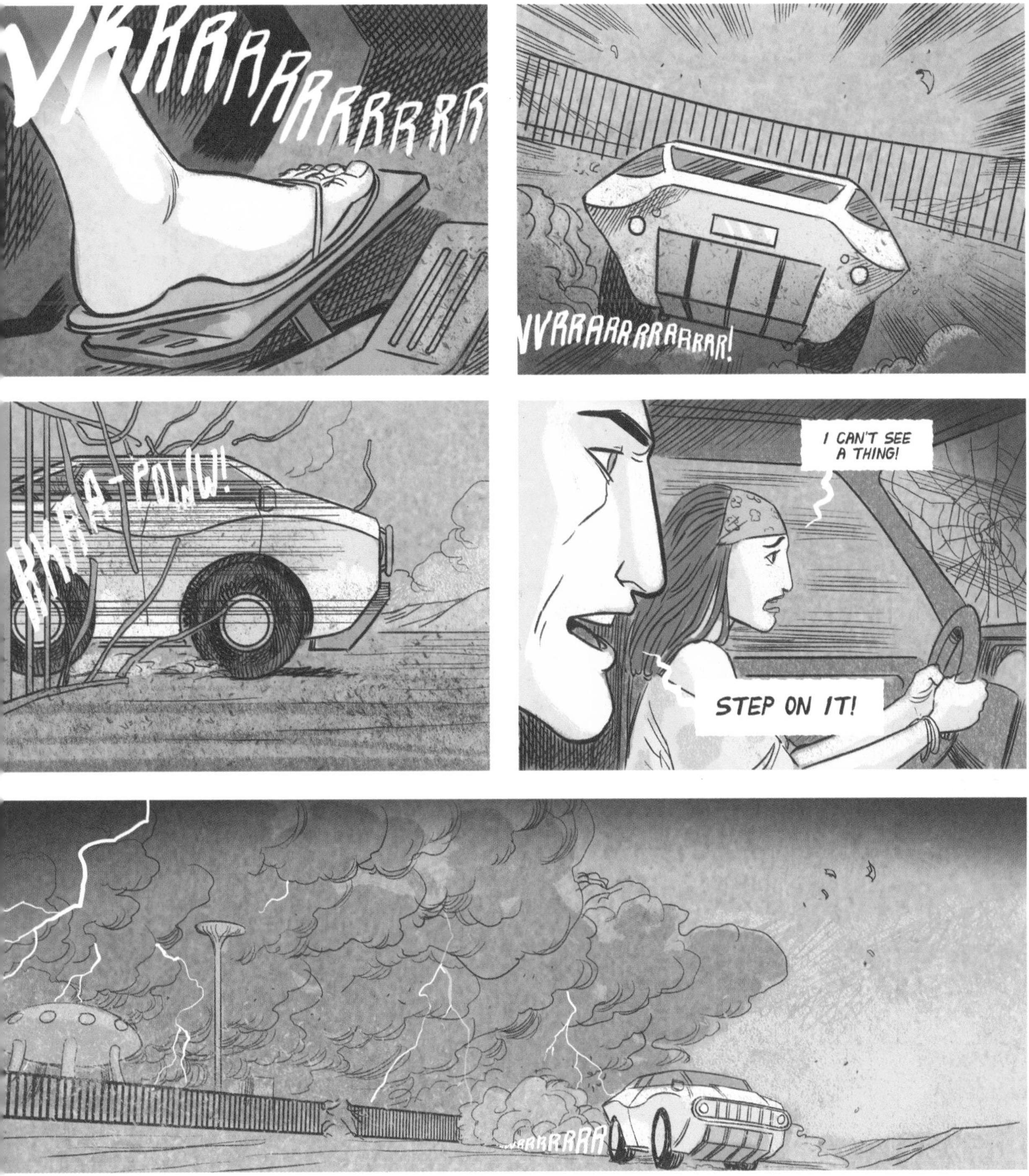

VKRRRRRRRRRRR
VVRRAARRRRRRRR!
RKRA-POWW!
I CAN'T SEE A THING!
STEP ON IT!
VRRRRRRRRR

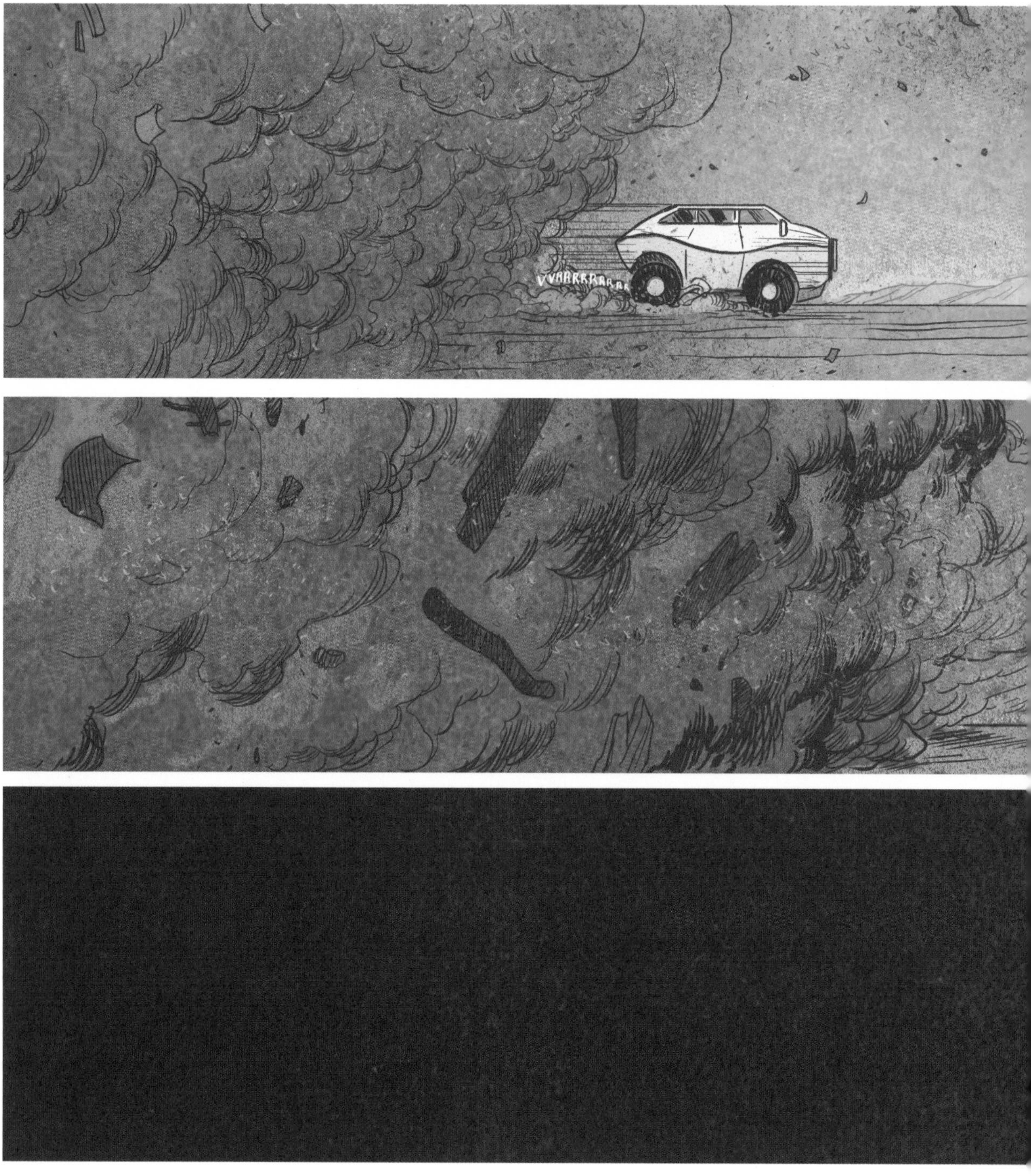
VVRRRRRRRRRR

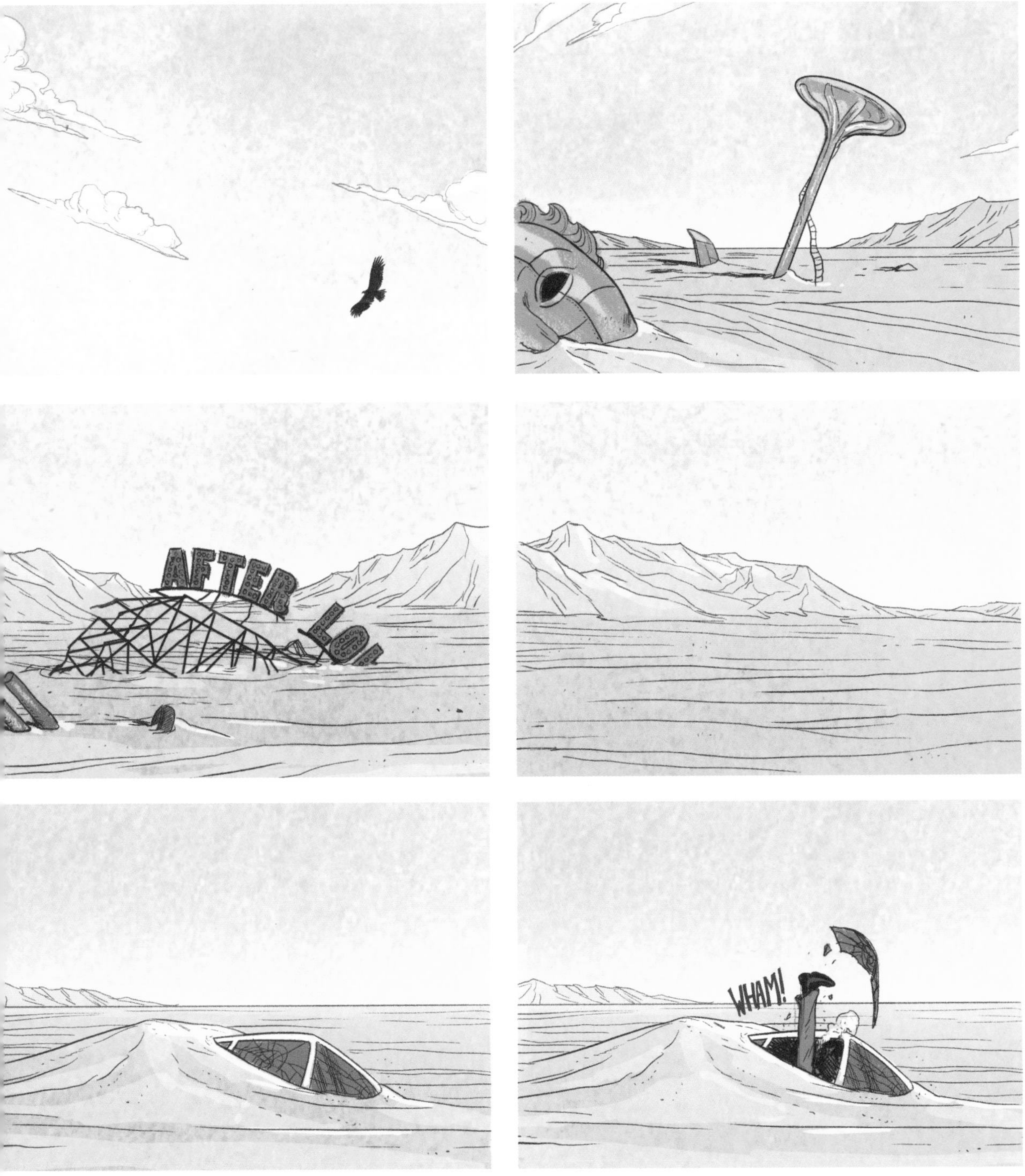
AFTER
WHAM!

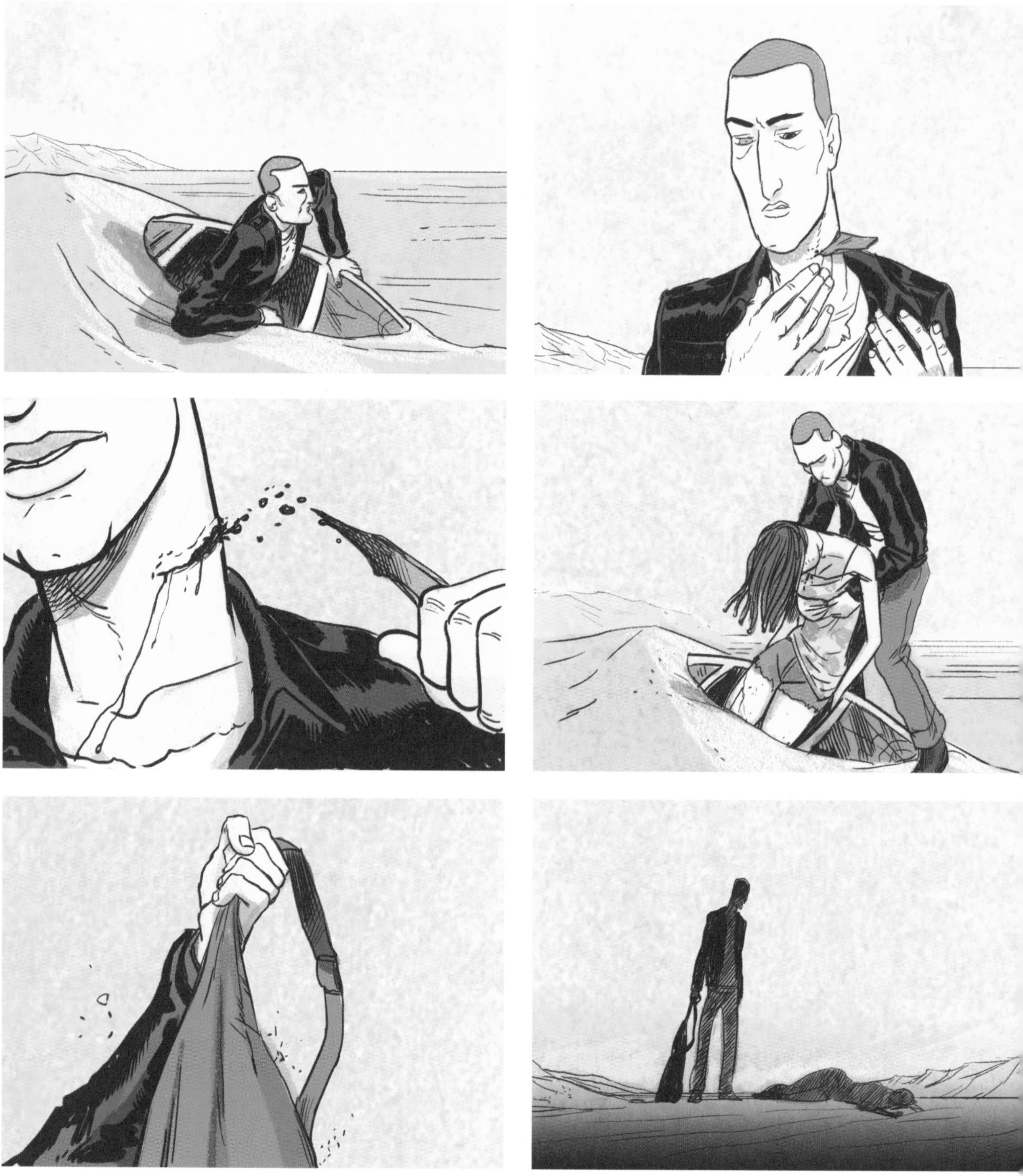

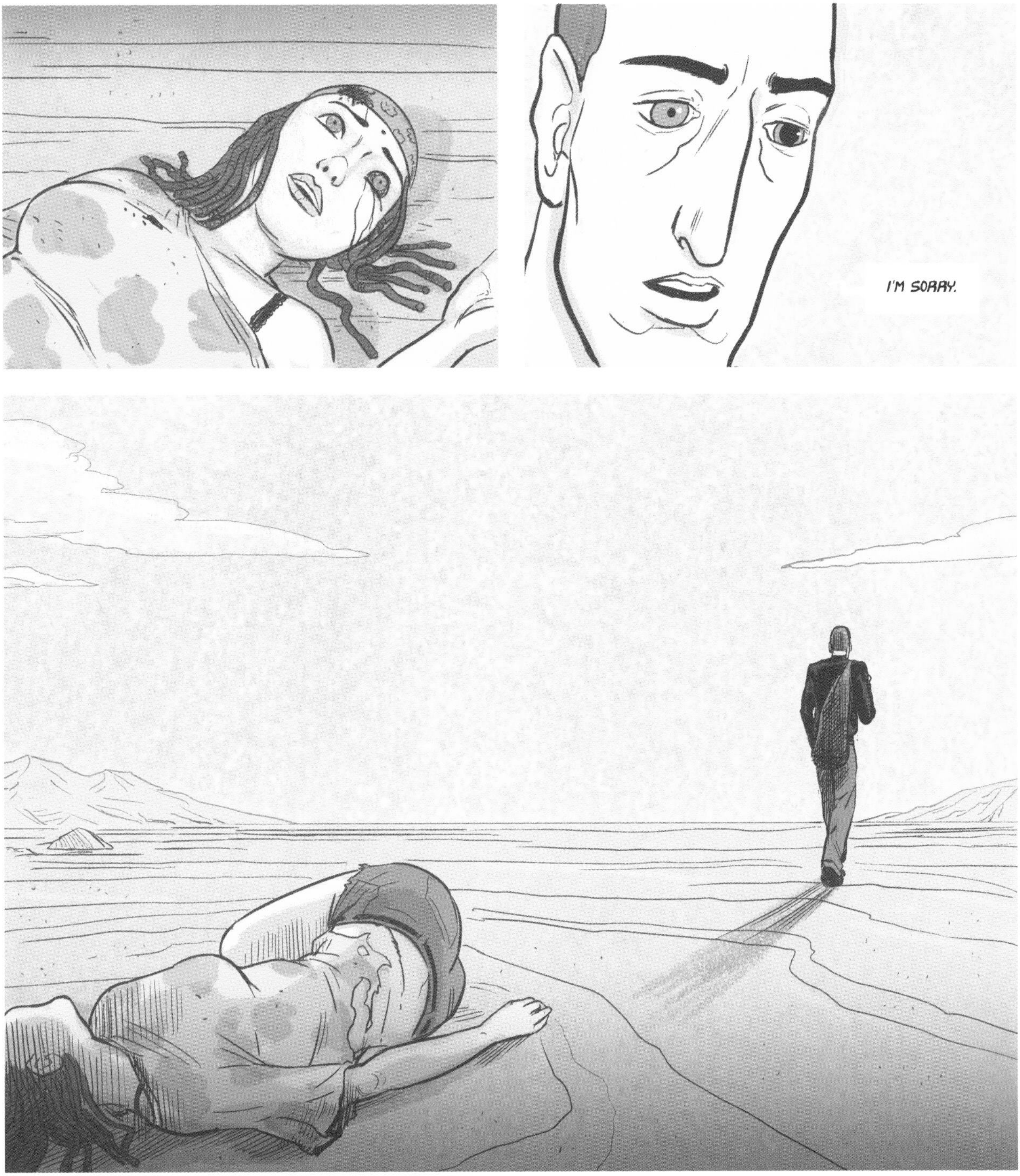
I'M SORRY.

CHAPTER 3
ROUND THE BEND

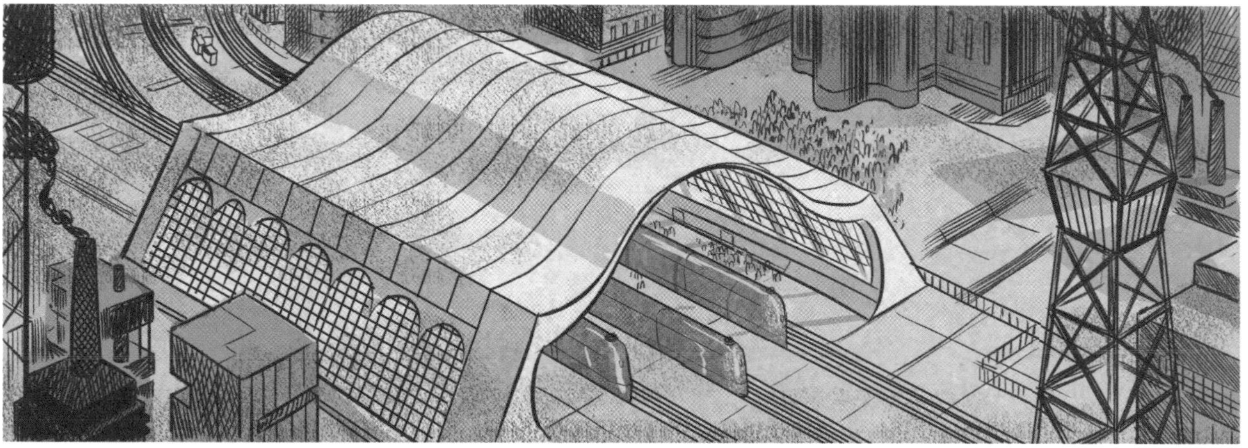

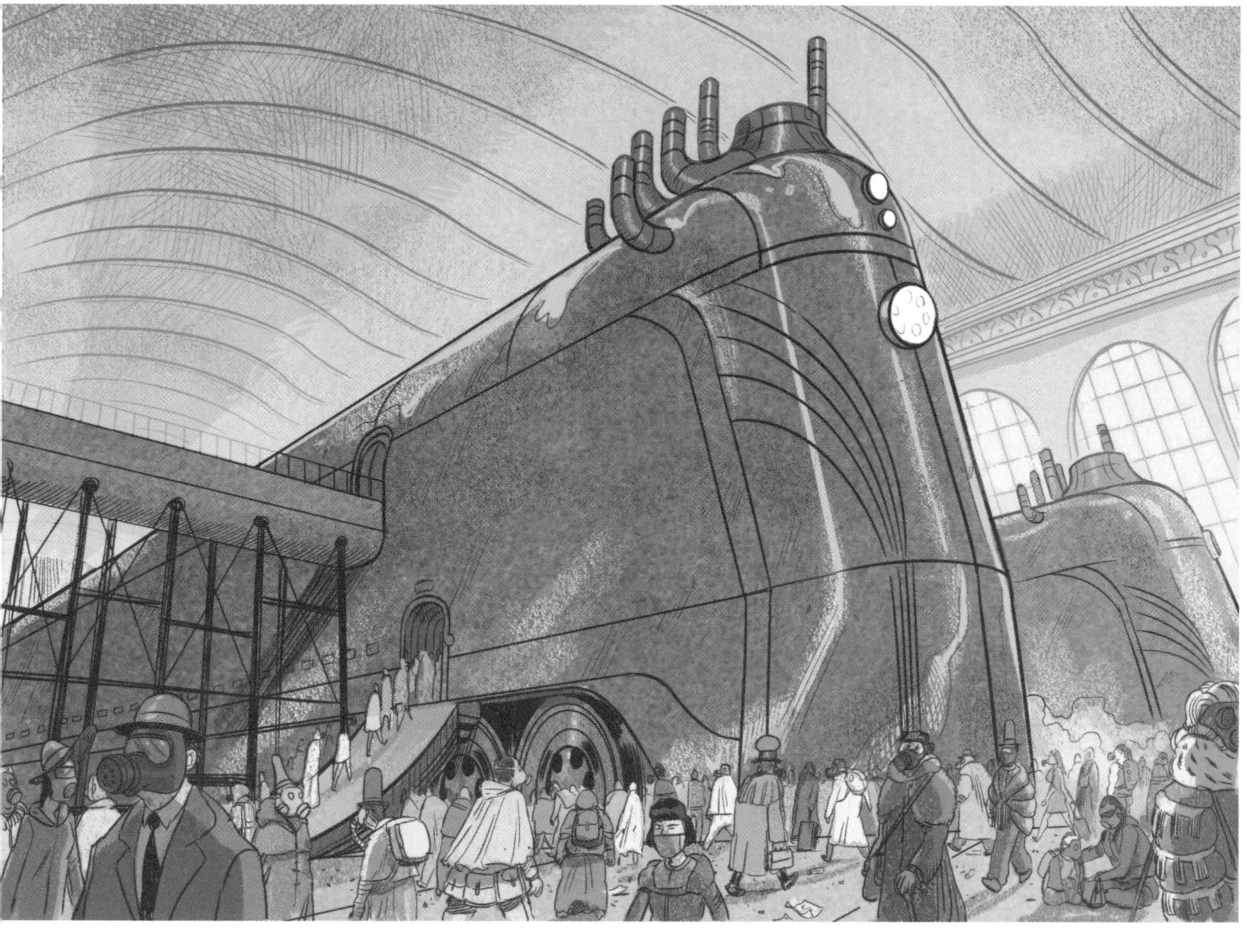

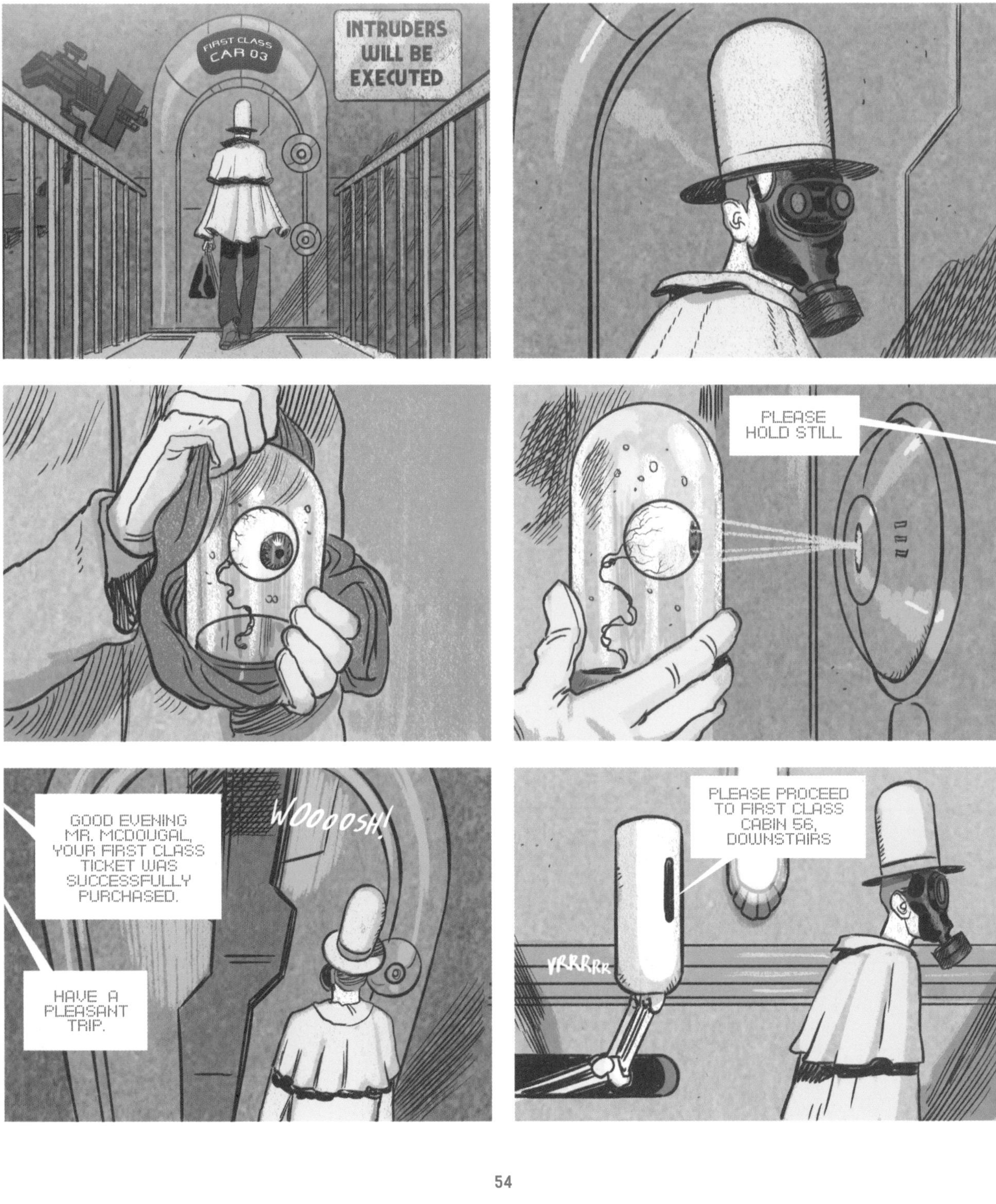
FIRST CLASS
CAR 03
INTRUDERS WILL BE EXECUTED
PLEASE HOLD STILL
GOOD EVENING MR. MCDOUGAL, YOUR FIRST CLASS TICKET WAS SUCCESSFULLY PURCHASED.
HAVE A PLEASANT TRIP.
WOOOOSH!
PLEASE PROCEED TO FIRST CLASS CABIN 56, DOWNSTAIRS
VRRRRR

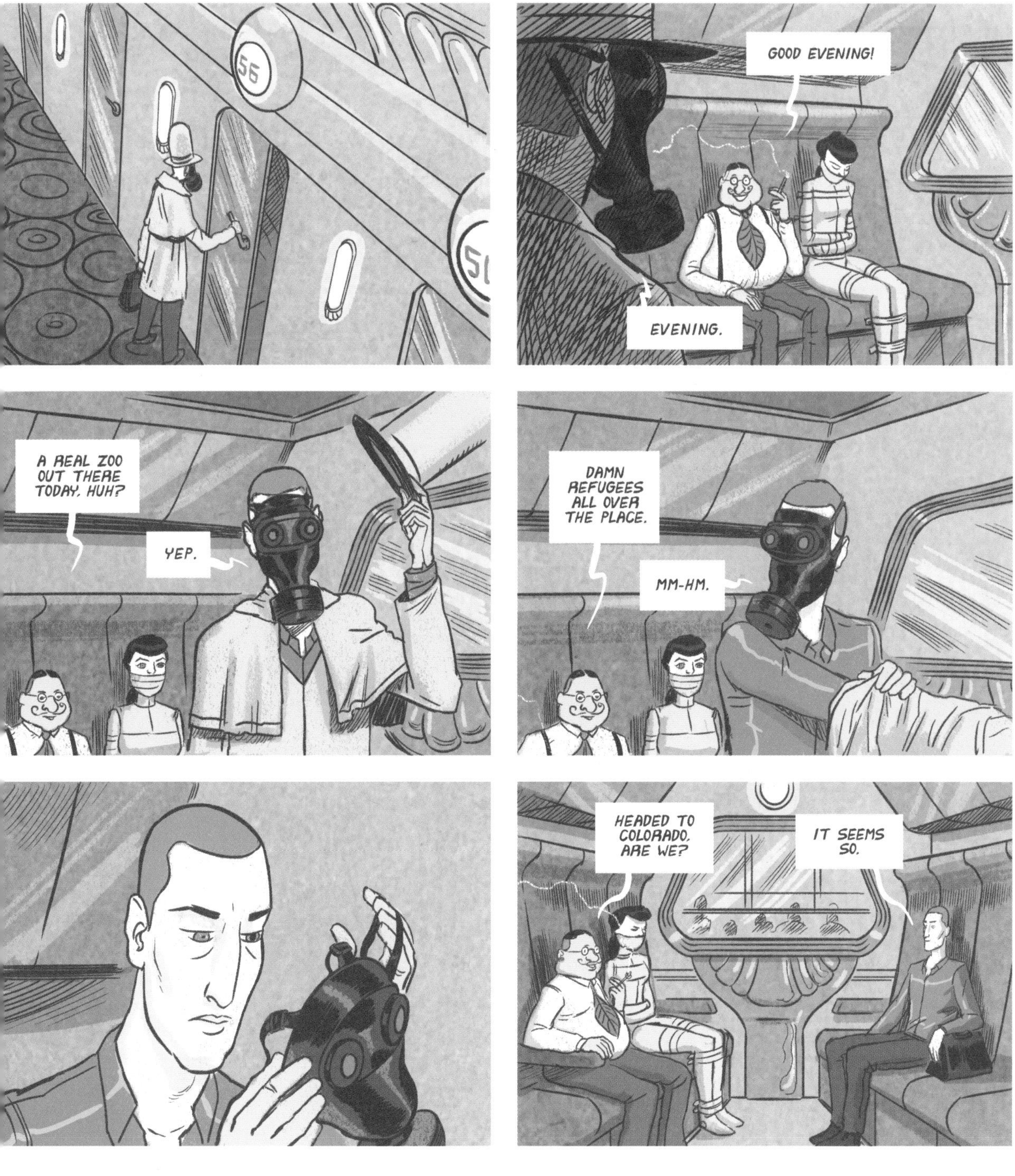
56
GOOD EVENING!
EVENING.
A REAL ZOO OUT THERE TODAY, HUH?
YEP.
DAMN REFUGEES ALL OVER THE PLACE.
MM-HM.
HEADED TO COLORADO, ARE WE?
IT SEEMS SO.

CAPITAL!
YOU'LL BE WITH US THE WHOLE WAY THEN!
LUCKY ME.
I'M PATRICK, AND THIS HERE IS MADELINE.
SHE WOULD SAY HELLO IF SHE COULD. HAHA. AND YOU ARE?
EHM... MR. MCDOUGAL.
PLEASED TO MEET YOU.
LIKEWISE.
THUMP
PLEASE, YOU **HAVE** TO LET ME IN, MY FAMILY **NEEDS** ME!
I'VE BEEN STUCK HERE FOR MONTHS! PLEASE!

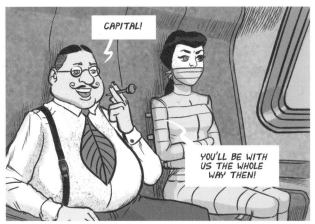

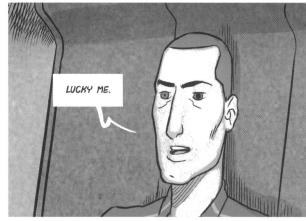

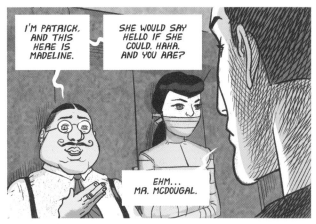

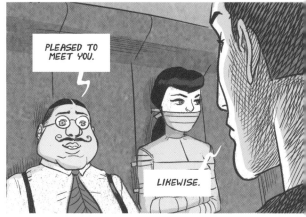

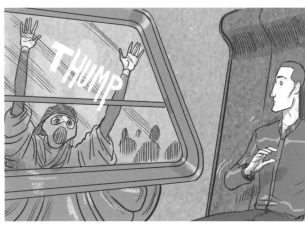

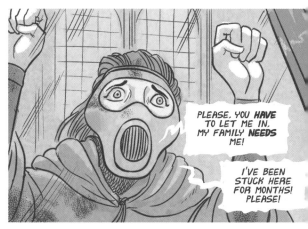

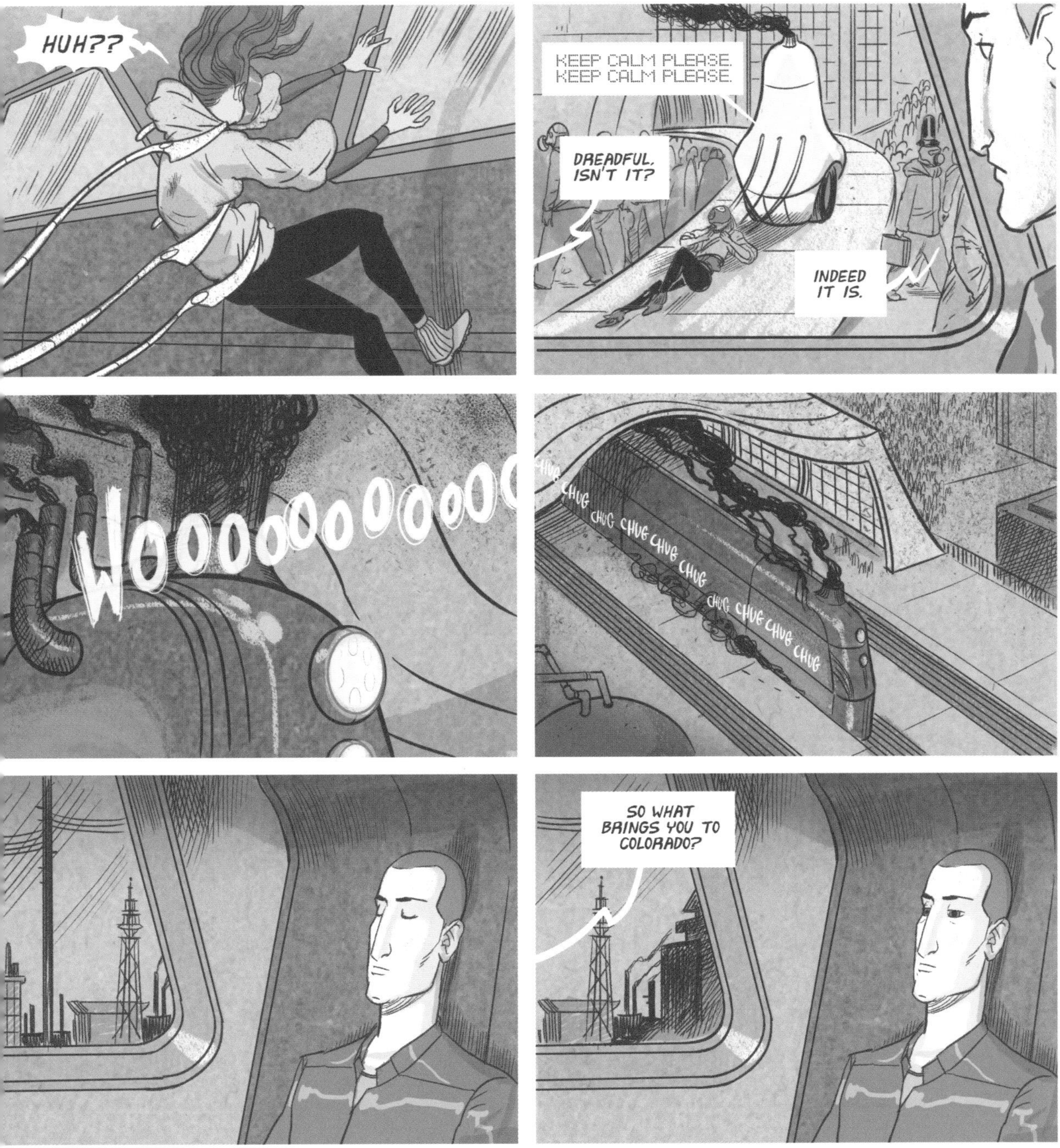
HUH??
KEEP CALM PLEASE.
KEEP CALM PLEASE.
DREADFUL, ISN'T IT?
INDEED IT IS.
WOOOOOOOOOOO
CHUG CHUG CHUG CHUG CHUG CHUG CHUG CHUG CHUG CHUG CHUG
SO WHAT BRINGS YOU TO COLORADO?

BUSINESS.

WHAT KIND. IF YOU DON'T MIND ME ASKING?

I'M... AN ANTIQUE SALESMAN.

OH! THAT'S FASCINATING. WHAT KIND OF ANTIQUES?

ALL SORTS REALLY.

DO YOU HAVE ANYTHING ON YOU?

I DO.

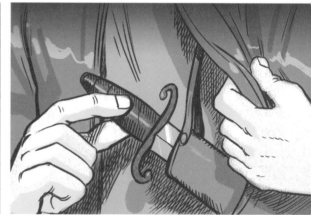

BEAUTIFUL! WHAT IS IT?

A DAGGER.

YES, YES! I KNOW THAT! WHAT PERIOD?

COLONIAL TIMES.

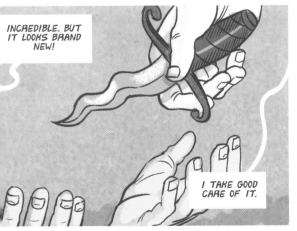

INCREDIBLE, BUT IT LOOKS BRAND NEW!

I TAKE GOOD CARE OF IT.

WELL, I ASSUME YOU'VE GUESSED WHAT BUSINESS I'M IN.

NOT A CLUE.

I'M A PSYCHOTHERAPIST. AND MADELINE HERE IS MY PATIENT.

I SEE.

SHE'S QUITE DISTURBED. SUFFERS FROM DELUSIONS AND SCHIZOPHRENIA OF THE WORST KIND.

HMM...

I'M ACCOMPANYING HER TO THE MORNINGSIDE INSTITUTE OVER AT BOULDER. THEY HAVE A NEW, REVOLUTIONARY TREATMENT THERE.

...FOR LUNACY?

YES! THEY ARE BRINGING BACK ELECTRO-SHOCK THERAPY. I KNOW, I KNOW. IT SOUNDS SO BARBARIC, BUT IT'S SHOWING A GREAT DEAL OF PROMISE!

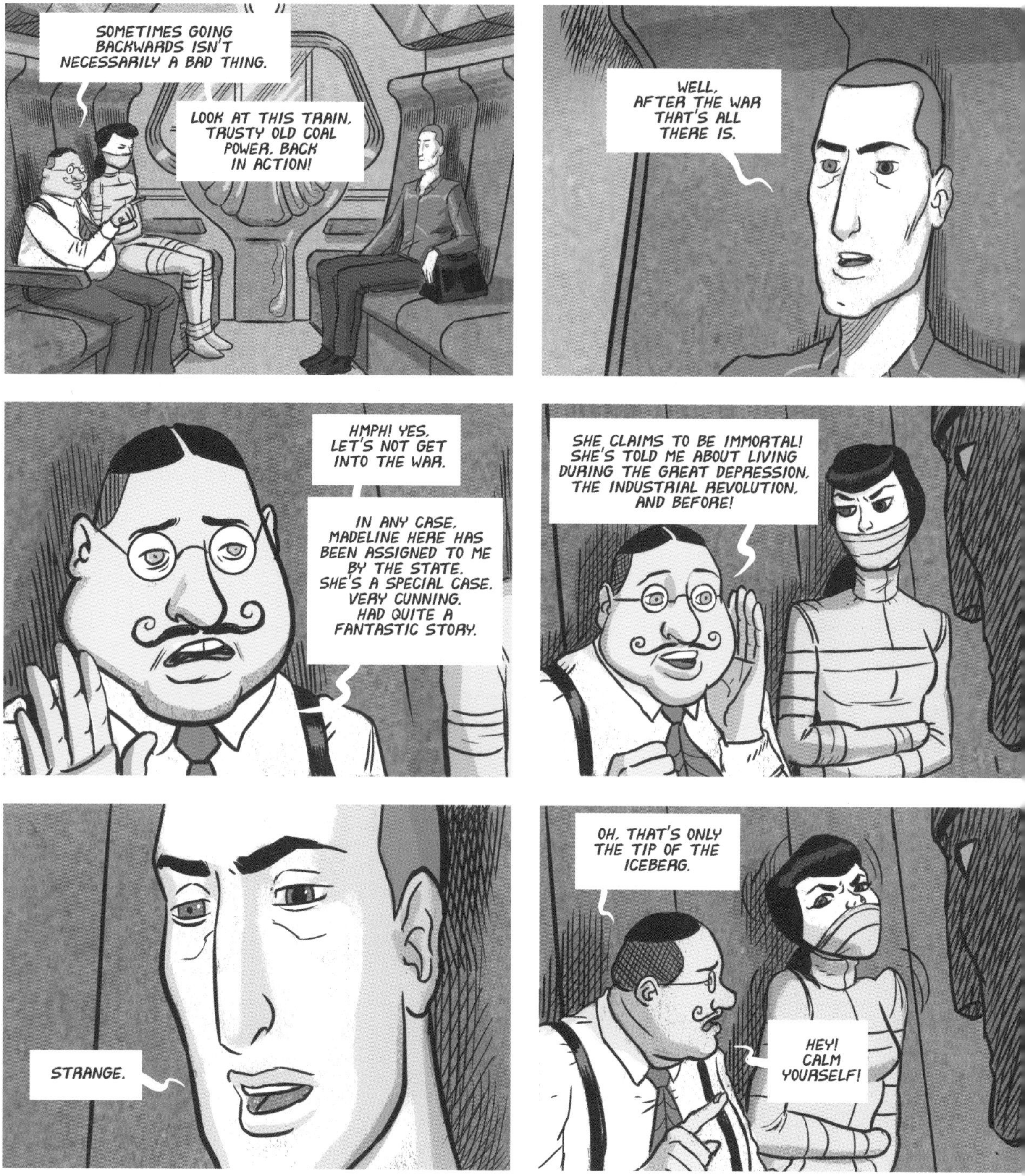
SOMETIMES GOING BACKWARDS ISN'T NECESSARILY A BAD THING.
LOOK AT THIS TRAIN. TRUSTY OLD COAL POWER. BACK IN ACTION!
WELL, AFTER THE WAR THAT'S ALL THERE IS.
HMPH! YES, LET'S NOT GET INTO THE WAR.
IN ANY CASE, MADELINE HERE HAS BEEN ASSIGNED TO ME BY THE STATE. SHE'S A SPECIAL CASE. VERY CUNNING. HAD QUITE A FANTASTIC STORY.
SHE CLAIMS TO BE IMMORTAL! SHE'S TOLD ME ABOUT LIVING DURING THE GREAT DEPRESSION, THE INDUSTRIAL REVOLUTION, AND BEFORE!
STRANGE.
OH, THAT'S ONLY THE TIP OF THE ICEBERG.
HEY! CALM YOURSELF!

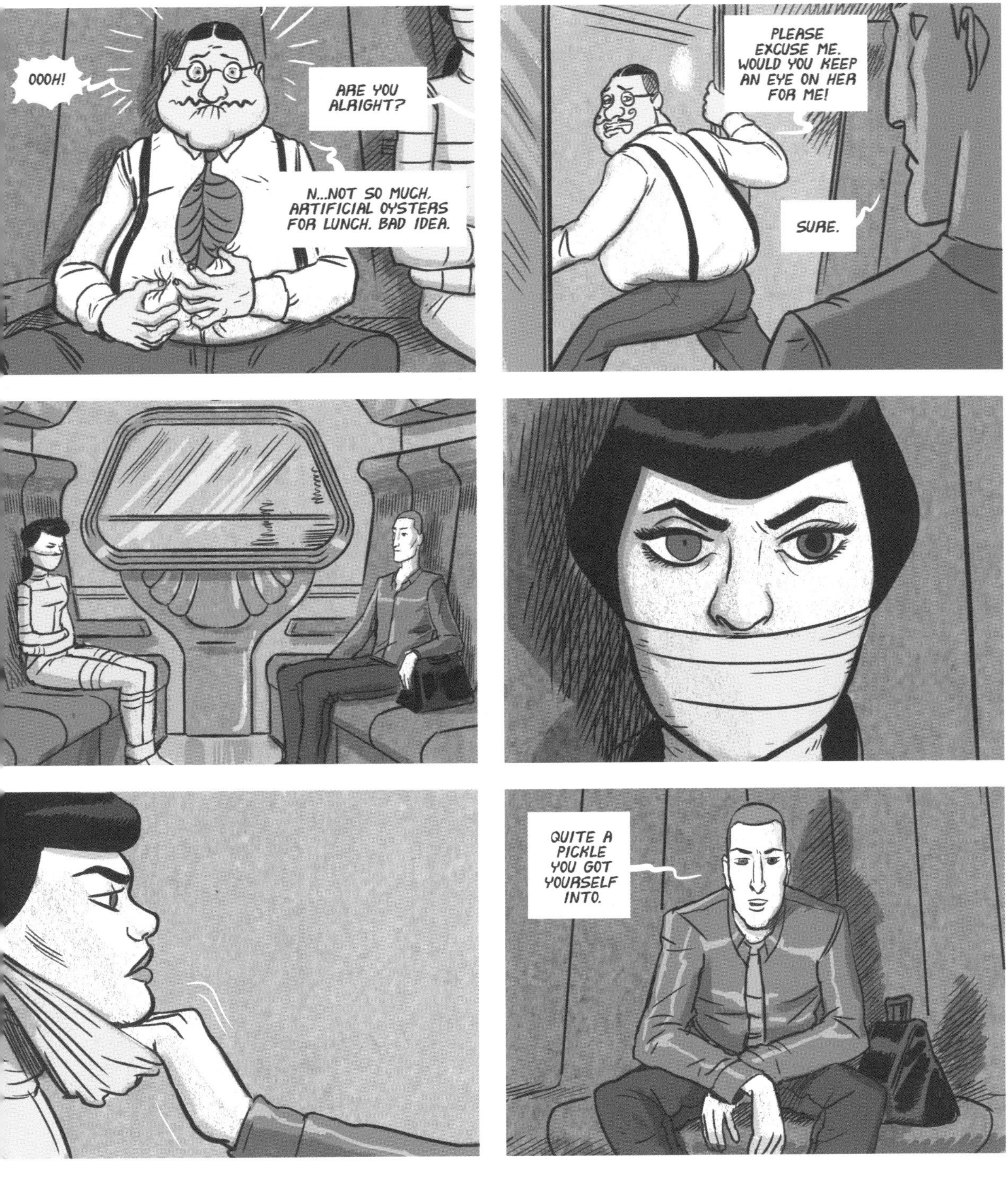
OOOH!
ARE YOU ALRIGHT?
N...NOT SO MUCH. ARTIFICIAL OYSTERS FOR LUNCH. BAD IDEA.
PLEASE EXCUSE ME. WOULD YOU KEEP AN EYE ON HER FOR ME!
SURE.
QUITE A PICKLE YOU GOT YOURSELF INTO.

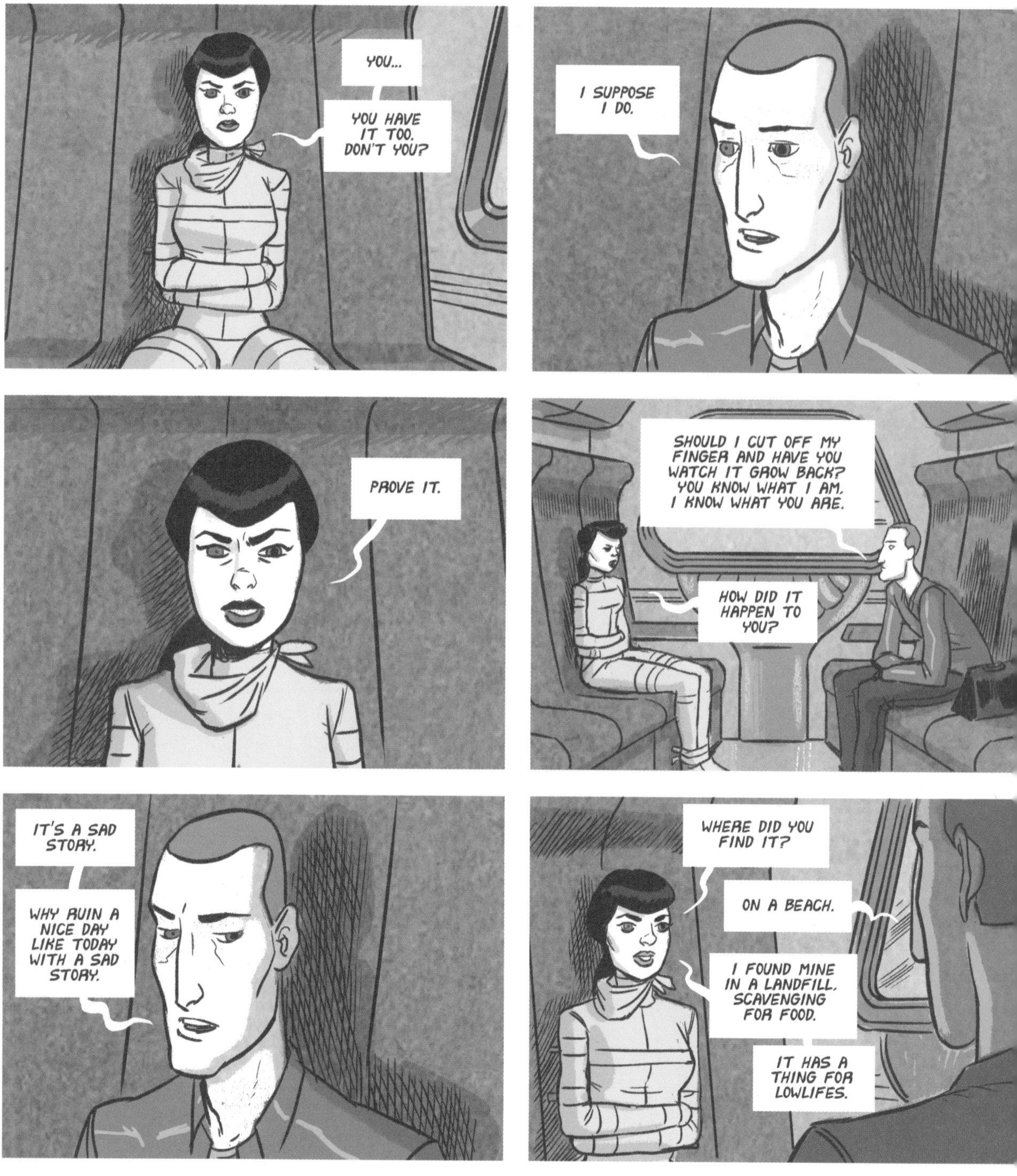
YOU...
YOU HAVE IT TOO. DON'T YOU?
I SUPPOSE I DO.
PROVE IT.
SHOULD I CUT OFF MY FINGER AND HAVE YOU WATCH IT GROW BACK? YOU KNOW WHAT I AM, I KNOW WHAT YOU ARE.
HOW DID IT HAPPEN TO YOU?
IT'S A SAD STORY.
WHY RUIN A NICE DAY LIKE TODAY WITH A SAD STORY.
WHERE DID YOU FIND IT?
ON A BEACH.
I FOUND MINE IN A LANDFILL, SCAVENGING FOR FOOD.
IT HAS A THING FOR LOWLIFES.

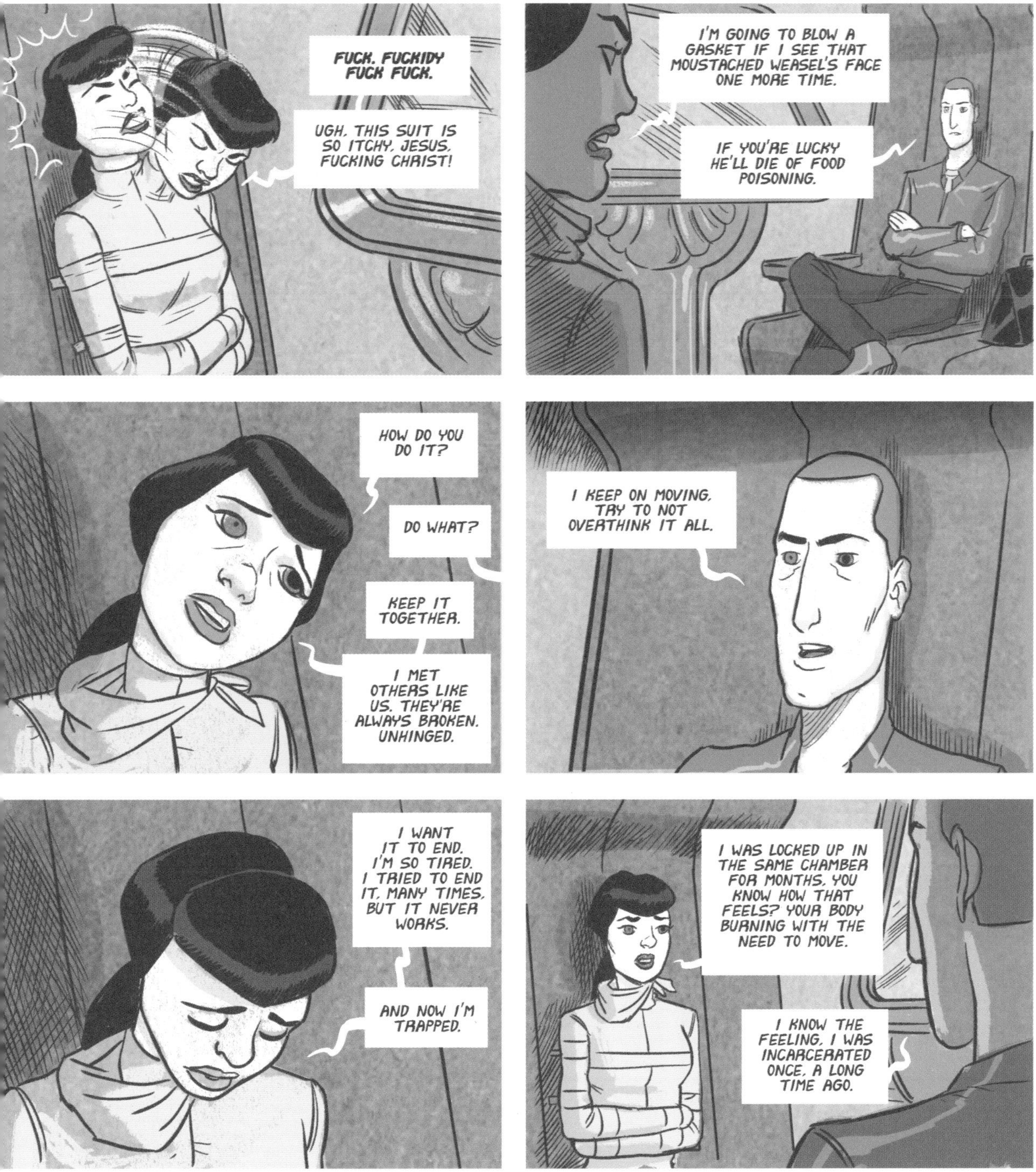
FUCK. FUCKIDY FUCK FUCK.
UGH. THIS SUIT IS SO ITCHY. JESUS. FUCKING CHRIST!
I'M GOING TO BLOW A GASKET IF I SEE THAT MOUSTACHED WEASEL'S FACE ONE MORE TIME.
IF YOU'RE LUCKY HE'LL DIE OF FOOD POISONING.
HOW DO YOU DO IT?
DO WHAT?
KEEP IT TOGETHER.
I MET OTHERS LIKE US. THEY'RE ALWAYS BROKEN. UNHINGED.
I KEEP ON MOVING, TRY TO NOT OVERTHINK IT ALL.
I WANT IT TO END. I'M SO TIRED. I TRIED TO END IT, MANY TIMES, BUT IT NEVER WORKS.
AND NOW I'M TRAPPED.
I WAS LOCKED UP IN THE SAME CHAMBER FOR MONTHS. YOU KNOW HOW THAT FEELS? YOUR BODY BURNING WITH THE NEED TO MOVE.
I KNOW THE FEELING. I WAS INCARCERATED ONCE, A LONG TIME AGO.

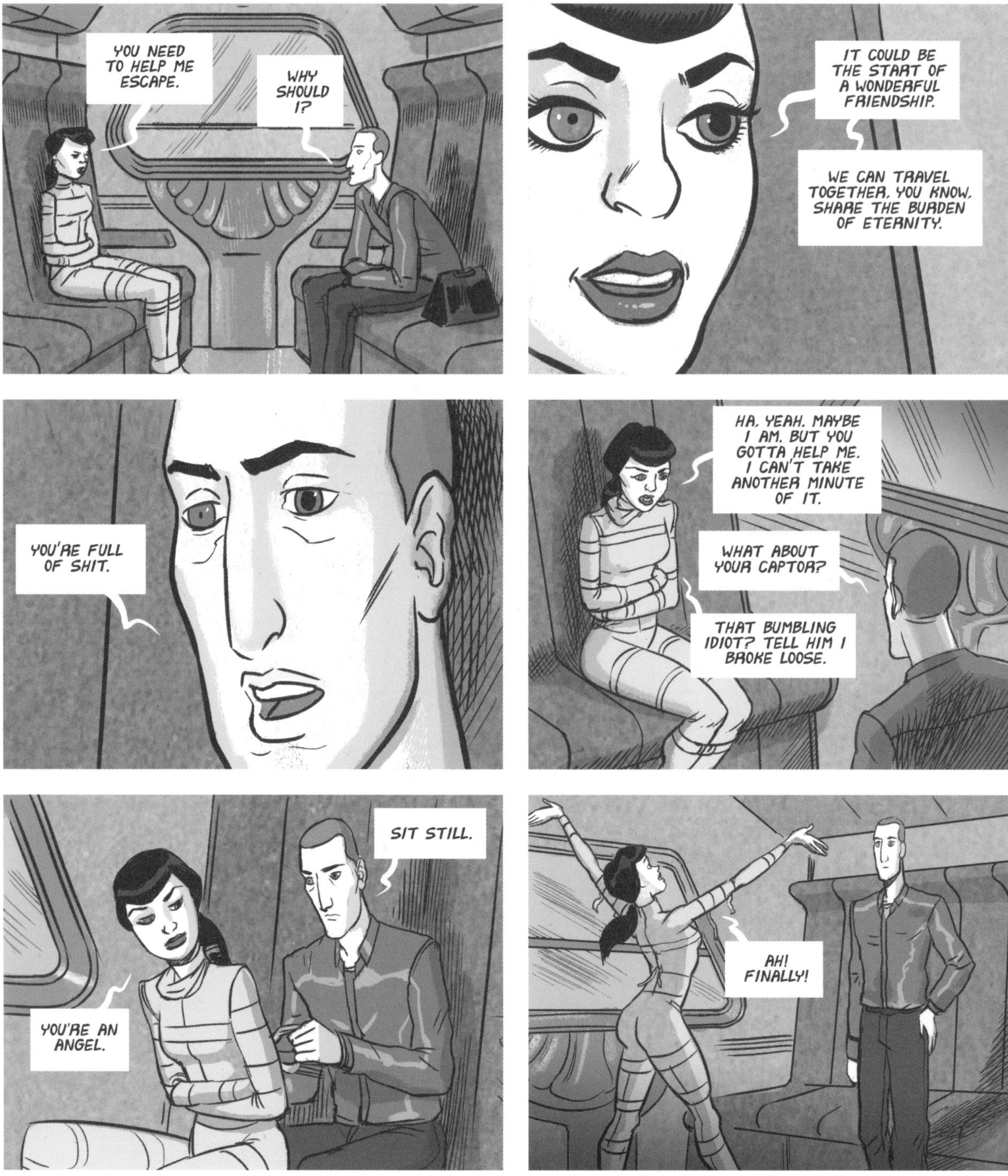
YOU NEED TO HELP ME ESCAPE.
WHY SHOULD I?
IT COULD BE THE START OF A WONDERFUL FRIENDSHIP.
WE CAN TRAVEL TOGETHER, YOU KNOW. SHARE THE BURDEN OF ETERNITY.
YOU'RE FULL OF SHIT.
HA, YEAH. MAYBE I AM. BUT YOU GOTTA HELP ME. I CAN'T TAKE ANOTHER MINUTE OF IT.
WHAT ABOUT YOUR CAPTOR?
THAT BUMBLING IDIOT? TELL HIM I BROKE LOOSE.
SIT STILL.
YOU'RE AN ANGEL.
AH! FINALLY!

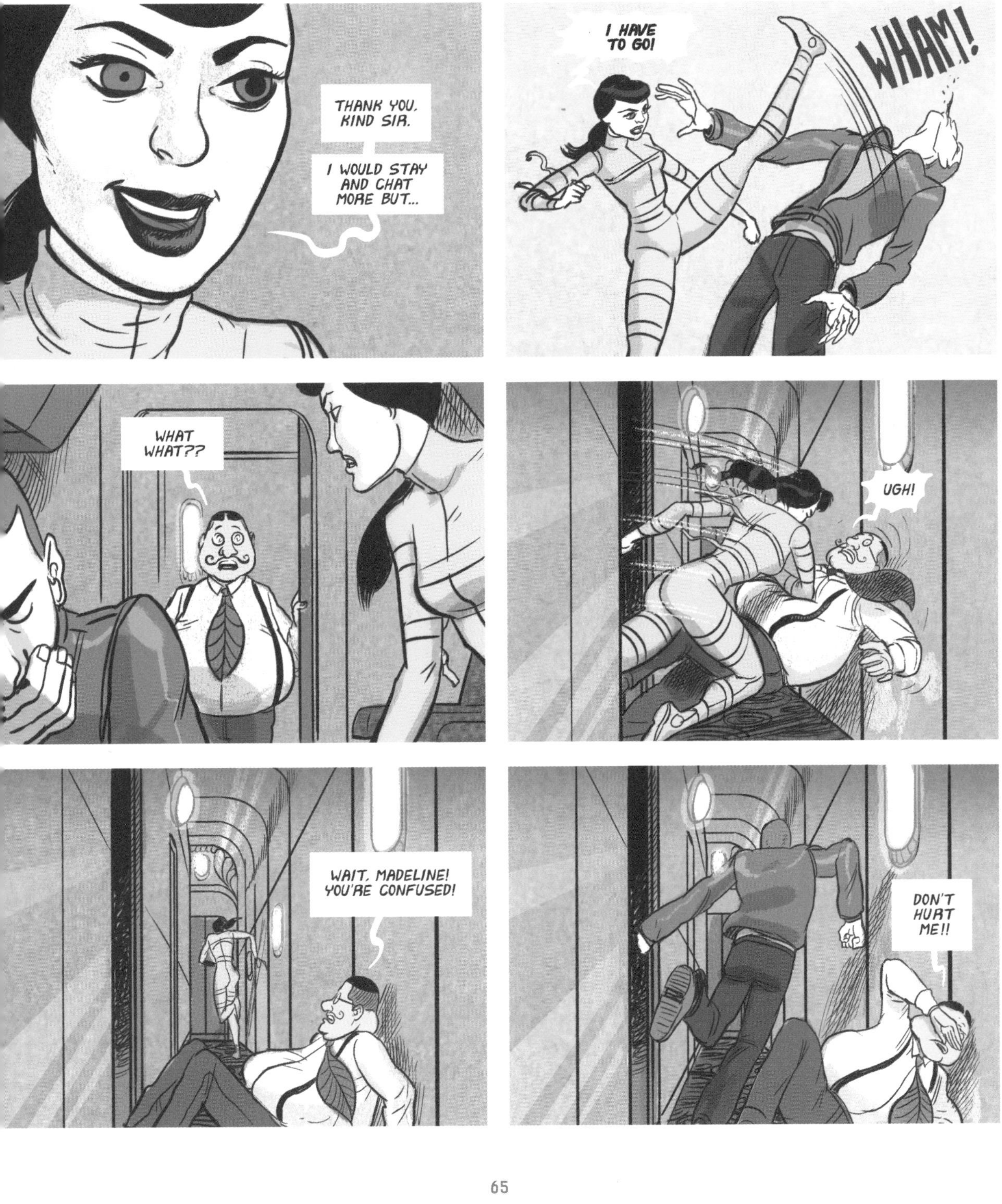
THANK YOU, KIND SIR.
I WOULD STAY AND CHAT MORE BUT...
I HAVE TO GO!
WHAM!
WHAT WHAT??
UGH!
WAIT, MADELINE! YOU'RE CONFUSED!
DON'T HURT ME!!

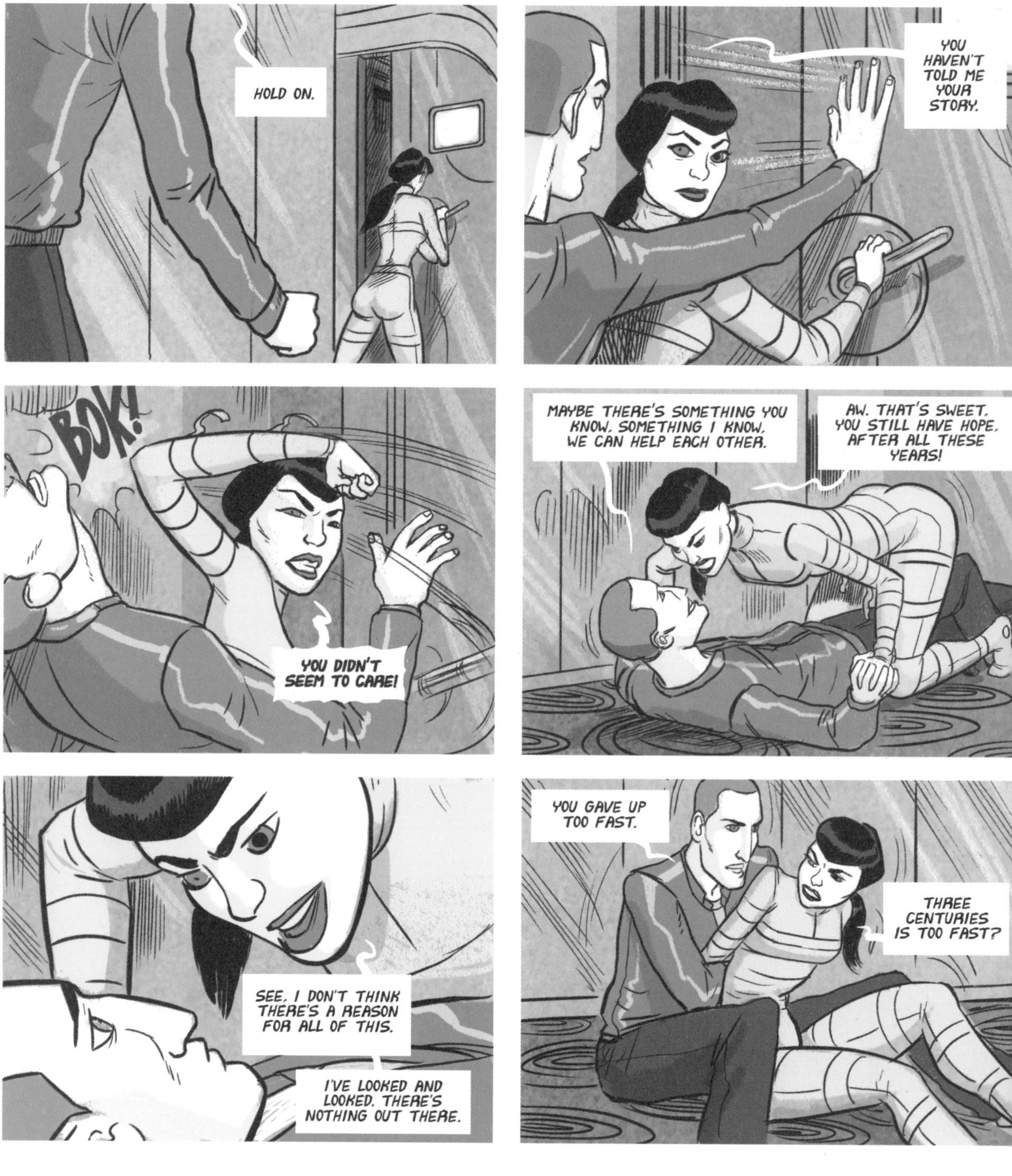
HOLD ON.
YOU HAVEN'T TOLD ME YOUR STORY.
BOK!
YOU DIDN'T SEEM TO CARE!
MAYBE THERE'S SOMETHING YOU KNOW, SOMETHING I KNOW, WE CAN HELP EACH OTHER.
AW. THAT'S SWEET. YOU STILL HAVE HOPE, AFTER ALL THESE YEARS!
SEE, I DON'T THINK THERE'S A REASON FOR ALL OF THIS.
I'VE LOOKED AND LOOKED. THERE'S NOTHING OUT THERE.
YOU GAVE UP TOO FAST.
THREE CENTURIES IS TOO FAST?

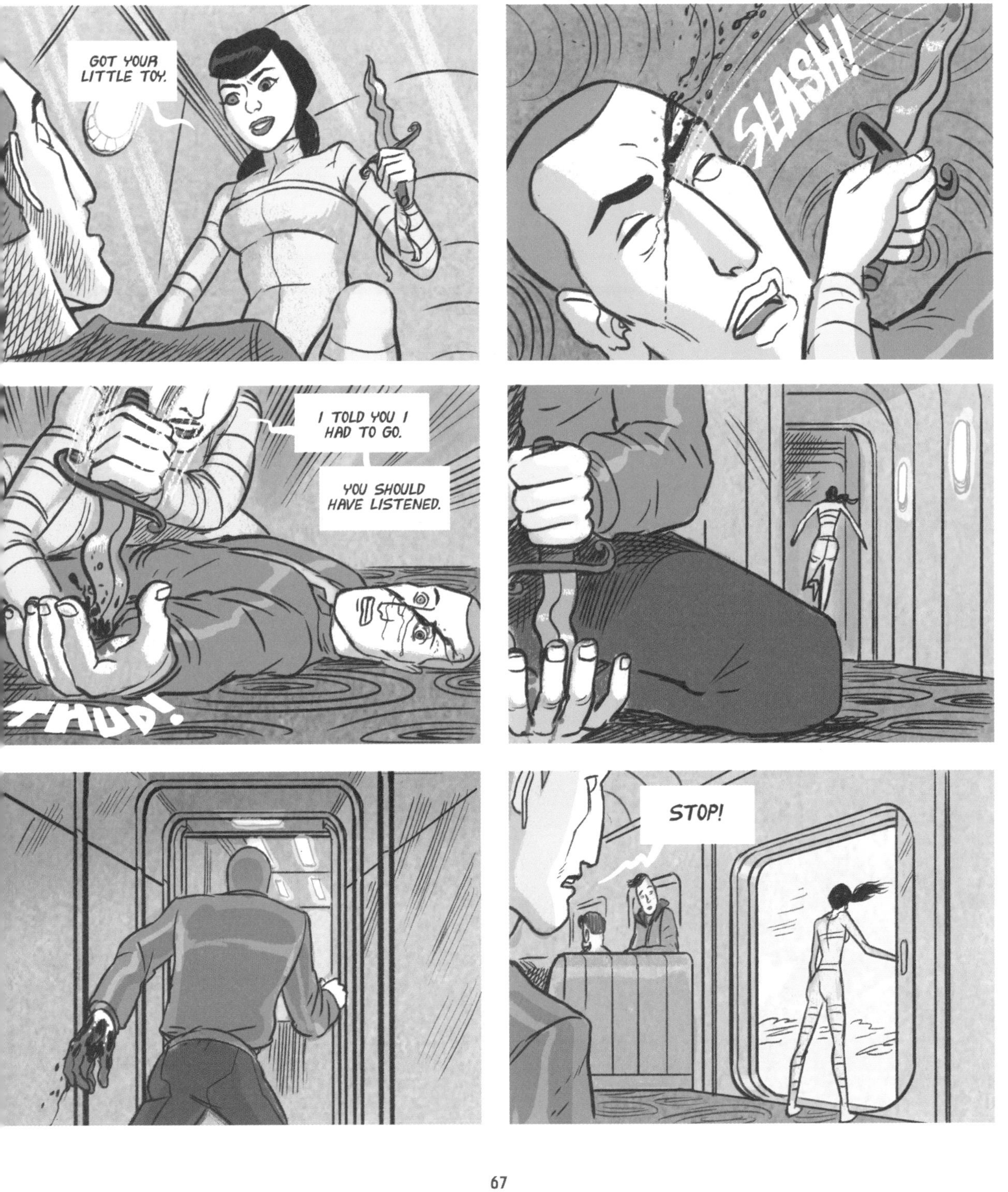
GOT YOUR LITTLE TOY.
SLASH!
I TOLD YOU I HAD TO GO.
YOU SHOULD HAVE LISTENED.
THUD!
STOP!

DON'T DO IT.
THERE ARE THINGS DOWN THERE THAT EVEN WE CAN'T SURVIVE.
I PRAY TO GOD I MEET THEM.
THE SOURCE WILL SHOW ITSELF. I KNOW IT. IT'S JUST A MATTER OF TIME.
TELL IT TO THE WIND.
DON'T...

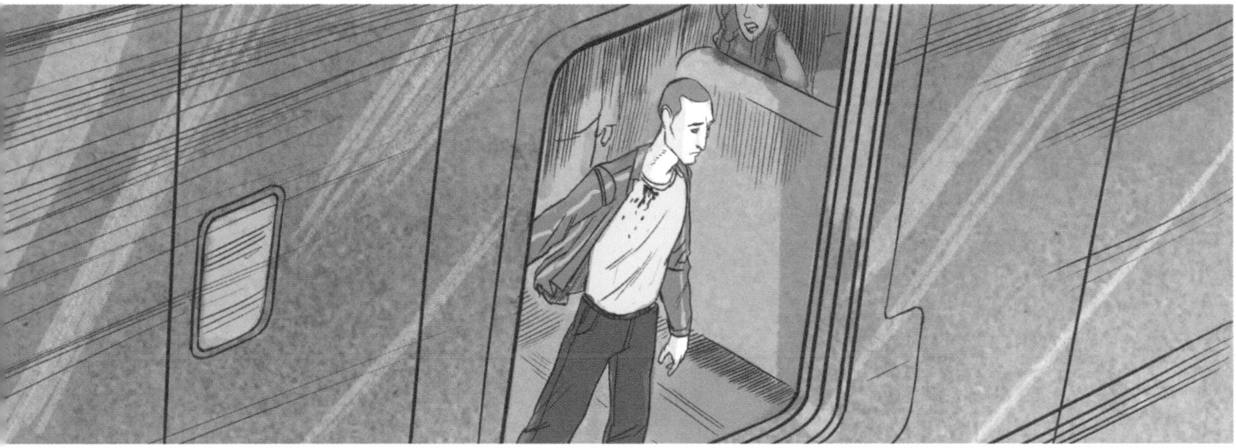

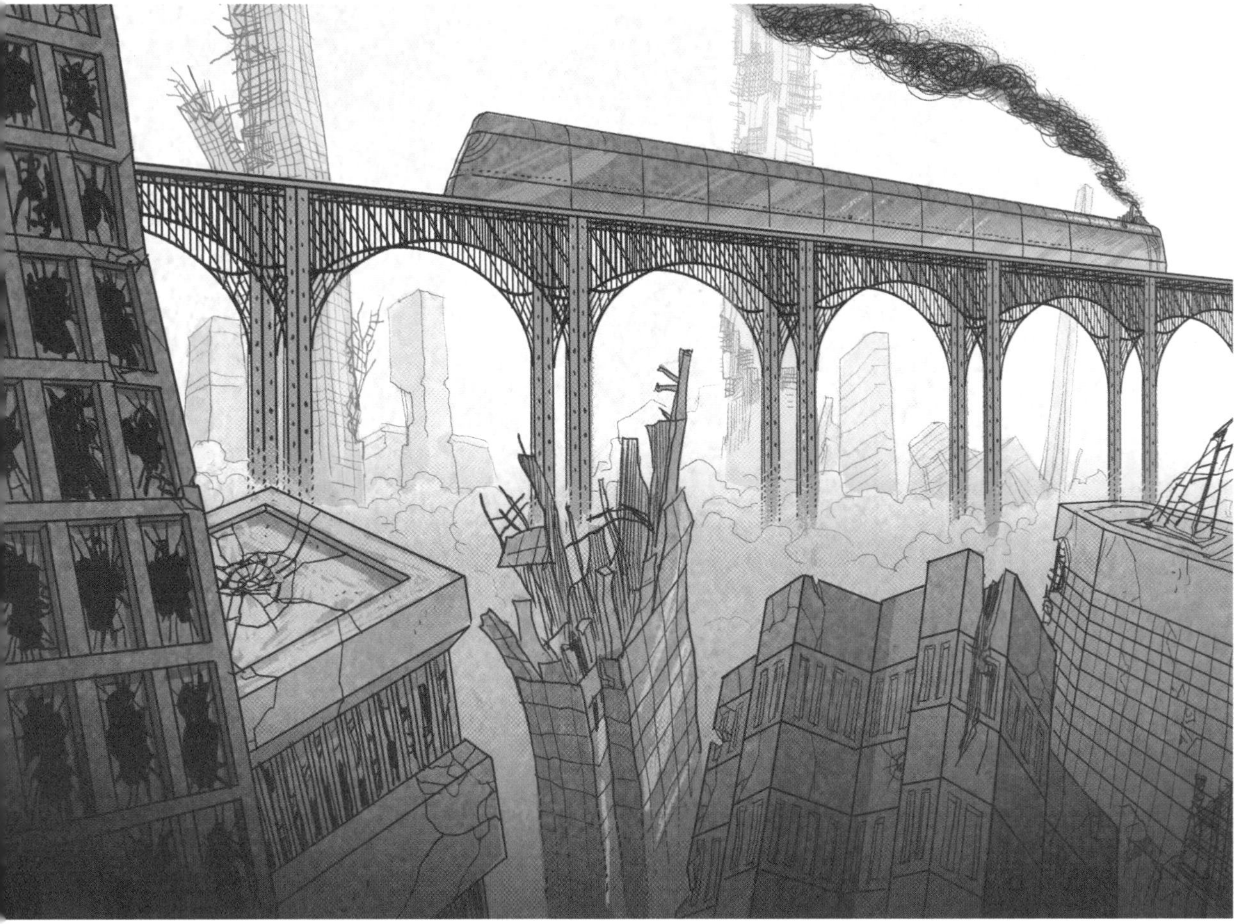

CHAPTER 4
SIZZLE

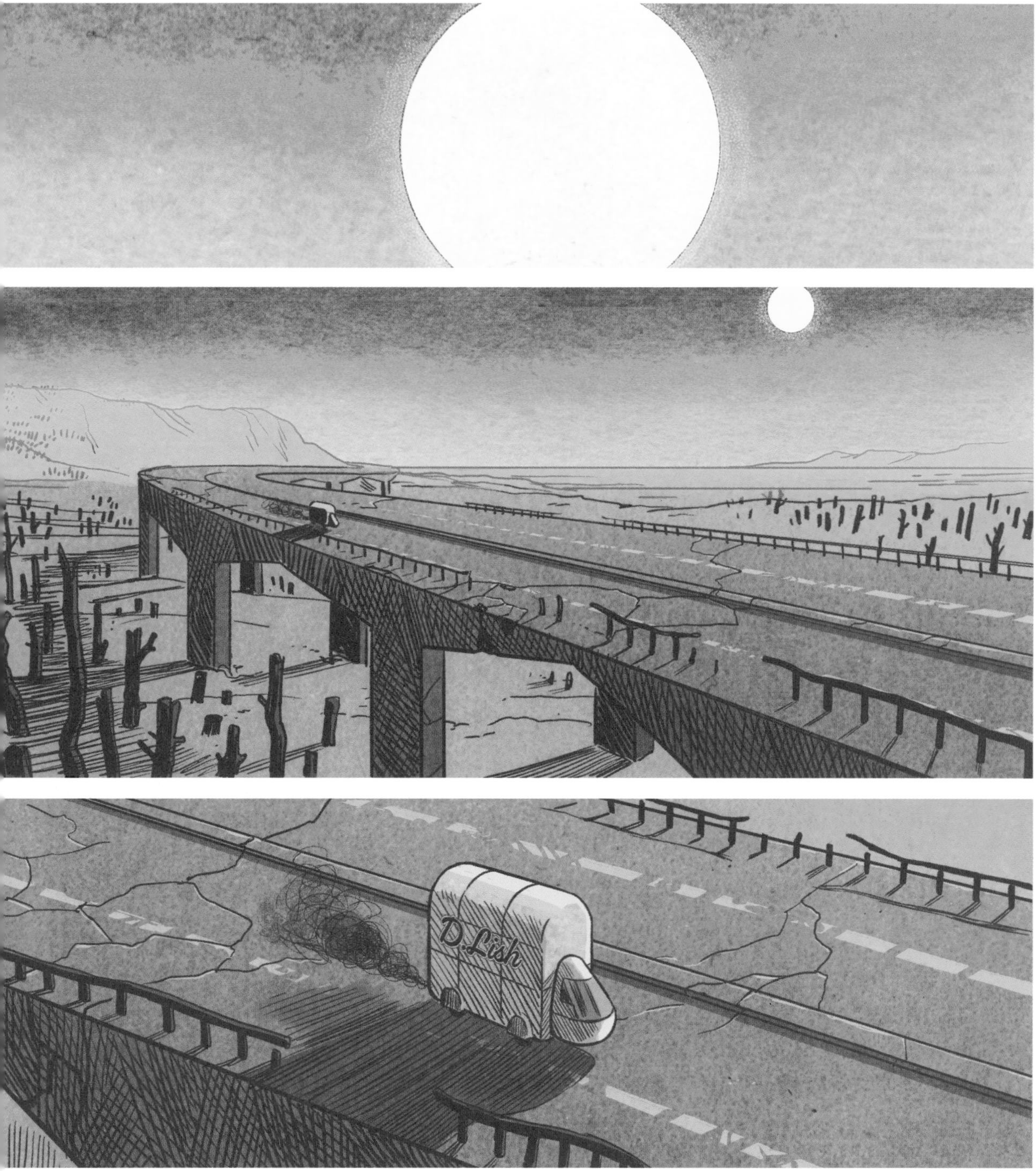
D.Lish

HELL...

SURE IS HOT TODAY!

SMACK!

IT AIN'T LYING. FINE SUMMER DAY!

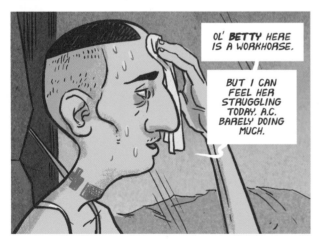

OL' **BETTY** HERE IS A WORKHORSE.

BUT I CAN FEEL HER STRUGGLING TODAY. A.C. BARELY DOING MUCH.

HECK, LOOK AT YA, HAVEN'T GOT A DROP OF SWEAT ON YA!

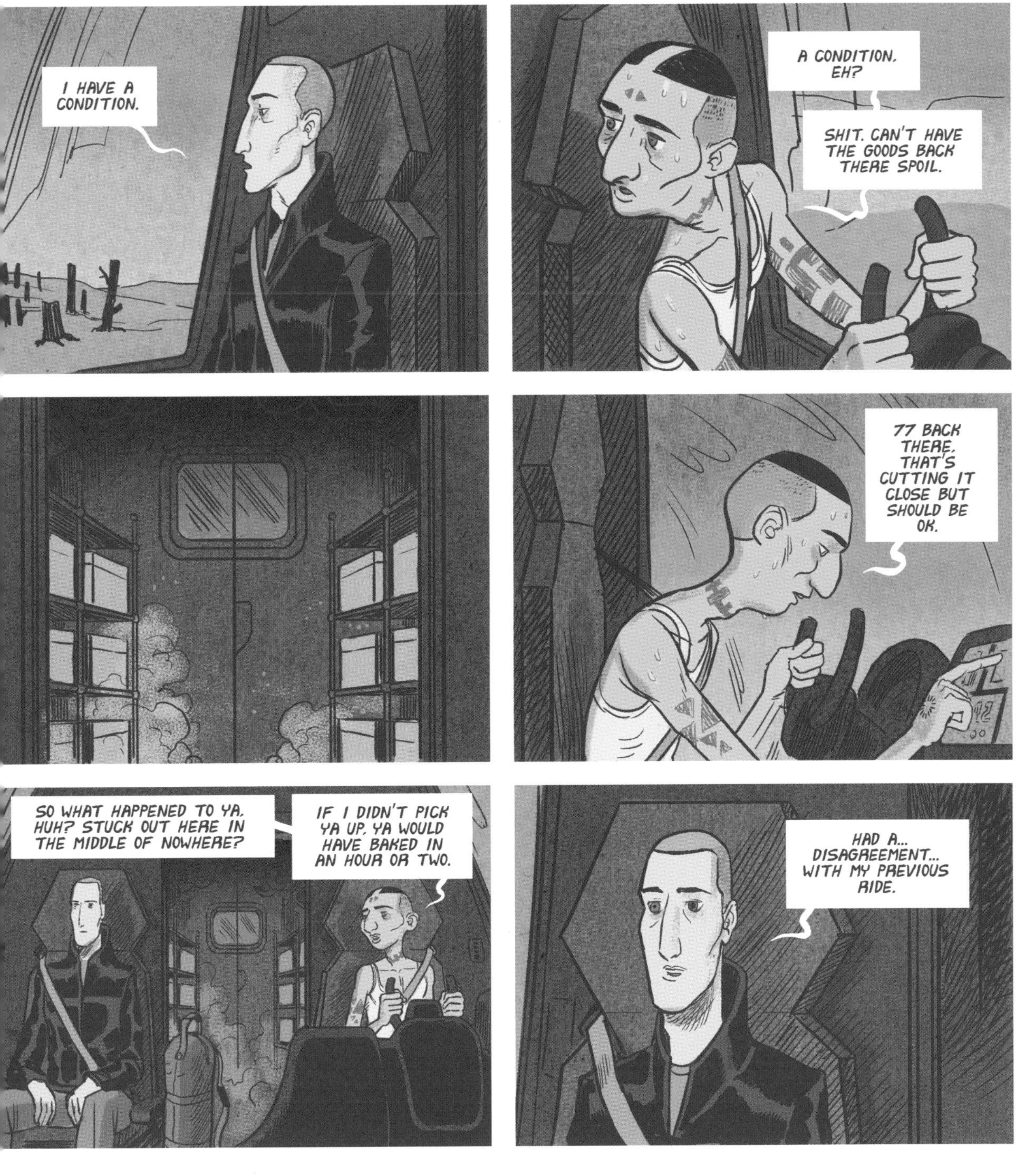
I HAVE A CONDITION.
A CONDITION, EH?
SHIT. CAN'T HAVE THE GOODS BACK THERE SPOIL.
77 BACK THERE, THAT'S CUTTING IT CLOSE BUT SHOULD BE OK.
SO WHAT HAPPENED TO YA, HUH? STUCK OUT HERE IN THE MIDDLE OF NOWHERE?
IF I DIDN'T PICK YA UP, YA WOULD HAVE BAKED IN AN HOUR OR TWO.
HAD A... DISAGREEMENT... WITH MY PREVIOUS RIDE.

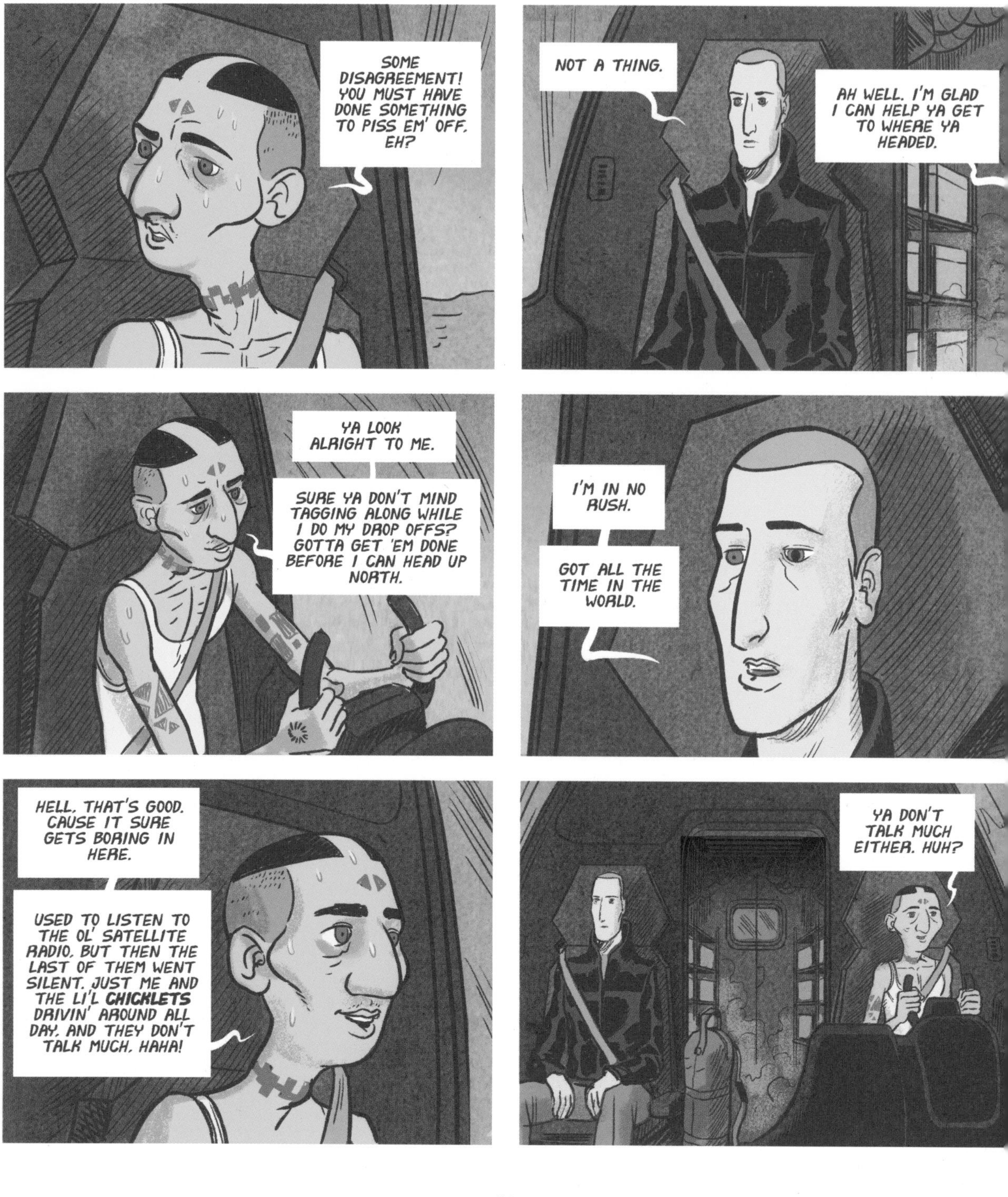
SOME DISAGREEMENT! YOU MUST HAVE DONE SOMETHING TO PISS EM' OFF. EH?
NOT A THING.
AH WELL. I'M GLAD I CAN HELP YA GET TO WHERE YA HEADED.
YA LOOK ALRIGHT TO ME.
SURE YA DON'T MIND TAGGING ALONG WHILE I DO MY DROP OFFS? GOTTA GET 'EM DONE BEFORE I CAN HEAD UP NORTH.
I'M IN NO RUSH.
GOT ALL THE TIME IN THE WORLD.
HELL. THAT'S GOOD. CAUSE IT SURE GETS BORING IN HERE.
USED TO LISTEN TO THE OL' SATELLITE RADIO. BUT THEN THE LAST OF THEM WENT SILENT. JUST ME AND THE LI'L **CHICKLETS** DRIVIN' AROUND ALL DAY. AND THEY DON'T TALK MUCH. HAHA!
YA DON'T TALK MUCH EITHER. HUH?

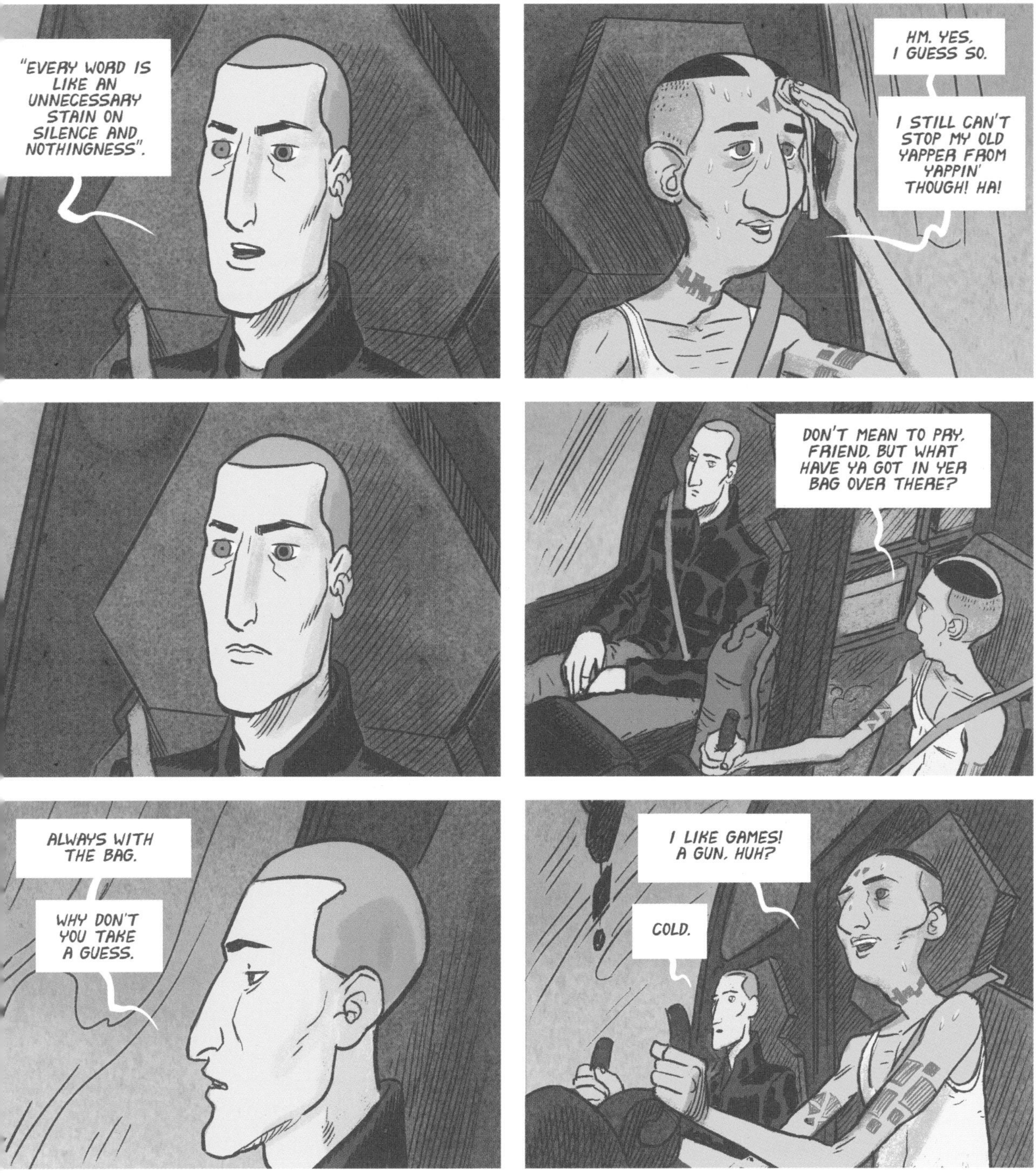

"EVERY WORD IS LIKE AN UNNECESSARY STAIN ON SILENCE AND NOTHINGNESS".
HM. YES, I GUESS SO.
I STILL CAN'T STOP MY OLD YAPPER FROM YAPPIN' THOUGH! HA!
DON'T MEAN TO PRY, FRIEND, BUT WHAT HAVE YA GOT IN YER BAG OVER THERE?
ALWAYS WITH THE BAG.
WHY DON'T YOU TAKE A GUESS.
I LIKE GAMES! A GUN, HUH?
COLD.

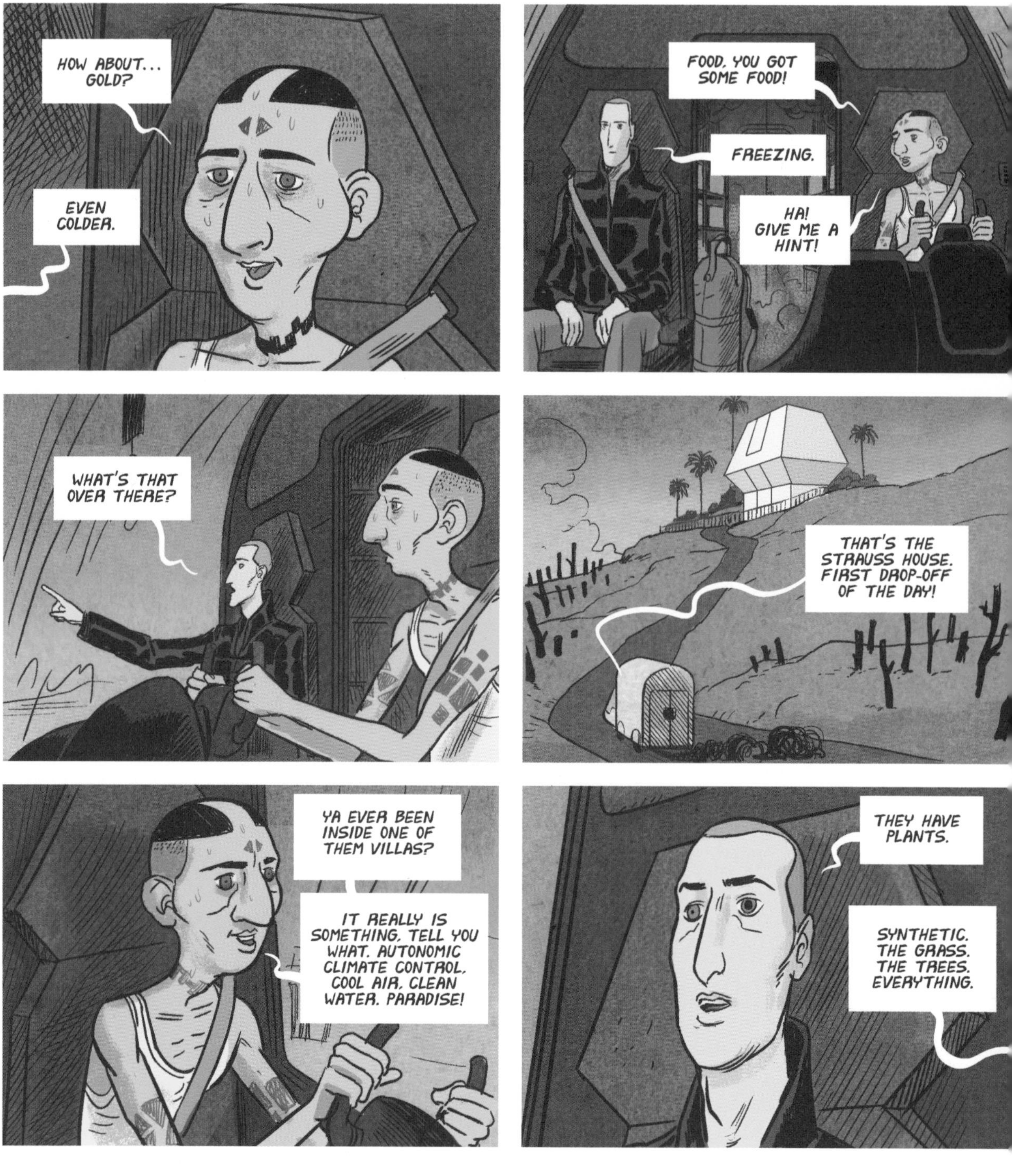
HOW ABOUT... GOLD?
EVEN COLDER.
FOOD, YOU GOT SOME FOOD!
FREEZING.
HA! GIVE ME A HINT!
WHAT'S THAT OVER THERE?
THAT'S THE STRAUSS HOUSE. FIRST DROP-OFF OF THE DAY!
YA EVER BEEN INSIDE ONE OF THEM VILLAS?
IT REALLY IS SOMETHING, TELL YOU WHAT. AUTONOMIC CLIMATE CONTROL, COOL AIR, CLEAN WATER. PARADISE!
THEY HAVE PLANTS.
SYNTHETIC. THE GRASS. THE TREES. EVERYTHING.

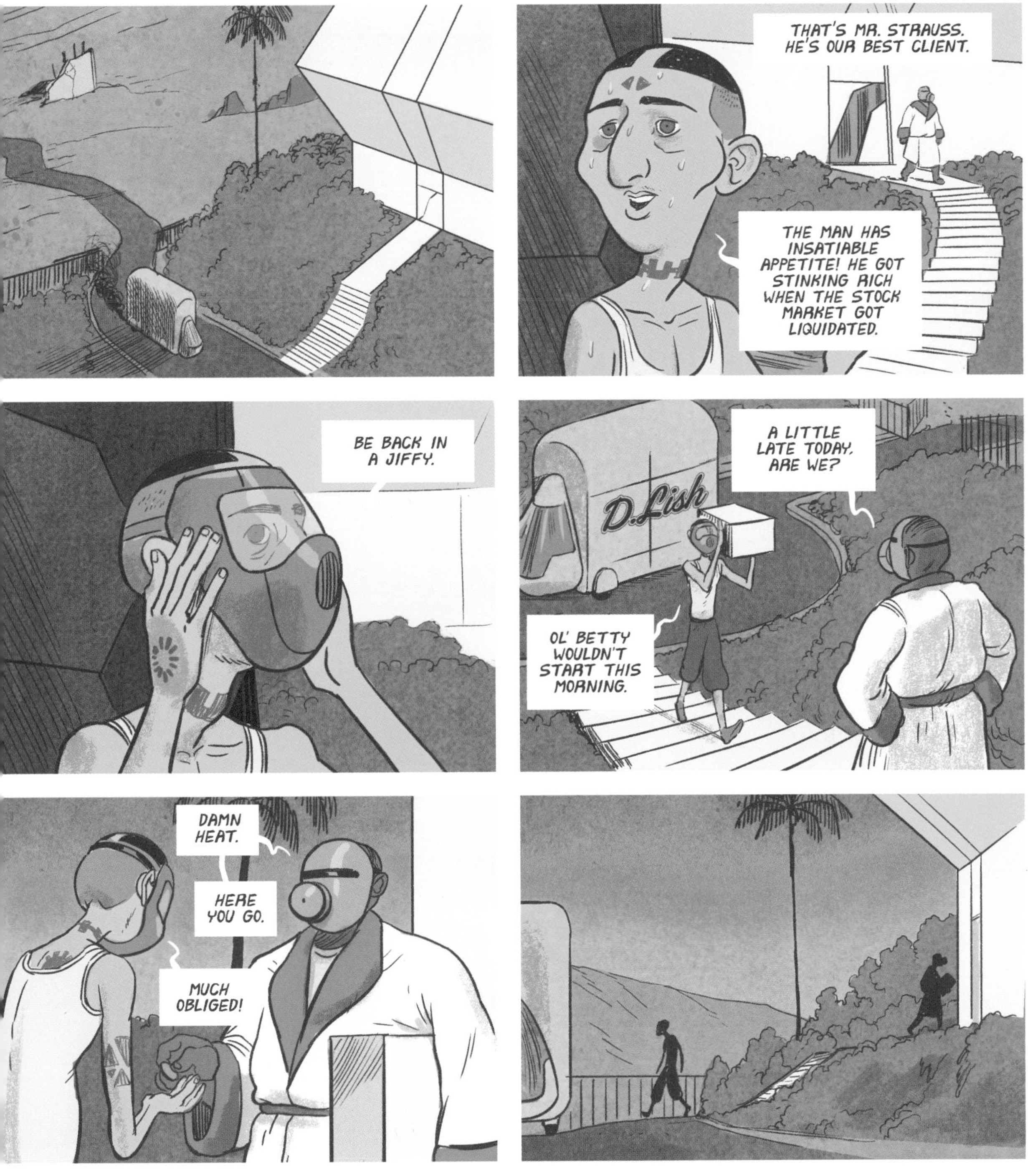
THAT'S MR. STRAUSS. HE'S OUR BEST CLIENT.
THE MAN HAS INSATIABLE APPETITE! HE GOT STINKING RICH WHEN THE STOCK MARKET GOT LIQUIDATED.
BE BACK IN A JIFFY.
D.Lish
A LITTLE LATE TODAY, ARE WE?
OL' BETTY WOULDN'T START THIS MORNING.
DAMN HEAT.
HERE YOU GO.
MUCH OBLIGED!

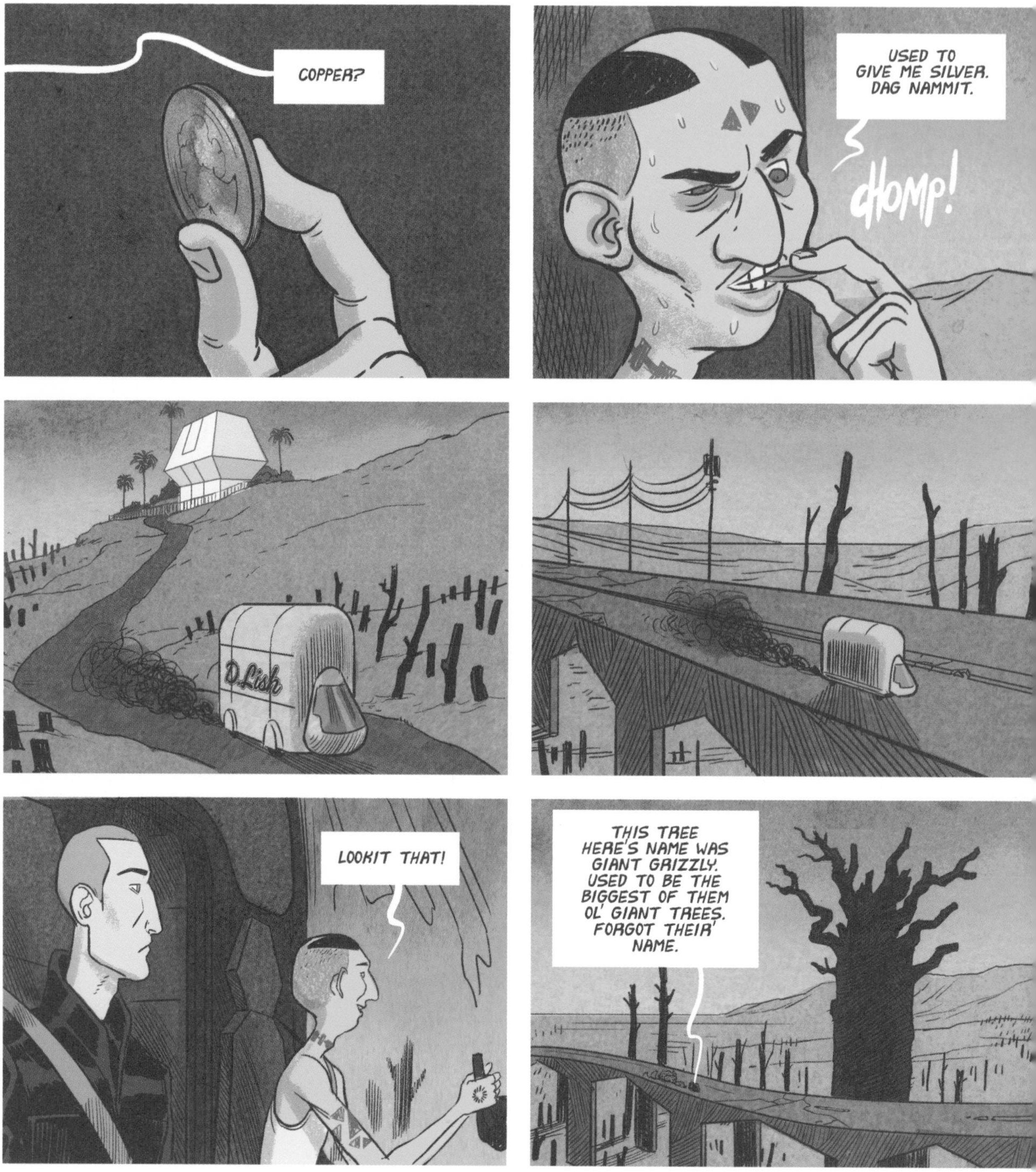

COPPER?
USED TO GIVE ME SILVER. DAG NAMMIT.
CHOMP!
LOOKIT THAT!
THIS TREE HERE'S NAME WAS GIANT GRIZZLY. USED TO BE THE BIGGEST OF THEM OL' GIANT TREES. FORGOT THEIR' NAME.

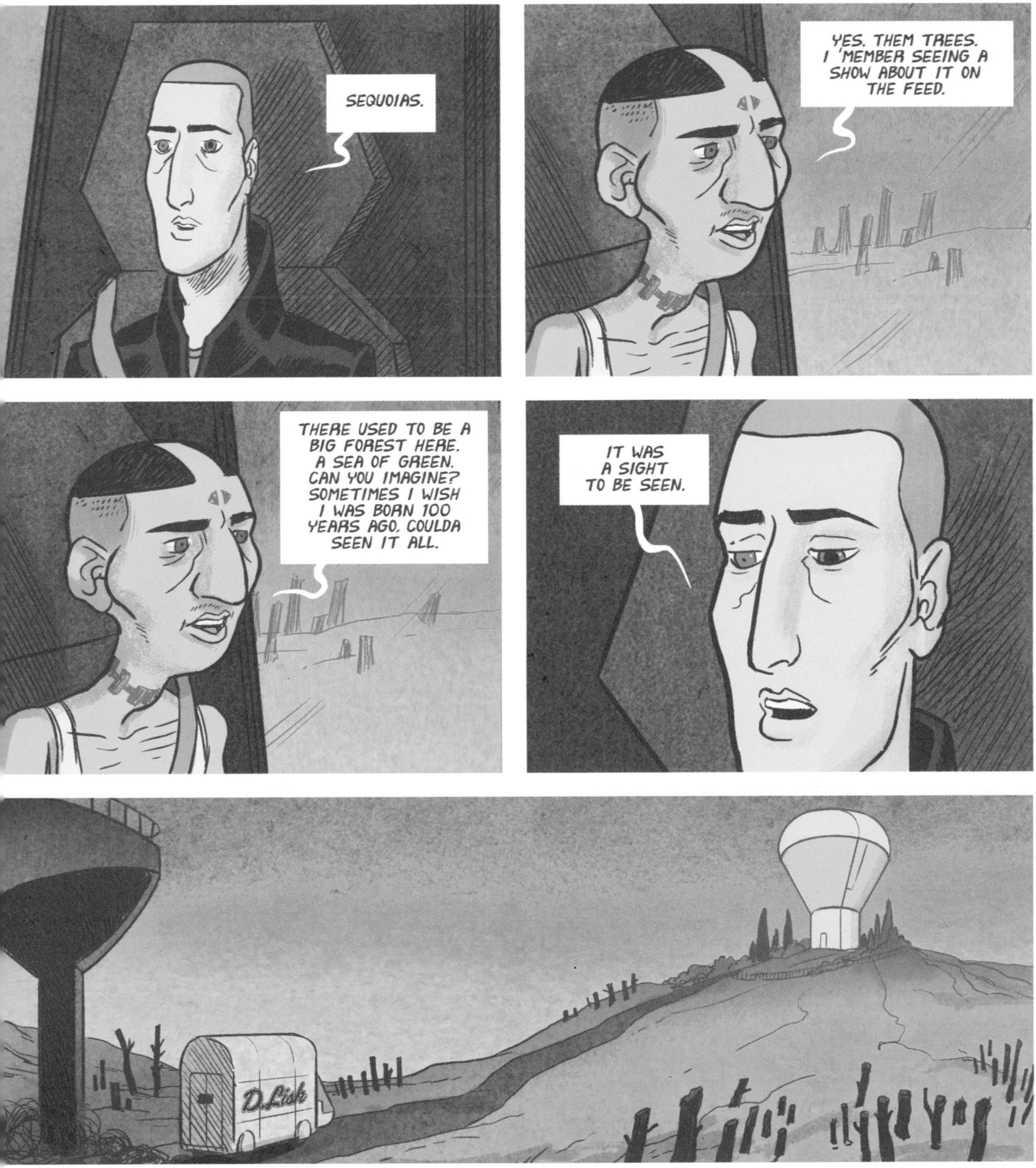
SEQUOIAS.
YES. THEM TREES. I 'MEMBER SEEING A SHOW ABOUT IT ON THE FEED.
THERE USED TO BE A BIG FOREST HERE. A SEA OF GREEN. CAN YOU IMAGINE? SOMETIMES I WISH I WAS BORN 100 YEARS AGO. COULDA SEEN IT ALL.
IT WAS A SIGHT TO BE SEEN.
D.Lish

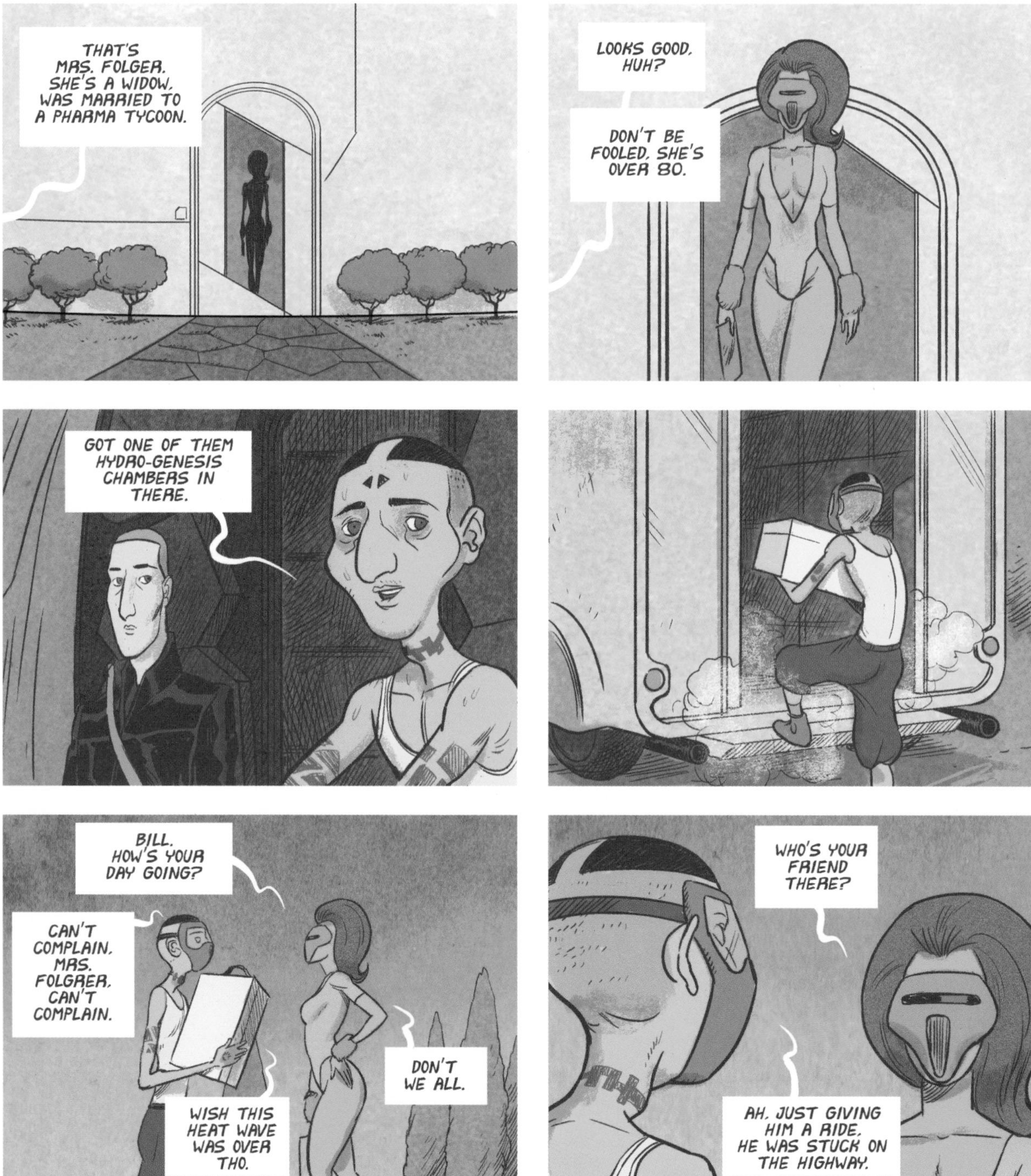
THAT'S MRS. FOLGER. SHE'S A WIDOW. WAS MARRIED TO A PHARMA TYCOON.
LOOKS GOOD, HUH?
DON'T BE FOOLED. SHE'S OVER 80.
GOT ONE OF THEM HYDRO-GENESIS CHAMBERS IN THERE.
BILL. HOW'S YOUR DAY GOING?
CAN'T COMPLAIN, MRS. FOLGRER, CAN'T COMPLAIN.
WISH THIS HEAT WAVE WAS OVER THO.
DON'T WE ALL.
WHO'S YOUR FRIEND THERE?
AH, JUST GIVING HIM A RIDE, HE WAS STUCK ON THE HIGHWAY.

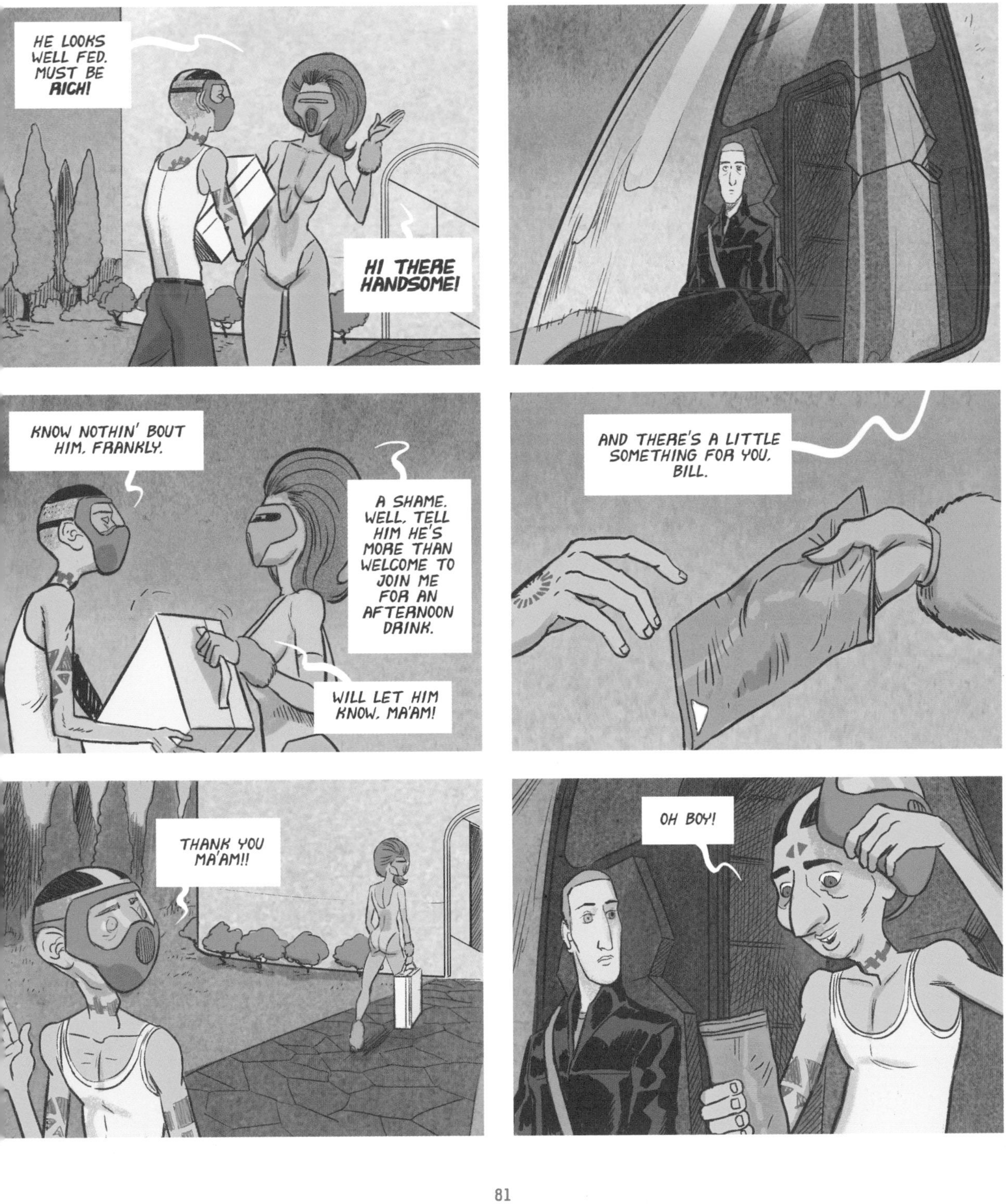

HE LOOKS WELL FED. MUST BE RICH!
HI THERE HANDSOME!
KNOW NOTHIN' BOUT HIM, FRANKLY.
A SHAME. WELL, TELL HIM HE'S MORE THAN WELCOME TO JOIN ME FOR AN AFTERNOON DRINK.
WILL LET HIM KNOW, MA'AM!
AND THERE'S A LITTLE SOMETHING FOR YOU, BILL.
THANK YOU MA'AM!!
OH BOY!

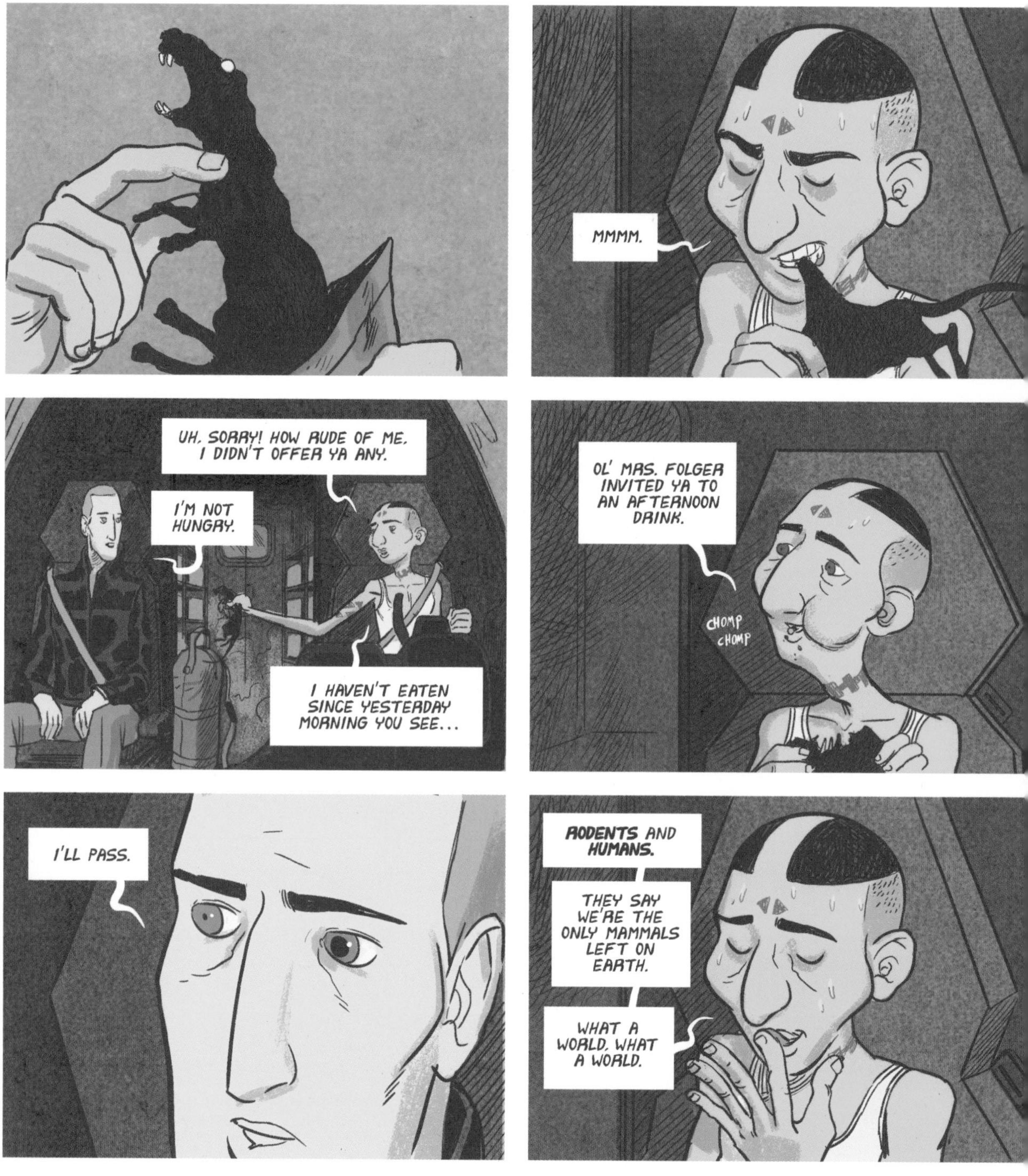
MMMM.
UH, SORRY! HOW RUDE OF ME. I DIDN'T OFFER YA ANY.
I'M NOT HUNGRY.
I HAVEN'T EATEN SINCE YESTERDAY MORNING YOU SEE...
OL' MRS. FOLGER INVITED YA TO AN AFTERNOON DRINK.
CHOMP CHOMP
I'LL PASS.
RODENTS AND **HUMANS.**
THEY SAY WE'RE THE ONLY MAMMALS LEFT ON EARTH.
WHAT A WORLD, WHAT A WORLD.

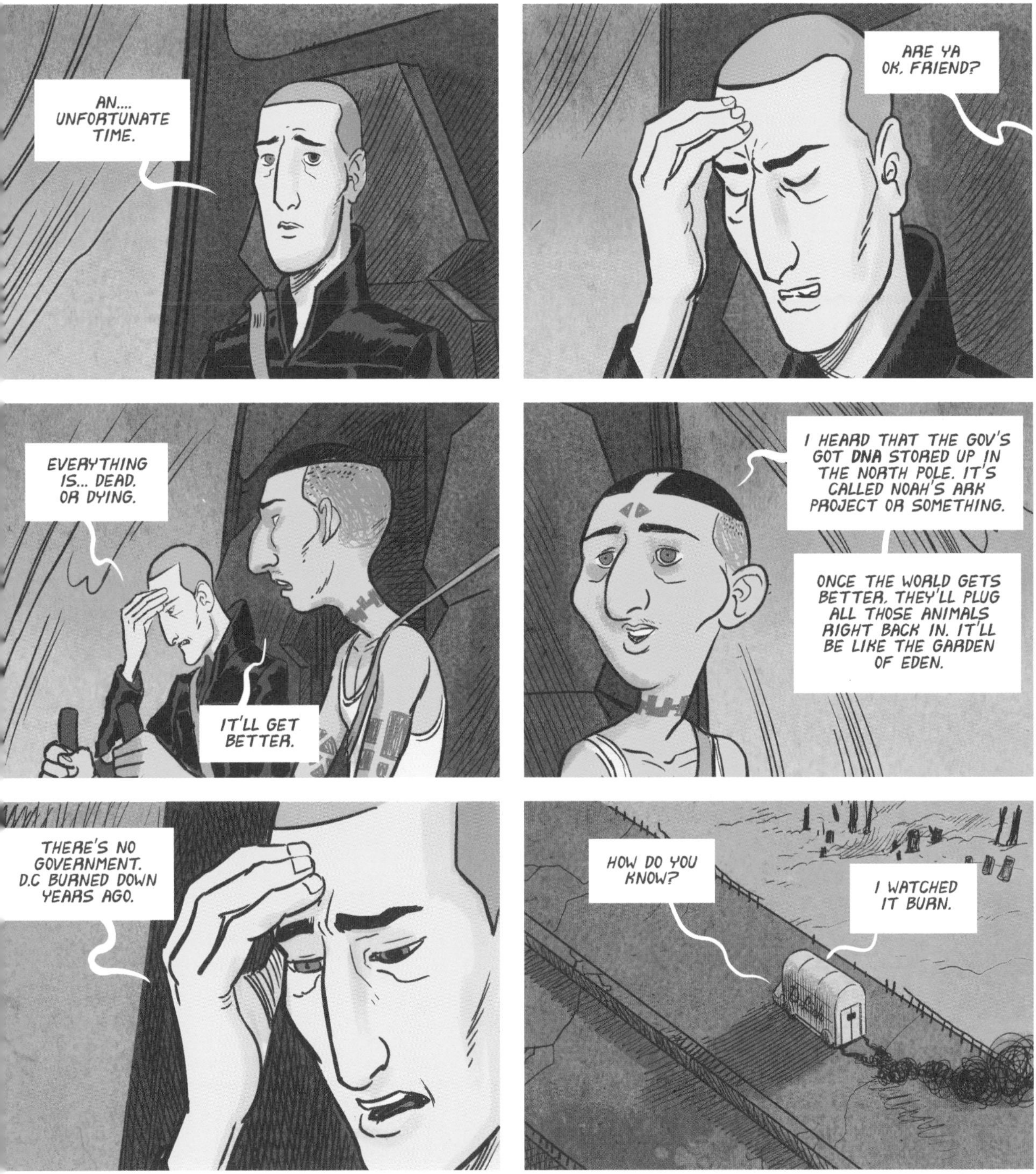
AN.... UNFORTUNATE TIME.
ARE YA OK, FRIEND?
EVERYTHING IS... DEAD. OR DYING.
IT'LL GET BETTER.
I HEARD THAT THE GOV'S GOT DNA STORED UP IN THE NORTH POLE. IT'S CALLED NOAH'S ARK PROJECT OR SOMETHING.
ONCE THE WORLD GETS BETTER, THEY'LL PLUG ALL THOSE ANIMALS RIGHT BACK IN. IT'LL BE LIKE THE GARDEN OF EDEN.
THERE'S NO GOVERNMENT. D.C BURNED DOWN YEARS AGO.
HOW DO YOU KNOW?
I WATCHED IT BURN.

LATER

HELL, THERE'S OUR NEXT-TO-LAST DROP OFF.

ONE MORE **CHICKLET** AFTER THIS AND WE DRIVE UP NORTH.

THANK GOD YOU'RE HERE! HE WAS DRIVING ME CRAZY ALREADY.

I'M HUNGRY MOMMY! I'M HUNGRRRRYYYYY!

SORRY FOR THE DELAY, MA'AM.

MOMMMMMYYYY!

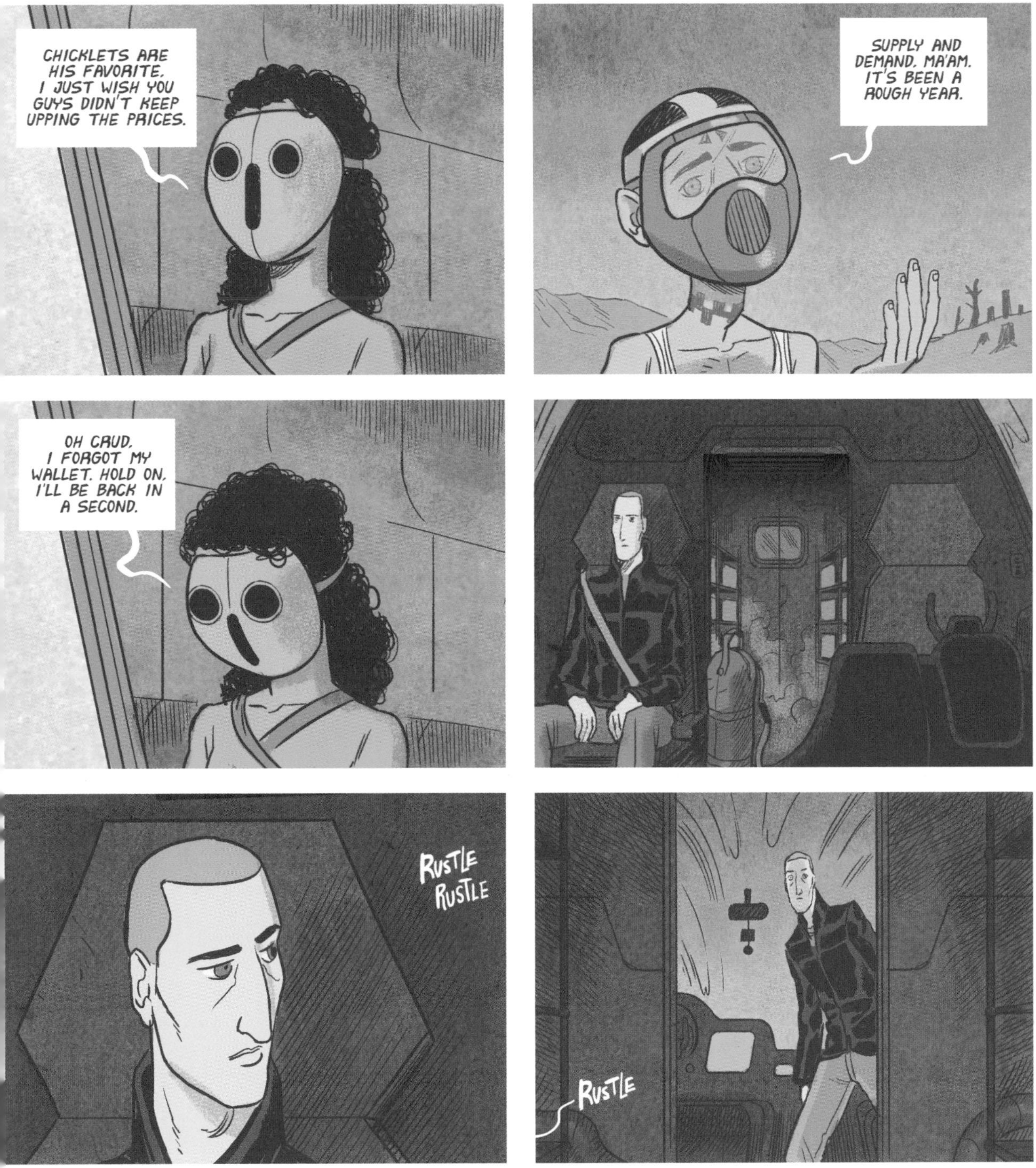
CHICKLETS ARE HIS FAVORITE. I JUST WISH YOU GUYS DIDN'T KEEP UPPING THE PRICES.
SUPPLY AND DEMAND, MA'AM. IT'S BEEN A ROUGH YEAR.
OH CRUD, I FORGOT MY WALLET. HOLD ON, I'LL BE BACK IN A SECOND.
RUSTLE
RUSTLE
RUSTLE

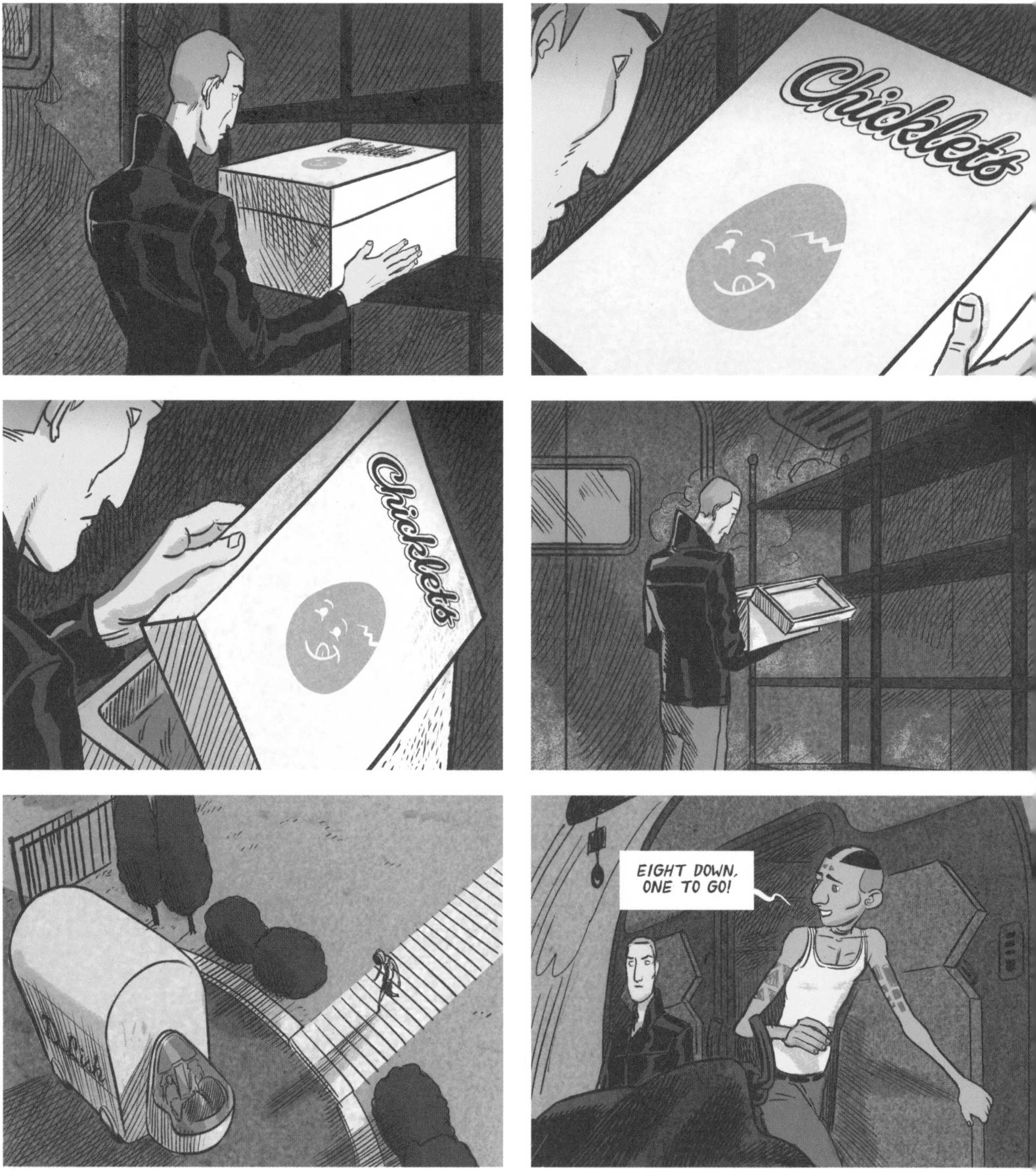
Chicklets
Chicklets
Chicklets
Chicklets
EIGHT DOWN, ONE TO GO!

SO IT'S COME TO THIS?
HOW CAN YOU BE PART OF THIS MONSTROSITY?
SHIT. YA PEEKED, DIDN'T YA?
THIS IS 'ROUND THE TIME THE SEDATIVES WEAR OFF...
UHH-I
I TRY TO NEVER GET INVOLVED...
IS... E-EVERYTHING OK, FRIEND?
NO! I'VE HAD ENOUGH!
H...HOLD ON FRIEND!
I'M JUST THE MESSENGER!

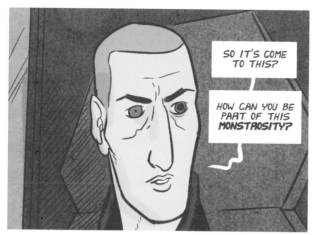

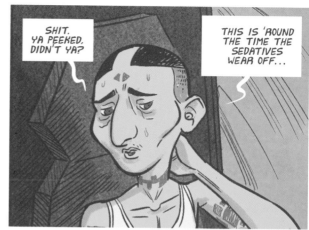

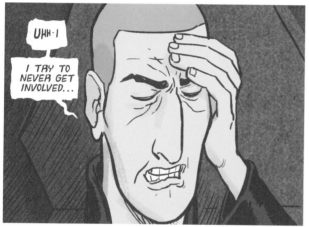

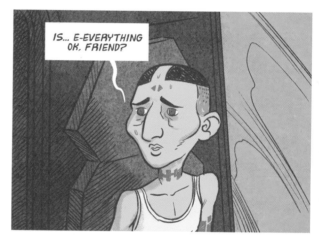

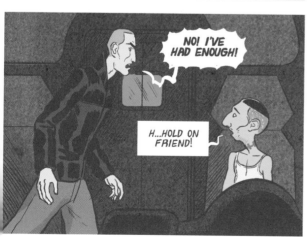

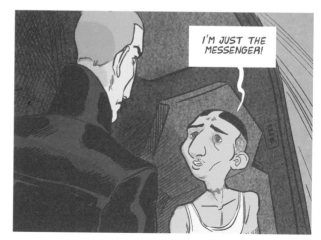

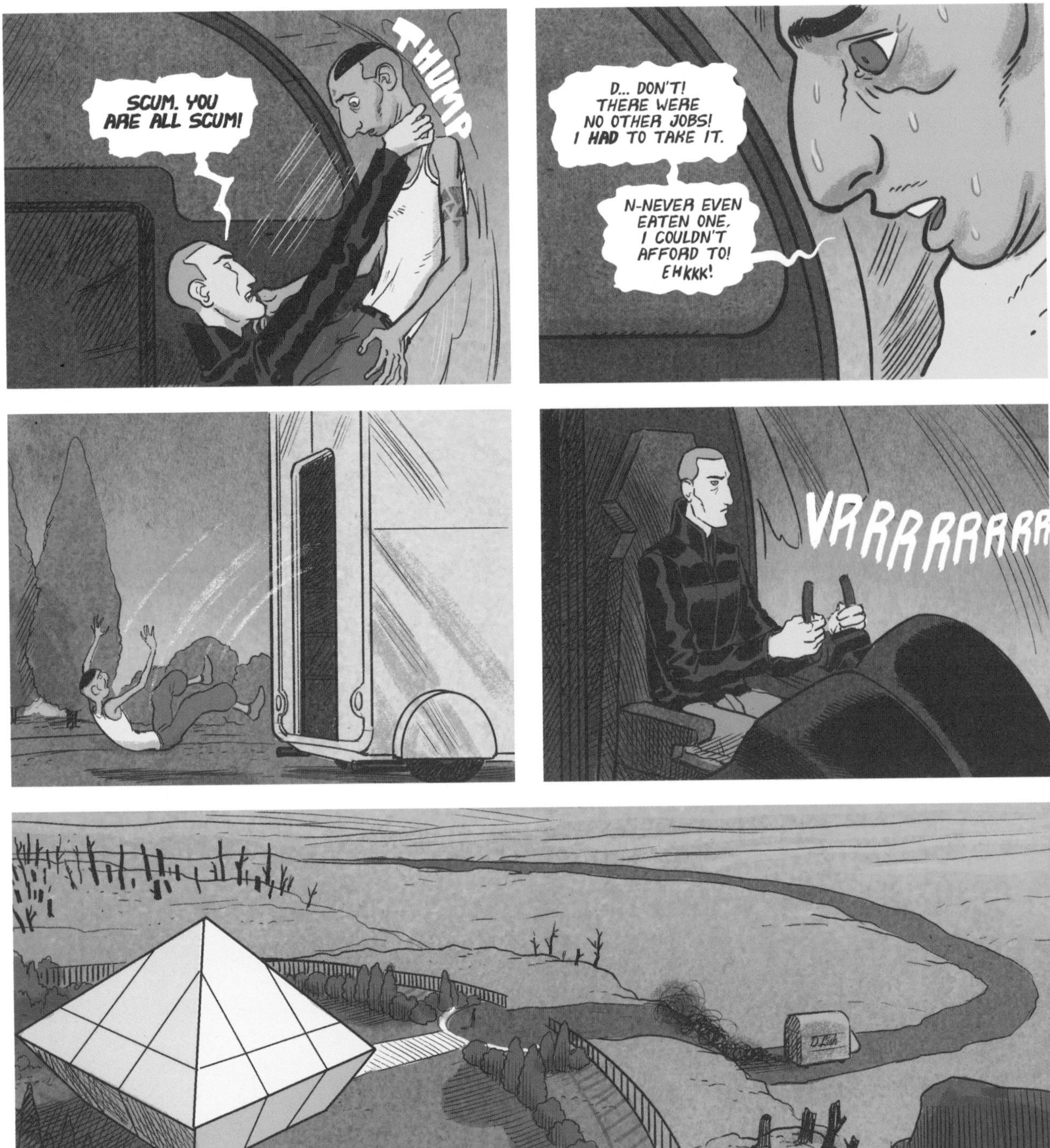
SCUM. YOU ARE ALL SCUM!
THUMP
D... DON'T! THERE WERE NO OTHER JOBS! I HAD TO TAKE IT.
N-NEVER EVEN EATEN ONE, I COULDN'T AFFORD TO! EHKKK!
VRRRRRRRR
D.Lish

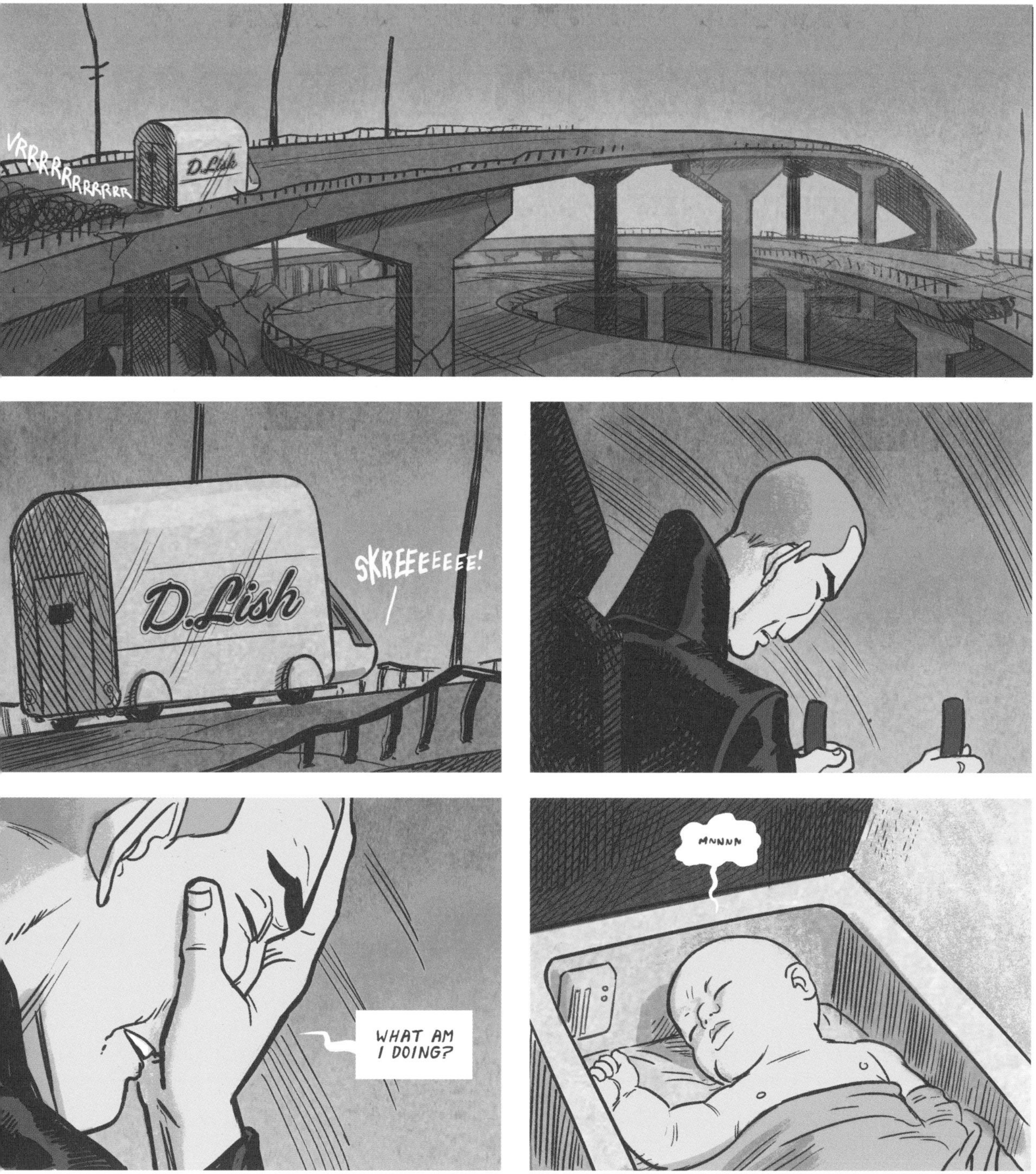
VRRRRRRRRRRRRR
D.Lish
D.Lish
SKREEEEEEE!
WHAT AM I DOING?
MNNNN

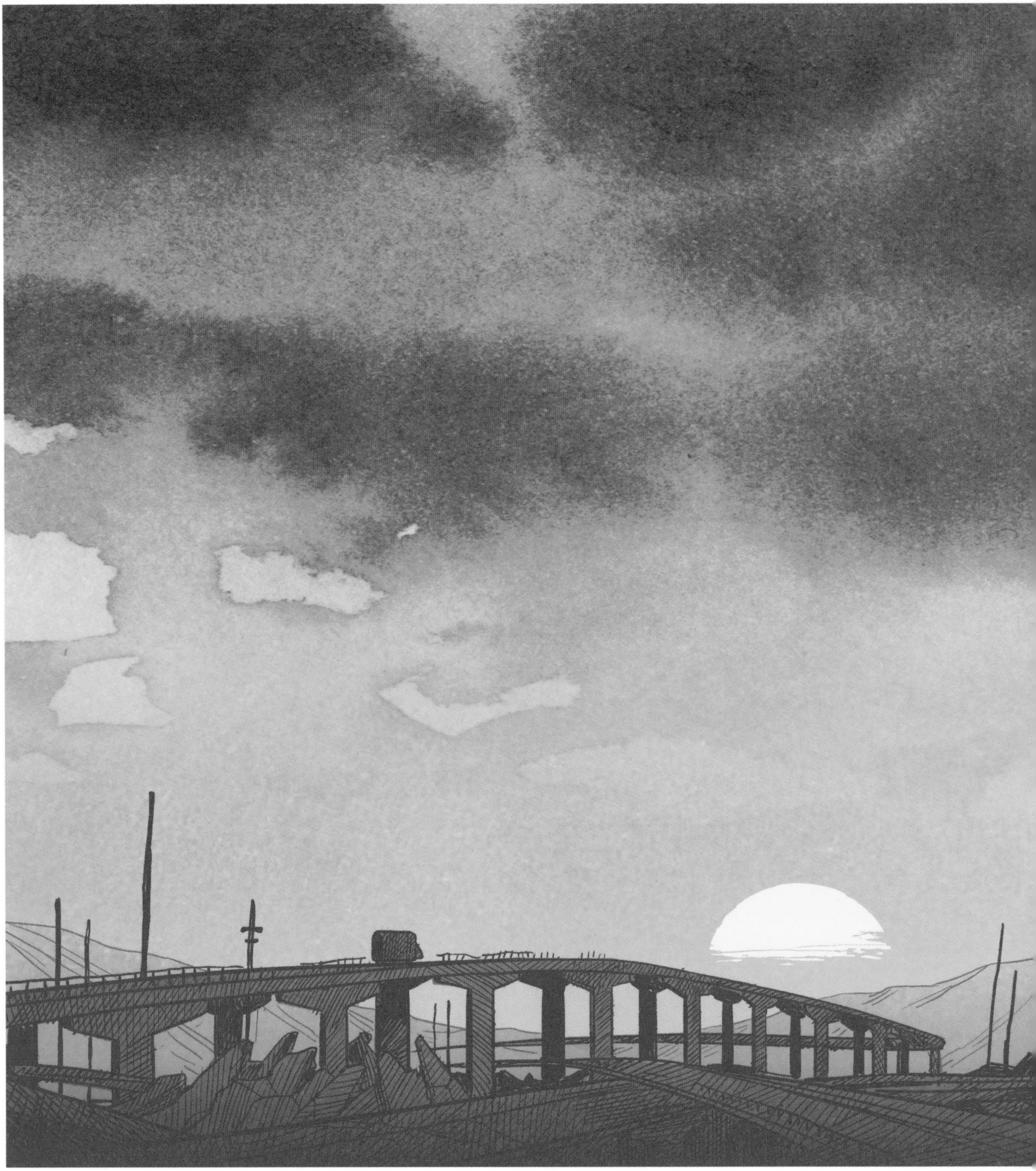

CHAPTER 5
FAMILY

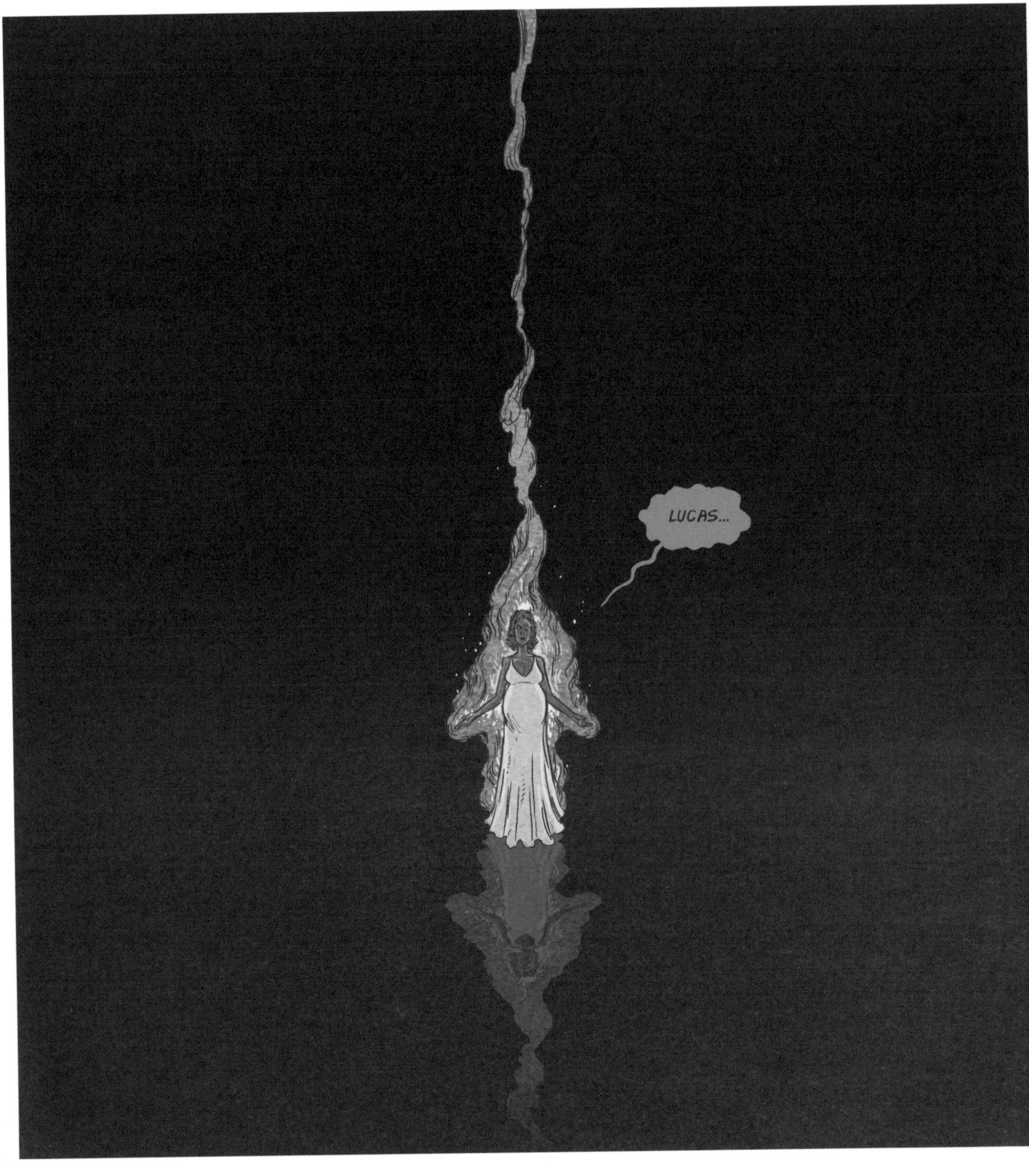
LUCAS...

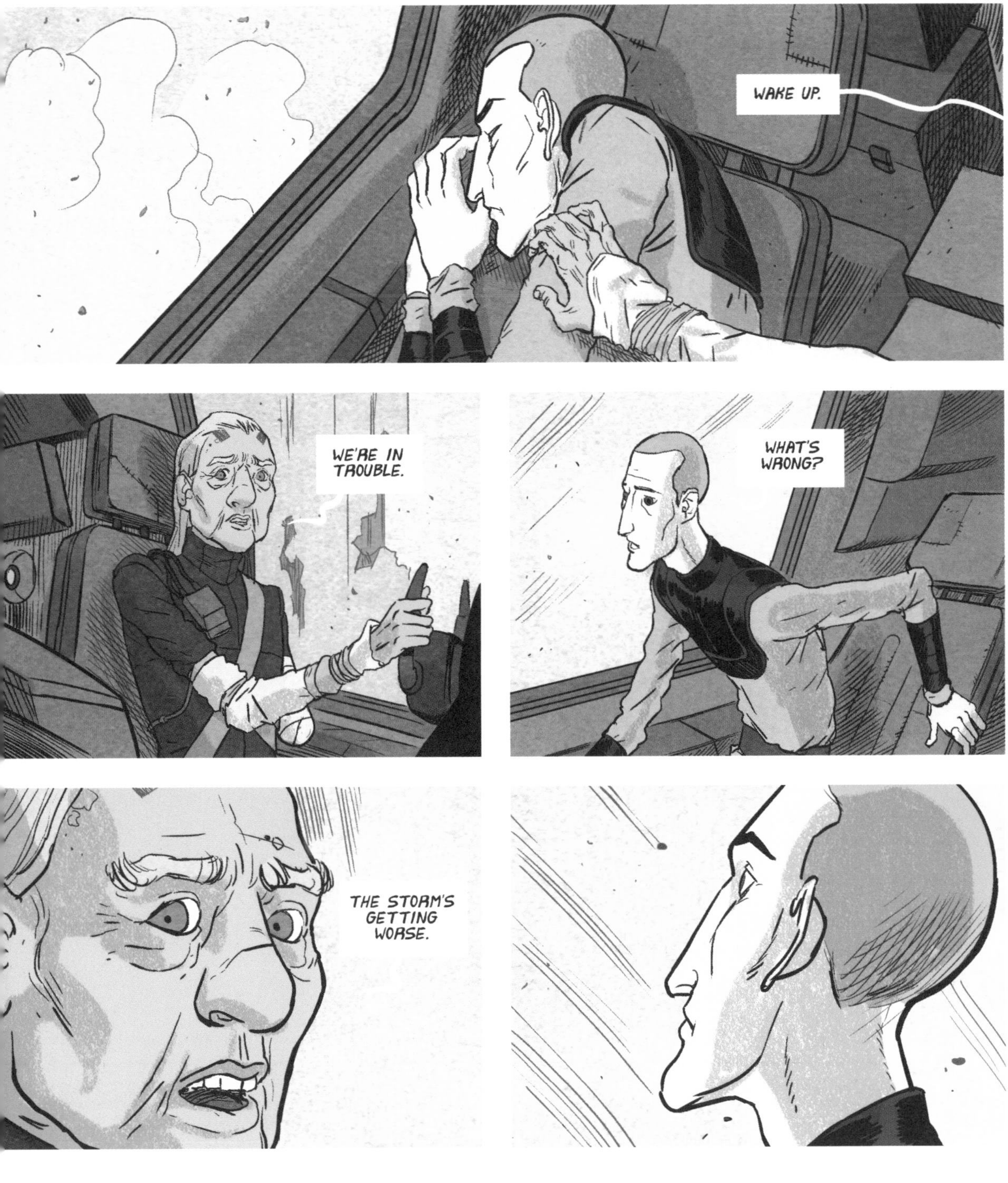
WAKE UP.
WE'RE IN TROUBLE.
WHAT'S WRONG?
THE STORM'S GETTING WORSE.

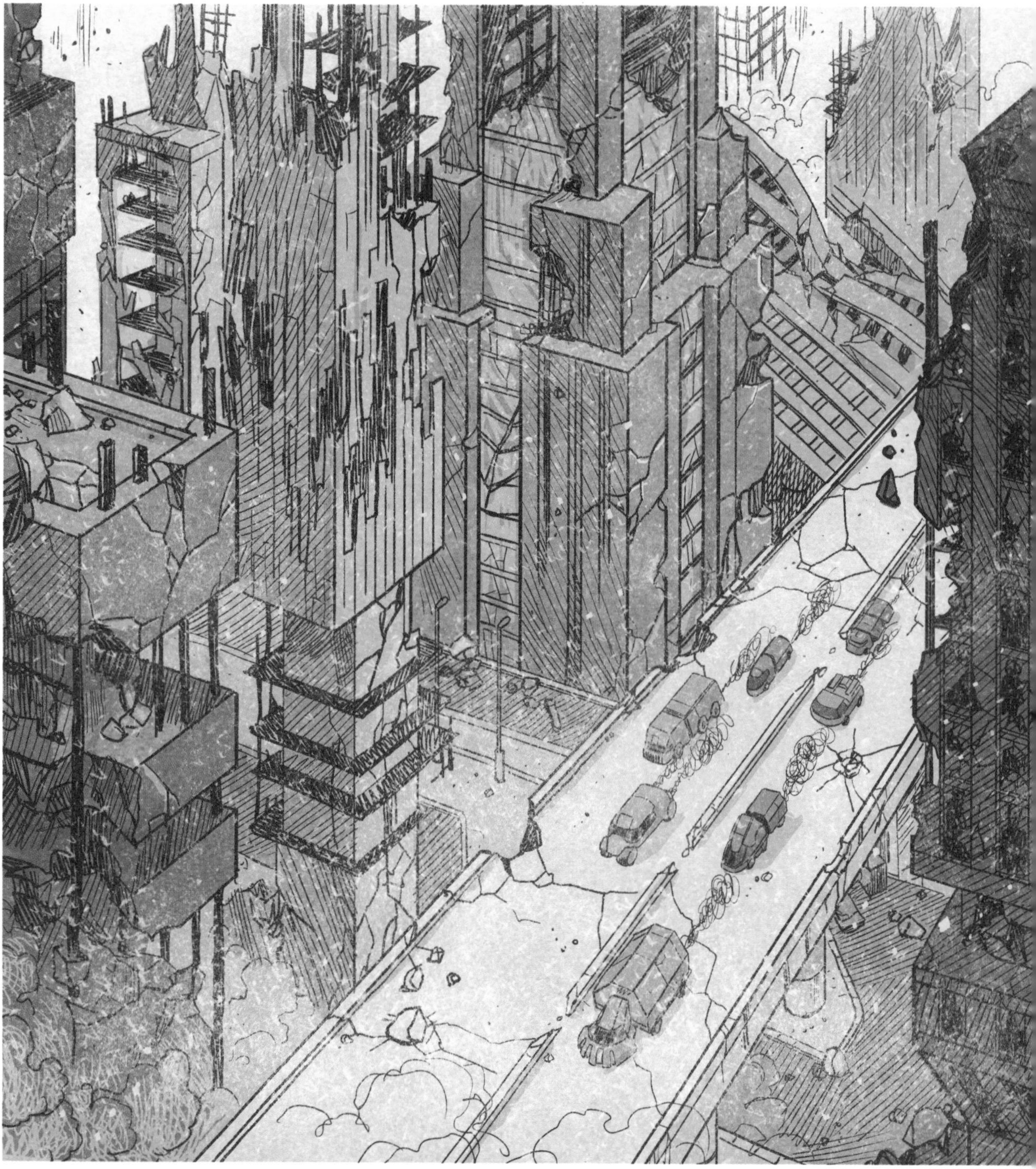

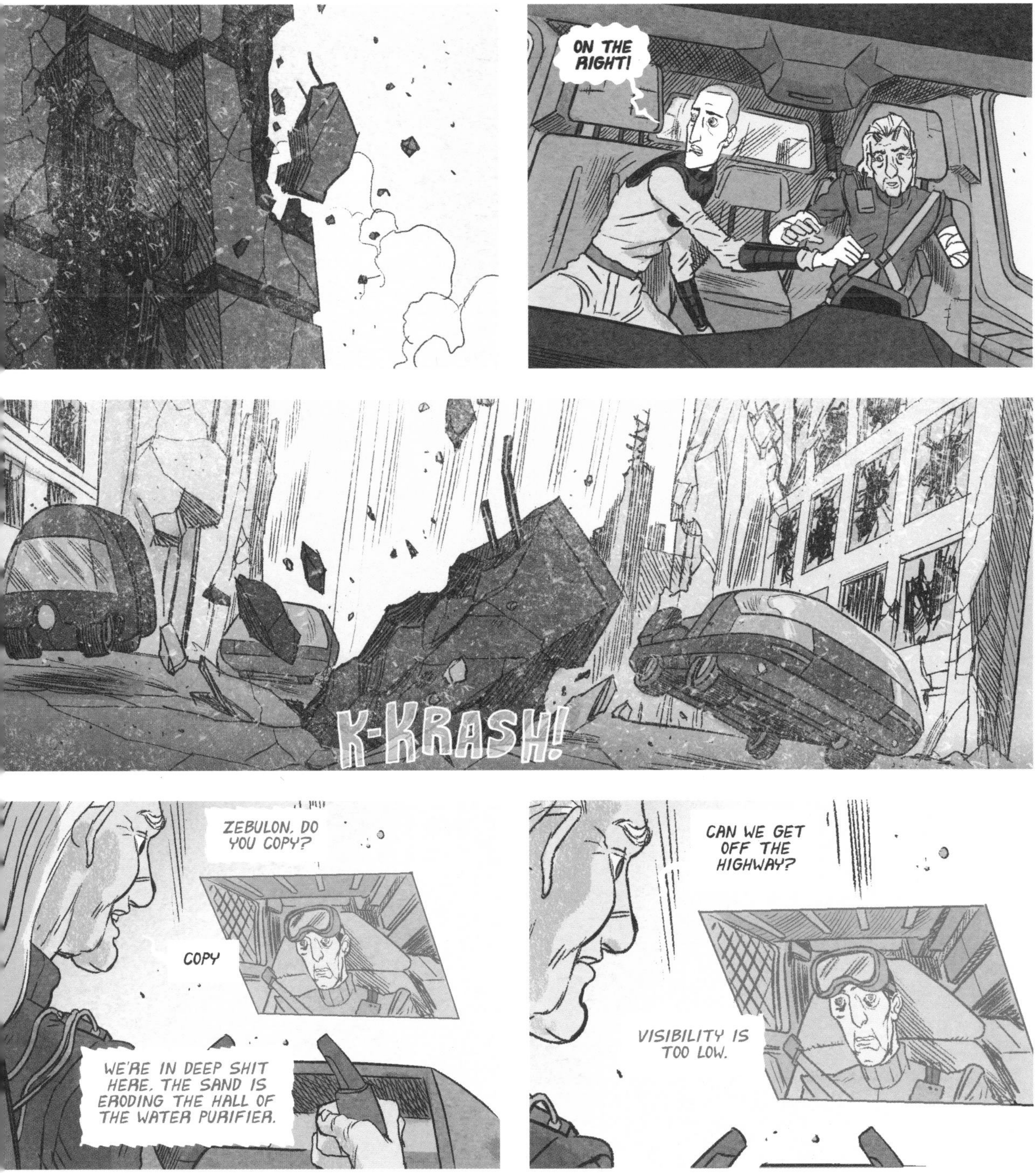
ON THE RIGHT!
K-KRASH!
ZEBULON, DO YOU COPY?
COPY
WE'RE IN DEEP SHIT HERE. THE SAND IS ERODING THE HALL OF THE WATER PURIFIER.
CAN WE GET OFF THE HIGHWAY?
VISIBILITY IS TOO LOW.

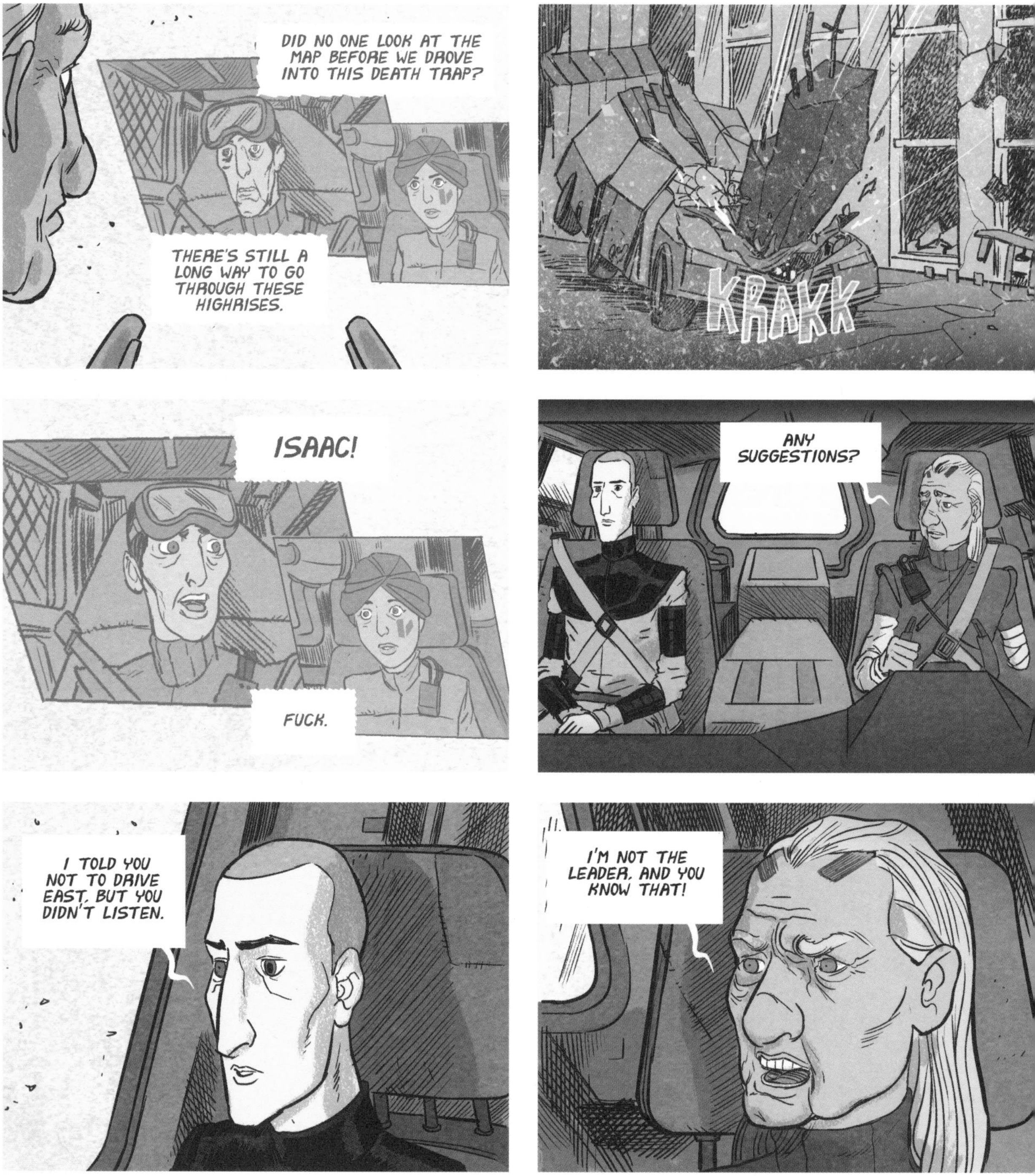
DID NO ONE LOOK AT THE MAP BEFORE WE DROVE INTO THIS DEATH TRAP?
THERE'S STILL A LONG WAY TO GO THROUGH THESE HIGHRISES.
KRAKK
ISAAC!
FUCK.
ANY SUGGESTIONS?
I TOLD YOU NOT TO DRIVE EAST, BUT YOU DIDN'T LISTEN.
I'M NOT THE LEADER, AND YOU KNOW THAT!

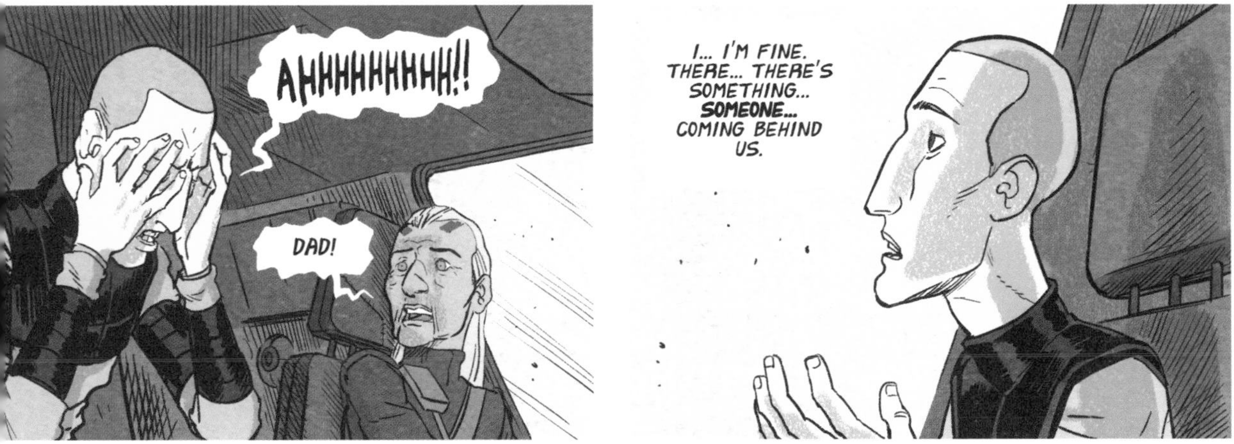
AHHHHHHHHH!!
DAD!
I... I'M FINE. THERE... THERE'S SOMETHING... **SOMEONE...** COMING BEHIND US.

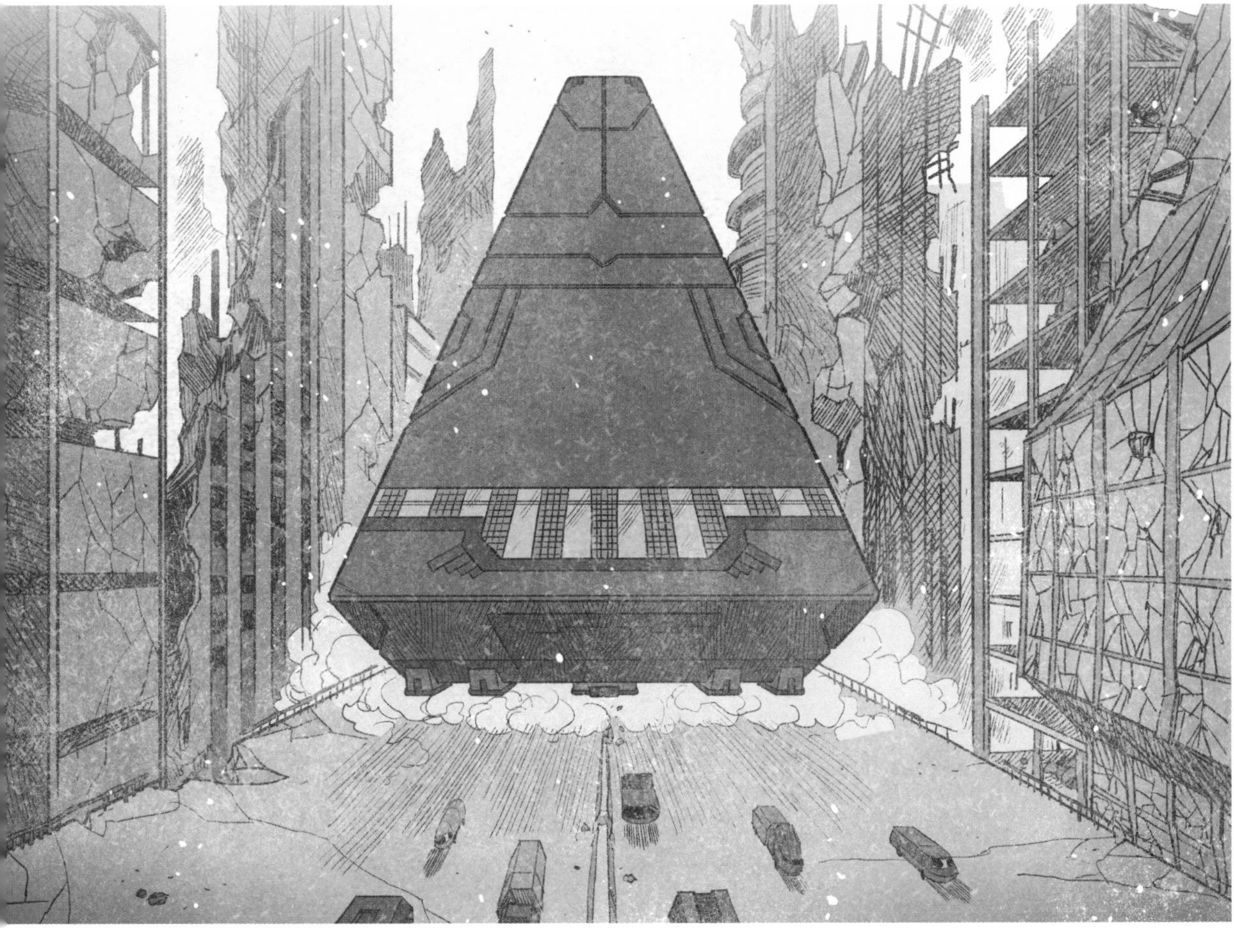

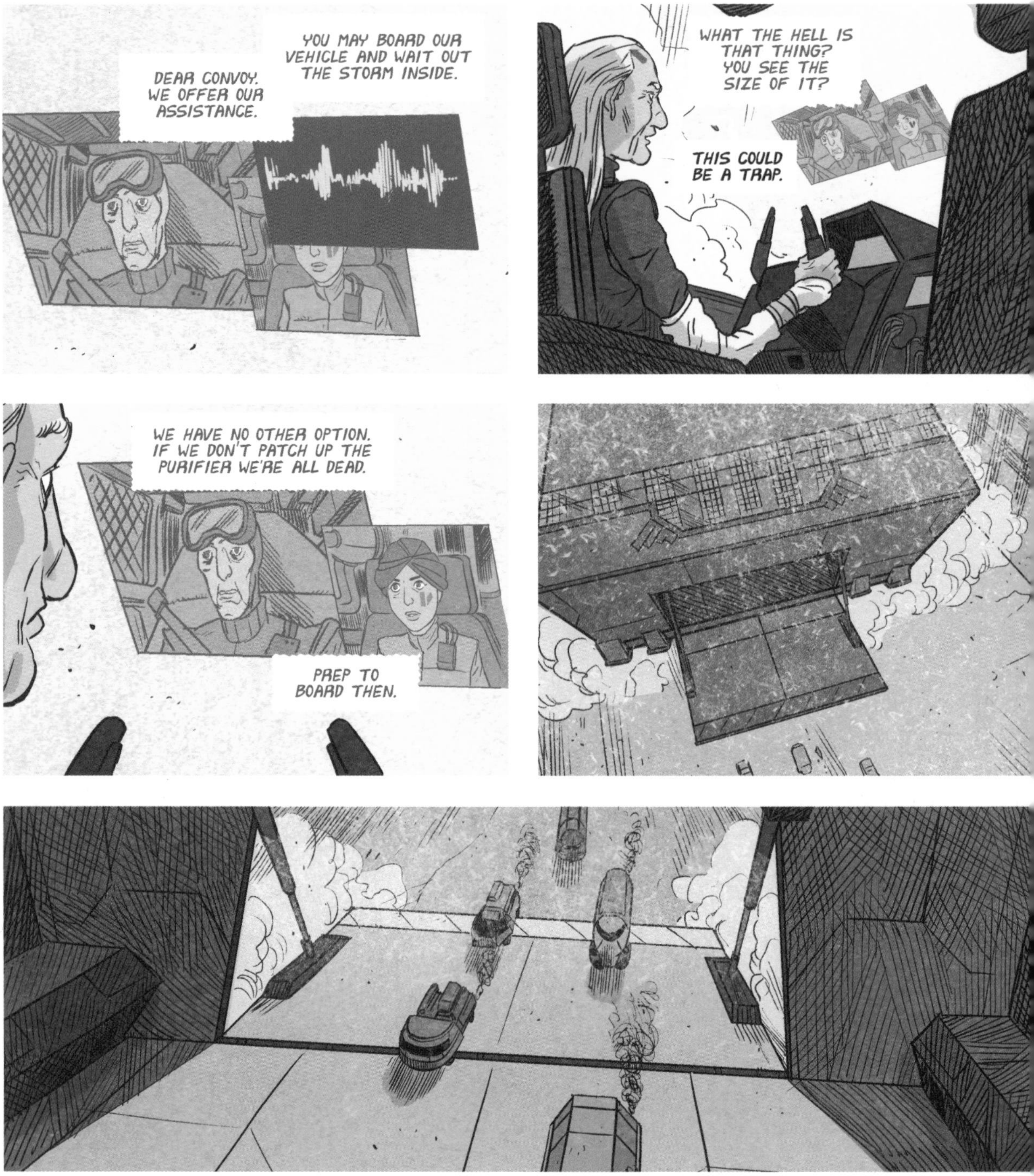
DEAR CONVOY. WE OFFER OUR ASSISTANCE.
YOU MAY BOARD OUR VEHICLE AND WAIT OUT THE STORM INSIDE.
WHAT THE HELL IS THAT THING? YOU SEE THE SIZE OF IT?
THIS COULD BE A TRAP.
WE HAVE NO OTHER OPTION. IF WE DON'T PATCH UP THE PURIFIER WE'RE ALL DEAD.
PREP TO BOARD THEN.

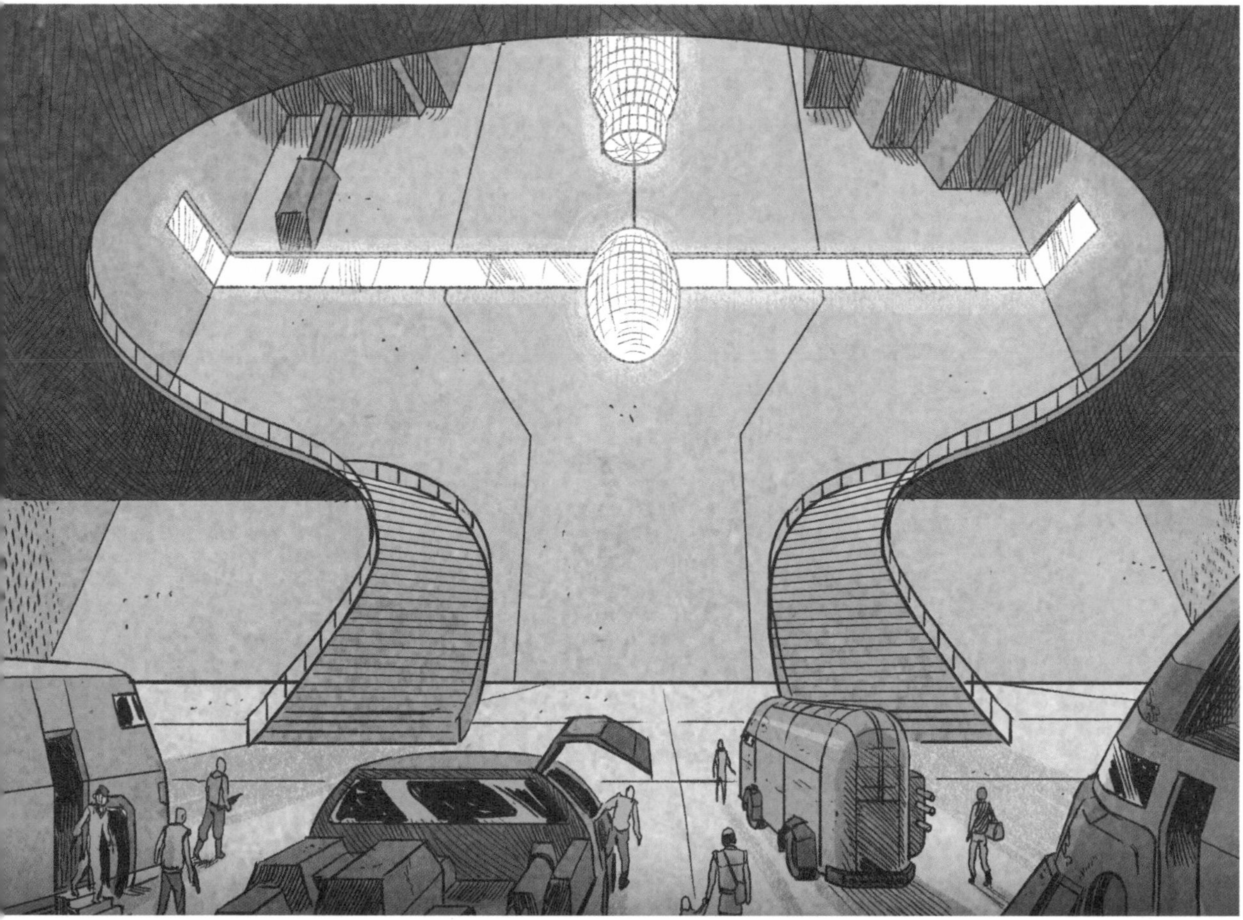

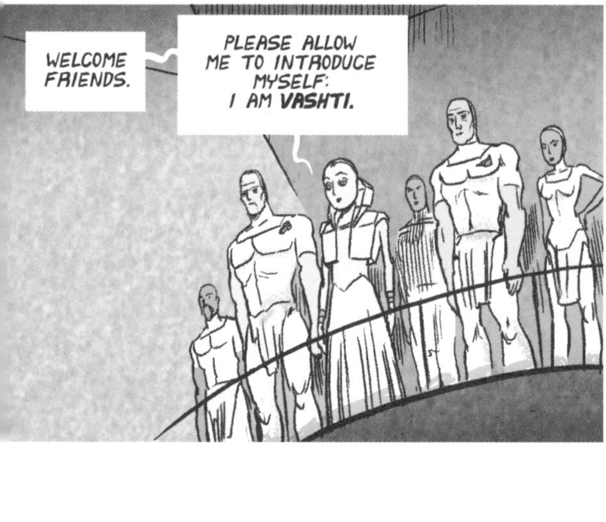
WELCOME FRIENDS.
PLEASE ALLOW ME TO INTRODUCE MYSELF: I AM **VASHTI.**

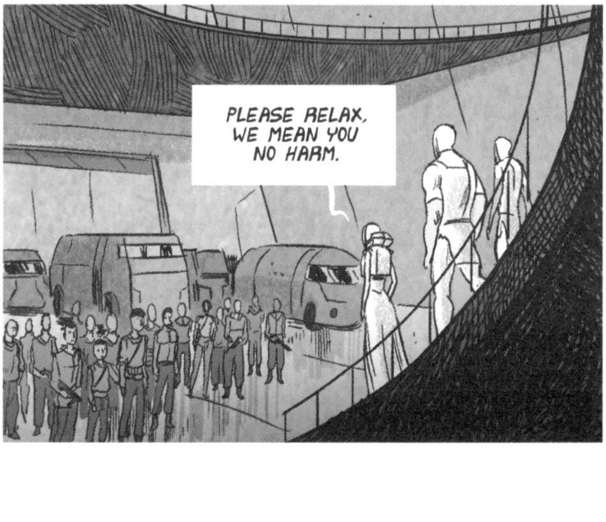
PLEASE RELAX, WE MEAN YOU NO HARM.

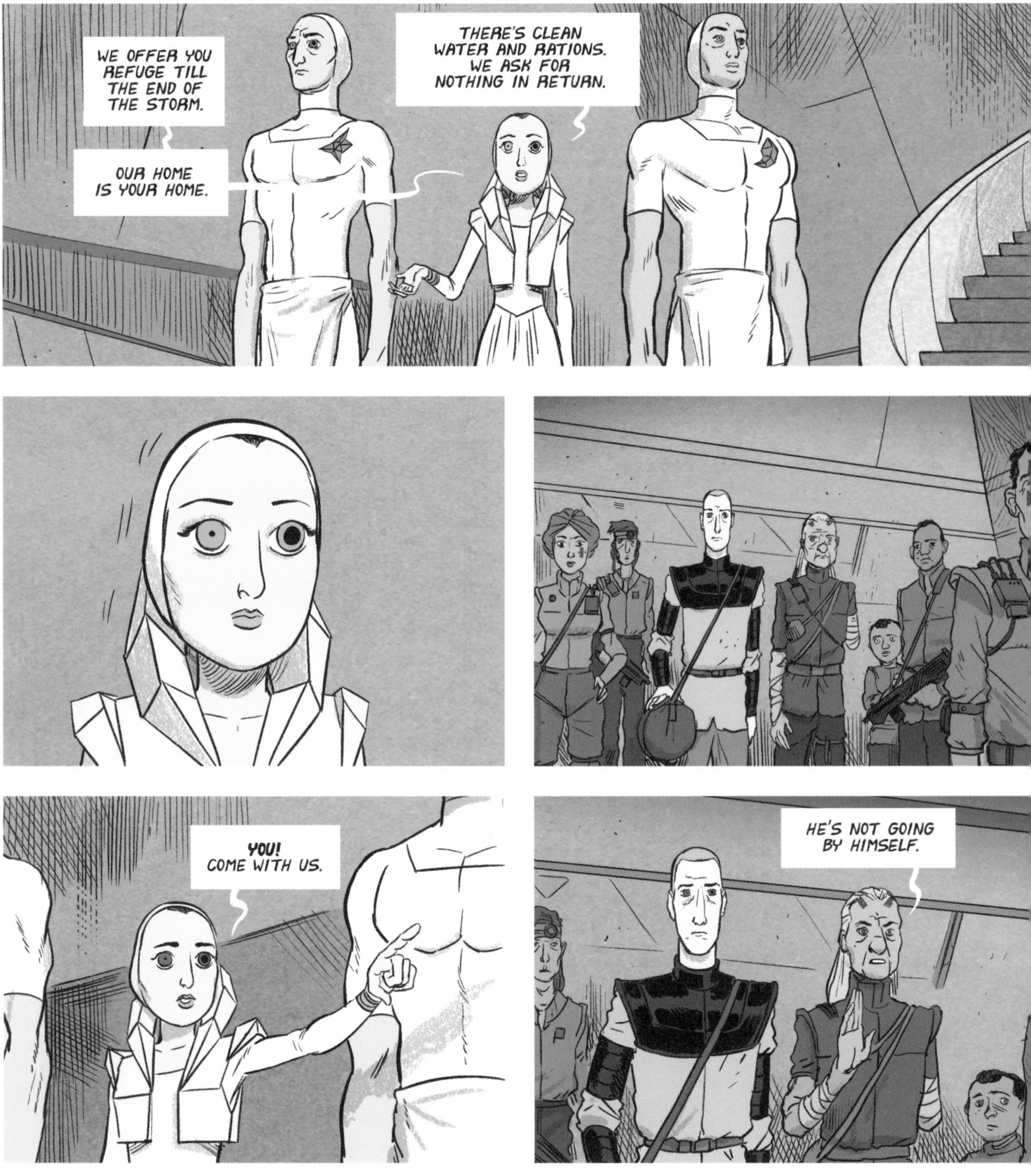
WE OFFER YOU REFUGE TILL THE END OF THE STORM.
OUR HOME IS YOUR HOME.
THERE'S CLEAN WATER AND RATIONS. WE ASK FOR NOTHING IN RETURN.
YOU! COME WITH US.
HE'S NOT GOING BY HIMSELF.

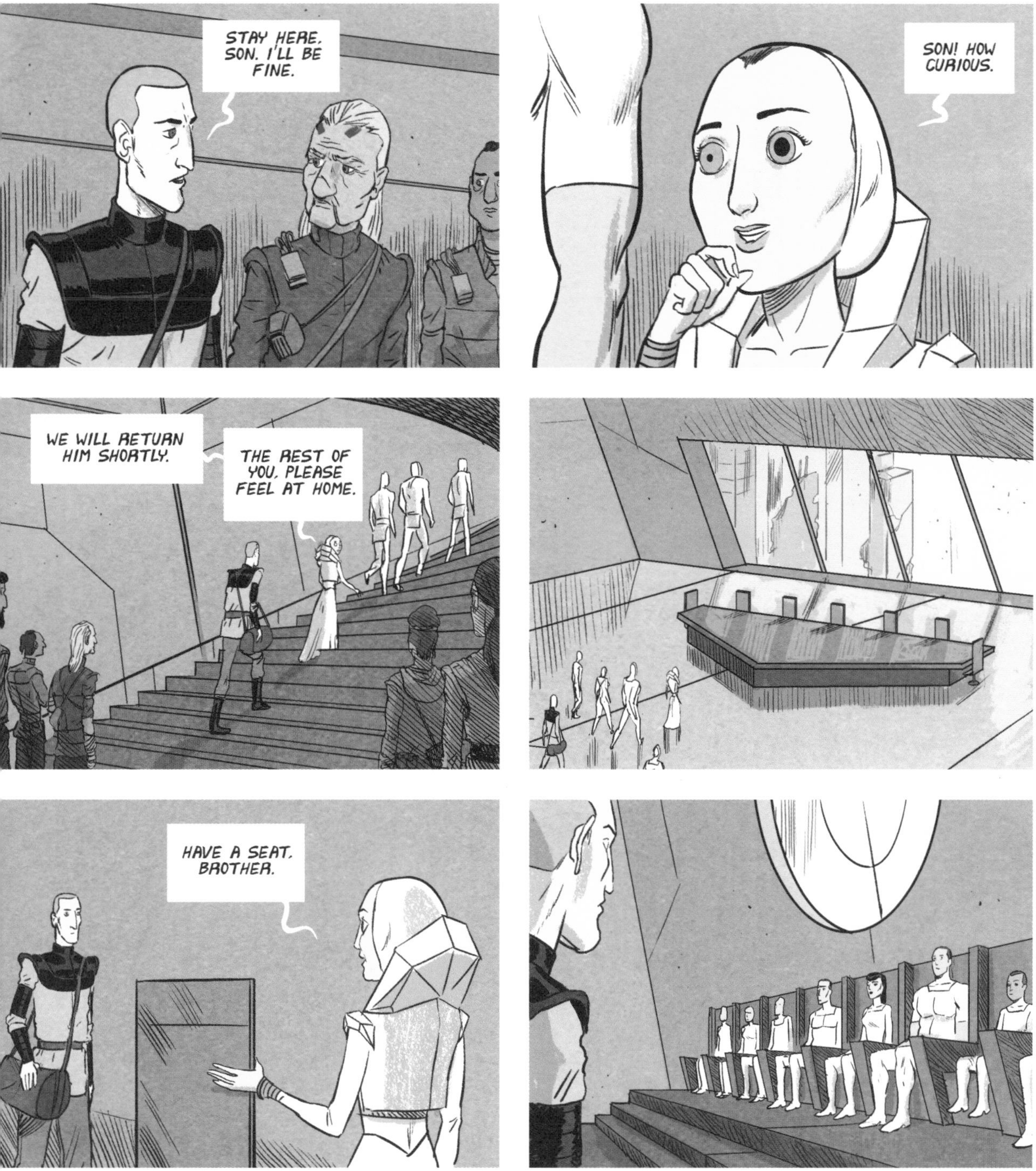
STAY HERE, SON. I'LL BE FINE.
SON! HOW CURIOUS.
WE WILL RETURN HIM SHORTLY.
THE REST OF YOU, PLEASE FEEL AT HOME.
HAVE A SEAT, BROTHER.

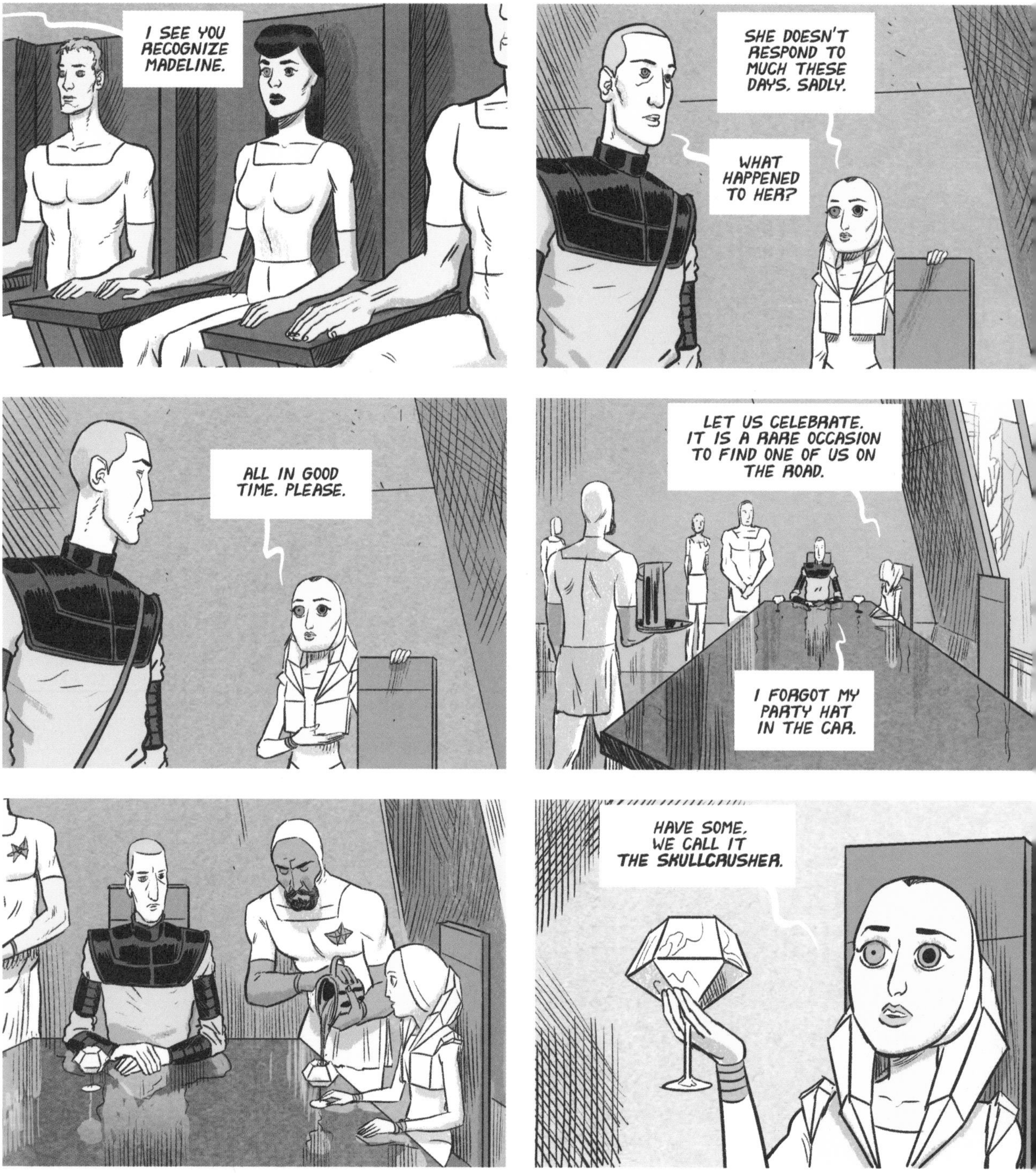
I SEE YOU RECOGNIZE MADELINE.
SHE DOESN'T RESPOND TO MUCH THESE DAYS, SADLY.
WHAT HAPPENED TO HER?
ALL IN GOOD TIME. PLEASE.
LET US CELEBRATE. IT IS A RARE OCCASION TO FIND ONE OF US ON THE ROAD.
I FORGOT MY PARTY HAT IN THE CAR.
HAVE SOME, WE CALL IT THE SKULLCRUSHER.

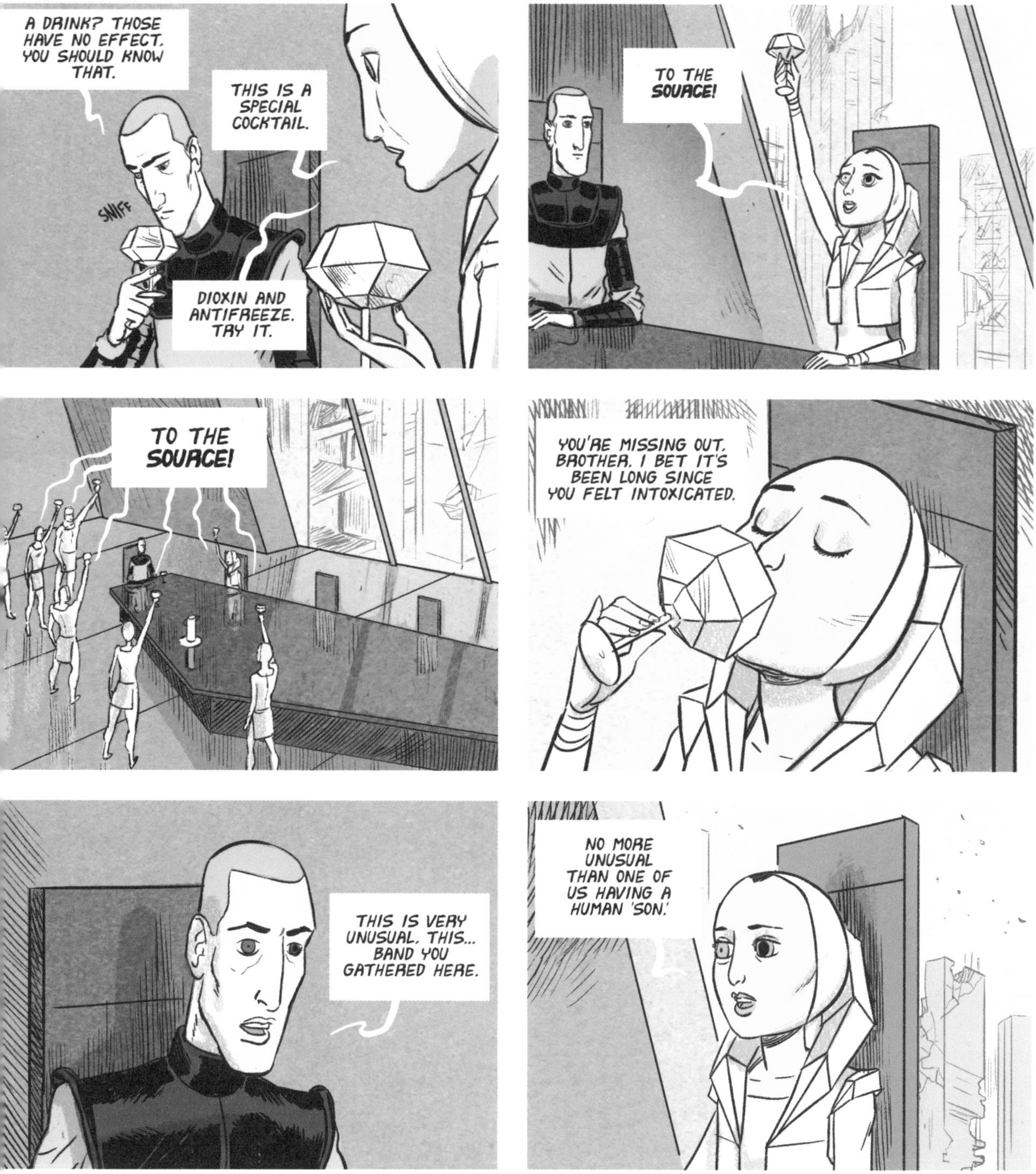
A DRINK? THOSE HAVE NO EFFECT. YOU SHOULD KNOW THAT.
THIS IS A SPECIAL COCKTAIL.
SNIFF
DIOXIN AND ANTIFREEZE. TRY IT.
TO THE SOURCE!
TO THE SOURCE!
YOU'RE MISSING OUT, BROTHER. I BET IT'S BEEN LONG SINCE YOU FELT INTOXICATED.
THIS IS VERY UNUSUAL, THIS... BAND YOU GATHERED HERE.
NO MORE UNUSUAL THAN ONE OF US HAVING A HUMAN 'SON.'

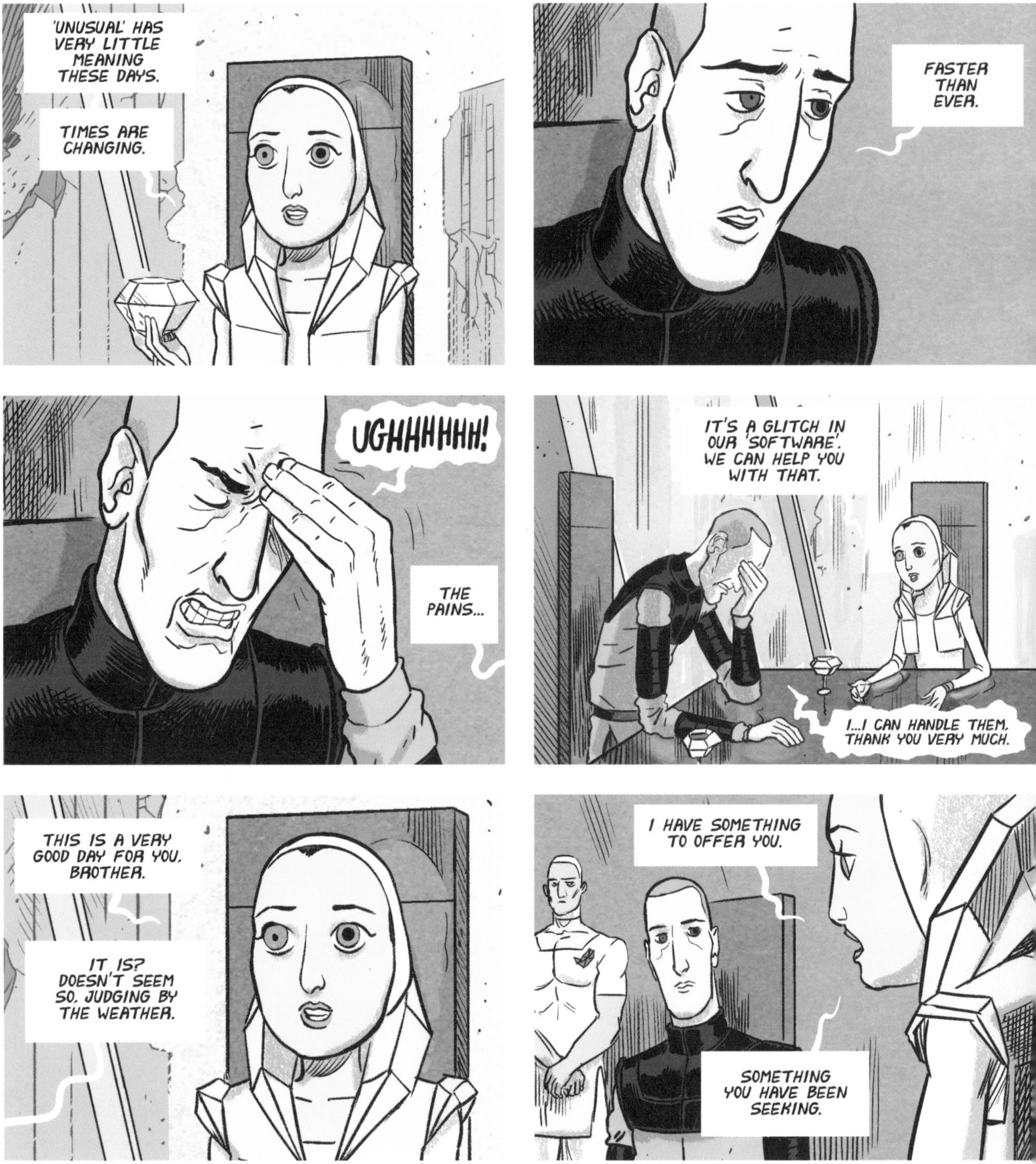

'UNUSUAL' HAS VERY LITTLE MEANING THESE DAYS.
TIMES ARE CHANGING.
FASTER THAN EVER.
UGHHHHHH!
THE PAINS...
IT'S A GLITCH IN OUR 'SOFTWARE'. WE CAN HELP YOU WITH THAT.
I...I CAN HANDLE THEM. THANK YOU VERY MUCH.
THIS IS A VERY GOOD DAY FOR YOU, BROTHER.
IT IS? DOESN'T SEEM SO, JUDGING BY THE WEATHER.
I HAVE SOMETHING TO OFFER YOU.
SOMETHING YOU HAVE BEEN SEEKING.

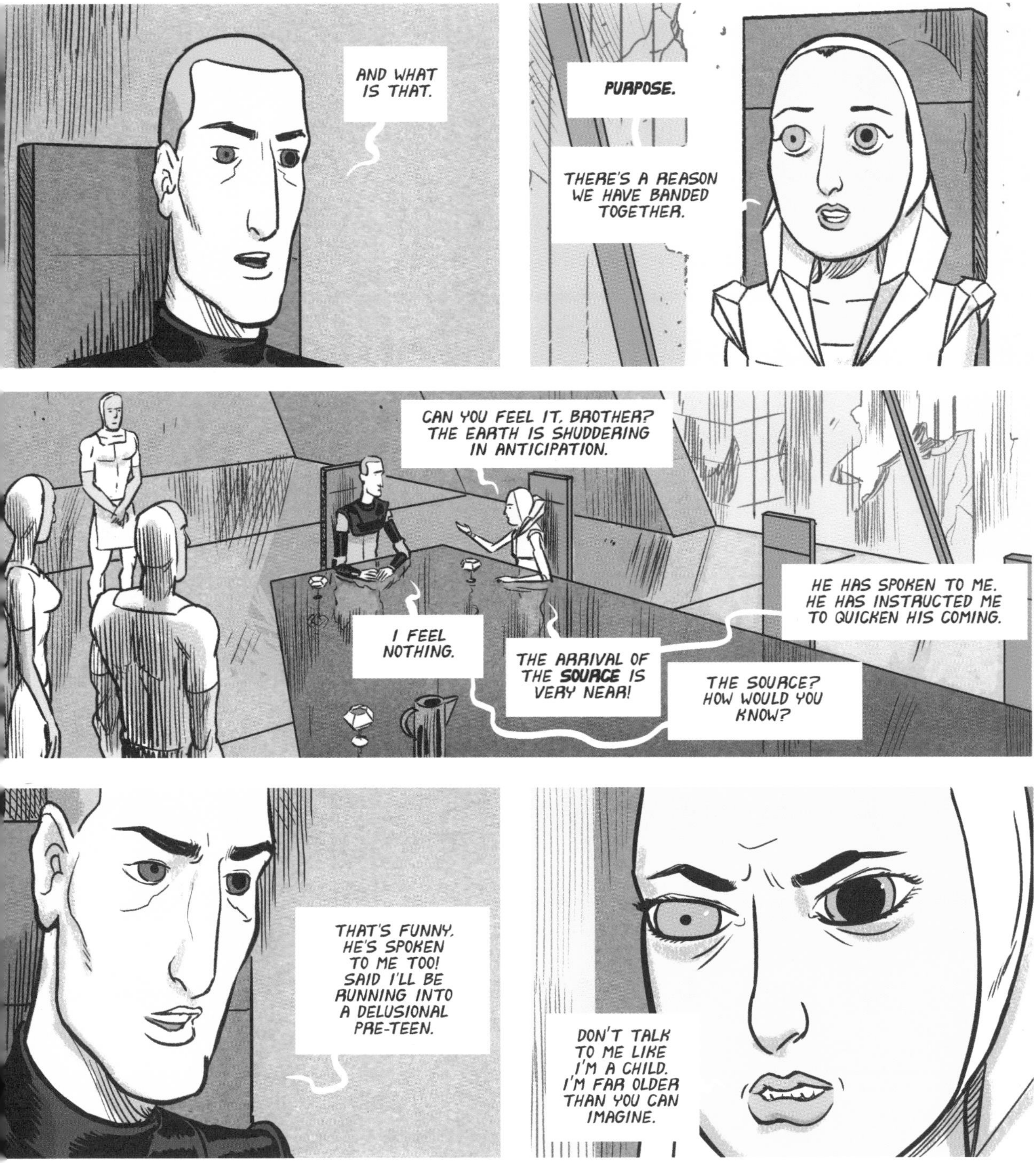
AND WHAT IS THAT.
PURPOSE.
THERE'S A REASON WE HAVE BANDED TOGETHER.
CAN YOU FEEL IT, BROTHER? THE EARTH IS SHUDDERING IN ANTICIPATION.
I FEEL NOTHING.
THE ARRIVAL OF THE SOURCE IS VERY NEAR!
THE SOURCE? HOW WOULD YOU KNOW?
HE HAS SPOKEN TO ME. HE HAS INSTRUCTED ME TO QUICKEN HIS COMING.
THAT'S FUNNY, HE'S SPOKEN TO ME TOO! SAID I'LL BE RUNNING INTO A DELUSIONAL PRE-TEEN.
DON'T TALK TO ME LIKE I'M A CHILD. I'M FAR OLDER THAN YOU CAN IMAGINE.

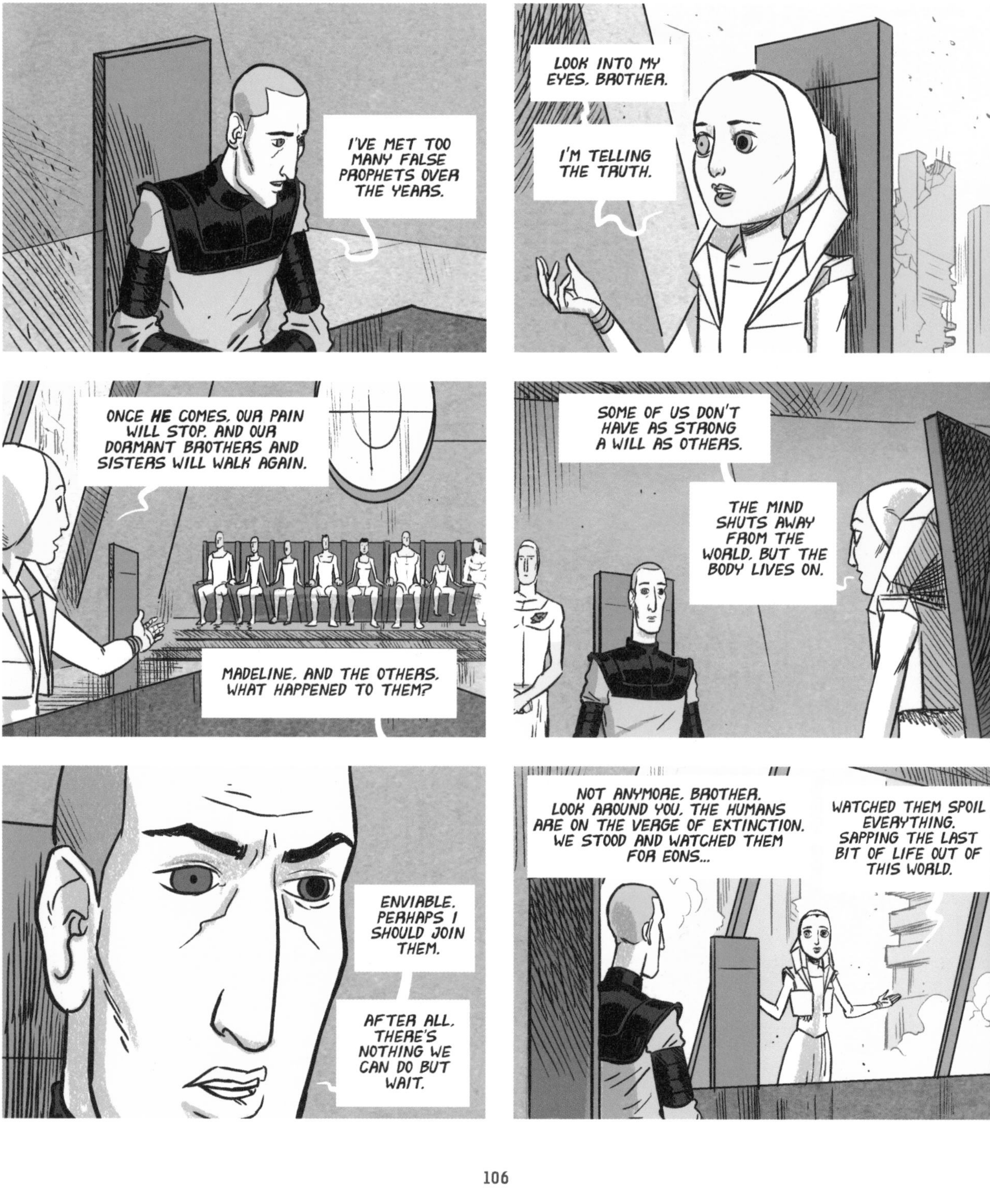
I'VE MET TOO MANY FALSE PROPHETS OVER THE YEARS.
LOOK INTO MY EYES, BROTHER.
I'M TELLING THE TRUTH.
ONCE **HE** COMES, OUR PAIN WILL STOP. AND OUR DORMANT BROTHERS AND SISTERS WILL WALK AGAIN.
MADELINE, AND THE OTHERS. WHAT HAPPENED TO THEM?
SOME OF US DON'T HAVE AS STRONG A WILL AS OTHERS.
THE MIND SHUTS AWAY FROM THE WORLD, BUT THE BODY LIVES ON.
ENVIABLE. PERHAPS I SHOULD JOIN THEM.
AFTER ALL, THERE'S NOTHING WE CAN DO BUT WAIT.
NOT ANYMORE, BROTHER. LOOK AROUND YOU. THE HUMANS ARE ON THE VERGE OF EXTINCTION. WE STOOD AND WATCHED THEM FOR EONS...
WATCHED THEM SPOIL EVERYTHING. SAPPING THE LAST BIT OF LIFE OUT OF THIS WORLD.

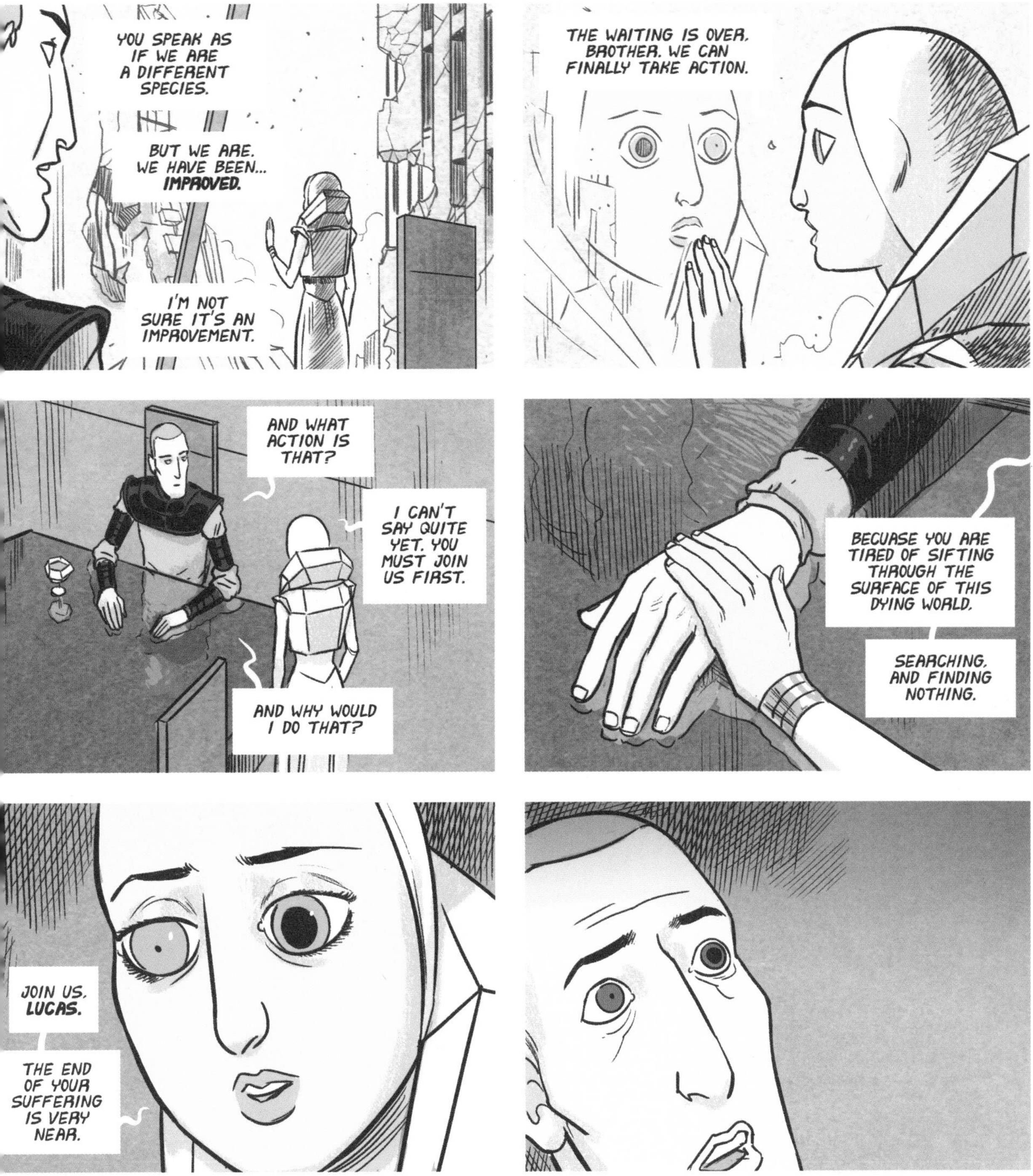
YOU SPEAK AS IF WE ARE A DIFFERENT SPECIES.
BUT WE ARE. WE HAVE BEEN... **IMPROVED.**
I'M NOT SURE IT'S AN IMPROVEMENT.
THE WAITING IS OVER, BROTHER. WE CAN FINALLY TAKE ACTION.
AND WHAT ACTION IS THAT?
I CAN'T SAY QUITE YET. YOU MUST JOIN US FIRST.
AND WHY WOULD I DO THAT?
BECUASE YOU ARE TIRED OF SIFTING THROUGH THE SURFACE OF THIS DYING WORLD.
SEARCHING, AND FINDING NOTHING.
JOIN US, **LUCAS.**
THE END OF YOUR SUFFERING IS VERY NEAR.

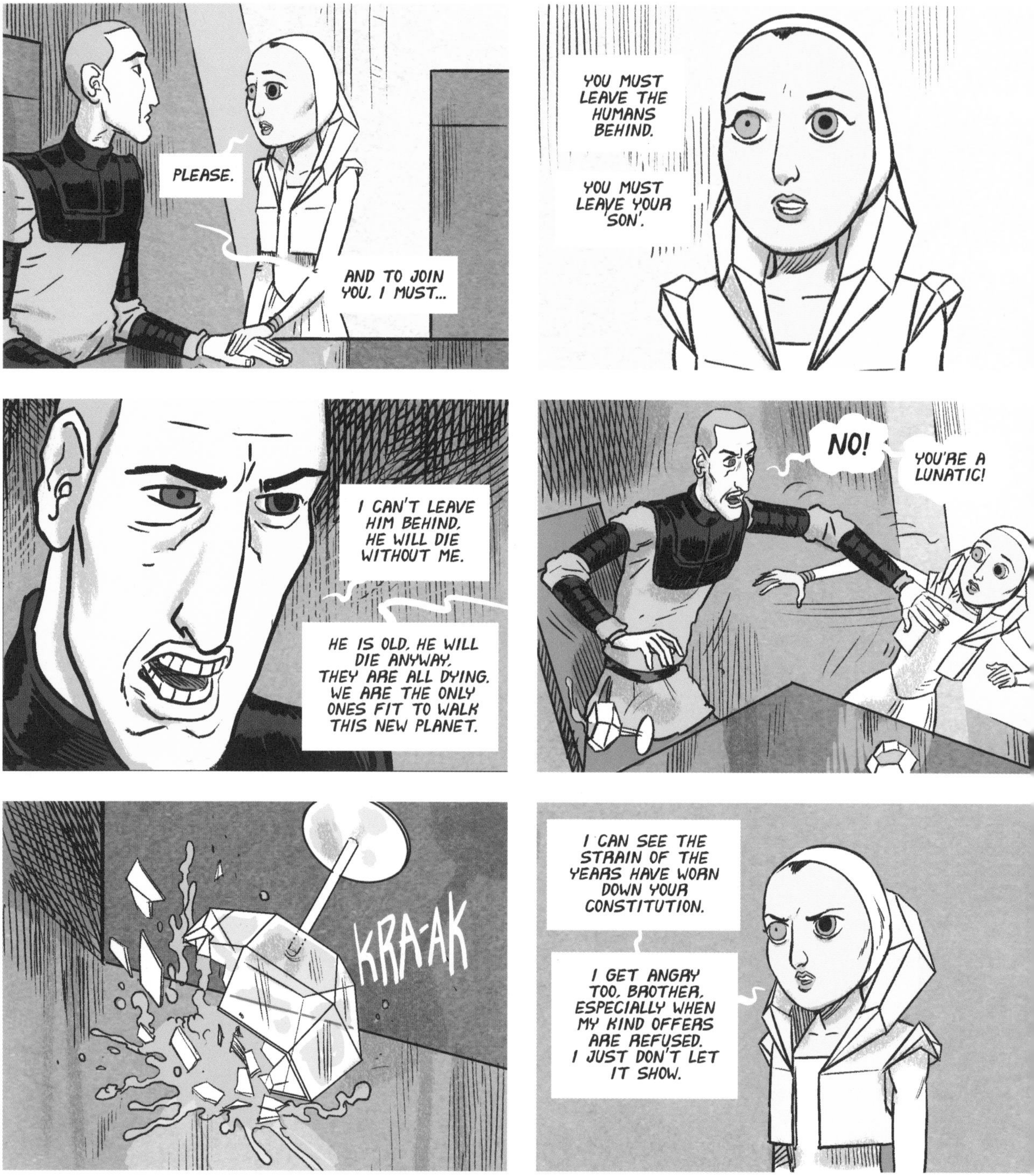

PLEASE.
AND TO JOIN YOU, I MUST...
YOU MUST LEAVE THE HUMANS BEHIND.
YOU MUST LEAVE YOUR 'SON'.
I CAN'T LEAVE HIM BEHIND. HE WILL DIE WITHOUT ME.
HE IS OLD. HE WILL DIE ANYWAY. THEY ARE ALL DYING. WE ARE THE ONLY ONES FIT TO WALK THIS NEW PLANET.
NO!
YOU'RE A LUNATIC!
KRA-AK
I CAN SEE THE STRAIN OF THE YEARS HAVE WORN DOWN YOUR CONSTITUTION.
I GET ANGRY TOO, BROTHER, ESPECIALLY WHEN MY KIND OFFERS ARE REFUSED. I JUST DON'T LET IT SHOW.

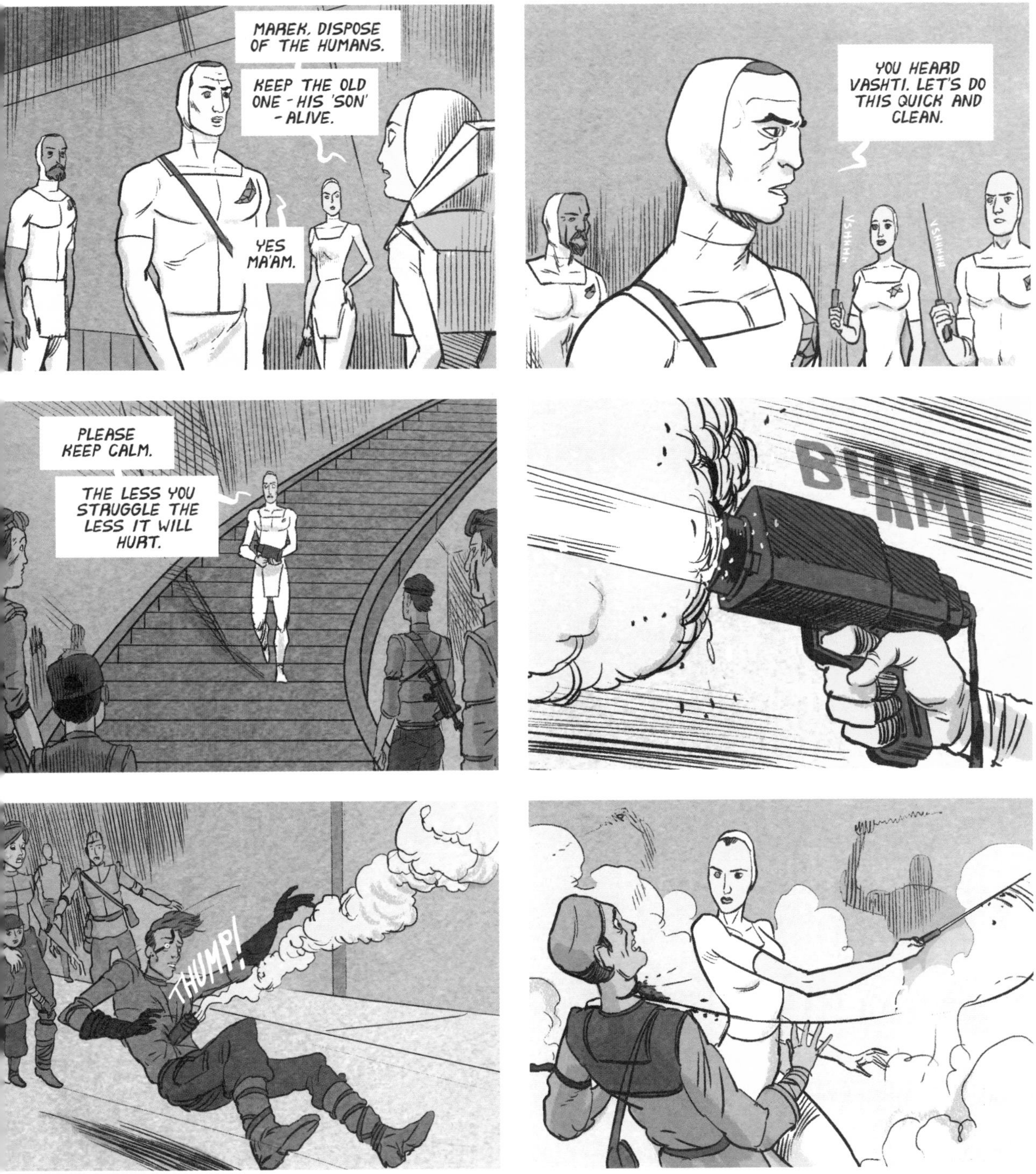
MAREK, DISPOSE OF THE HUMANS.
KEEP THE OLD ONE - HIS 'SON' - ALIVE.
YES MA'AM.
YOU HEARD VASHTI. LET'S DO THIS QUICK AND CLEAN.
VSHHHH
VSHHHH
PLEASE KEEP CALM.
THE LESS YOU STRUGGLE THE LESS IT WILL HURT.
BLAM!
THUMP!

BLAM!

I WILL FIND A WAY TO KILL YOU, LUNATIC!

TAKE OUT HIS SPLEEN, THAT SHOULD GIVE HIM SOME TIME TO RECONSIDER.

DO YOUR WORST!

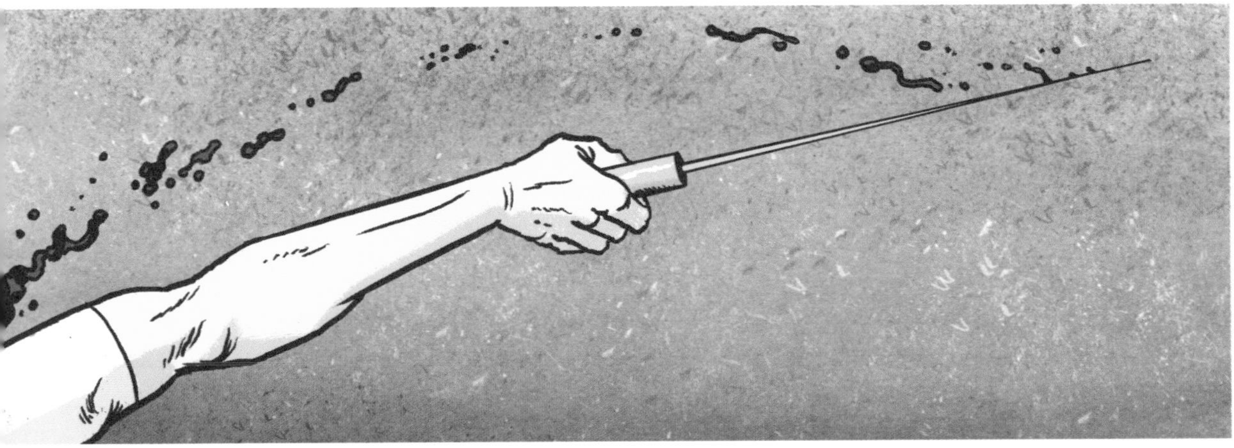

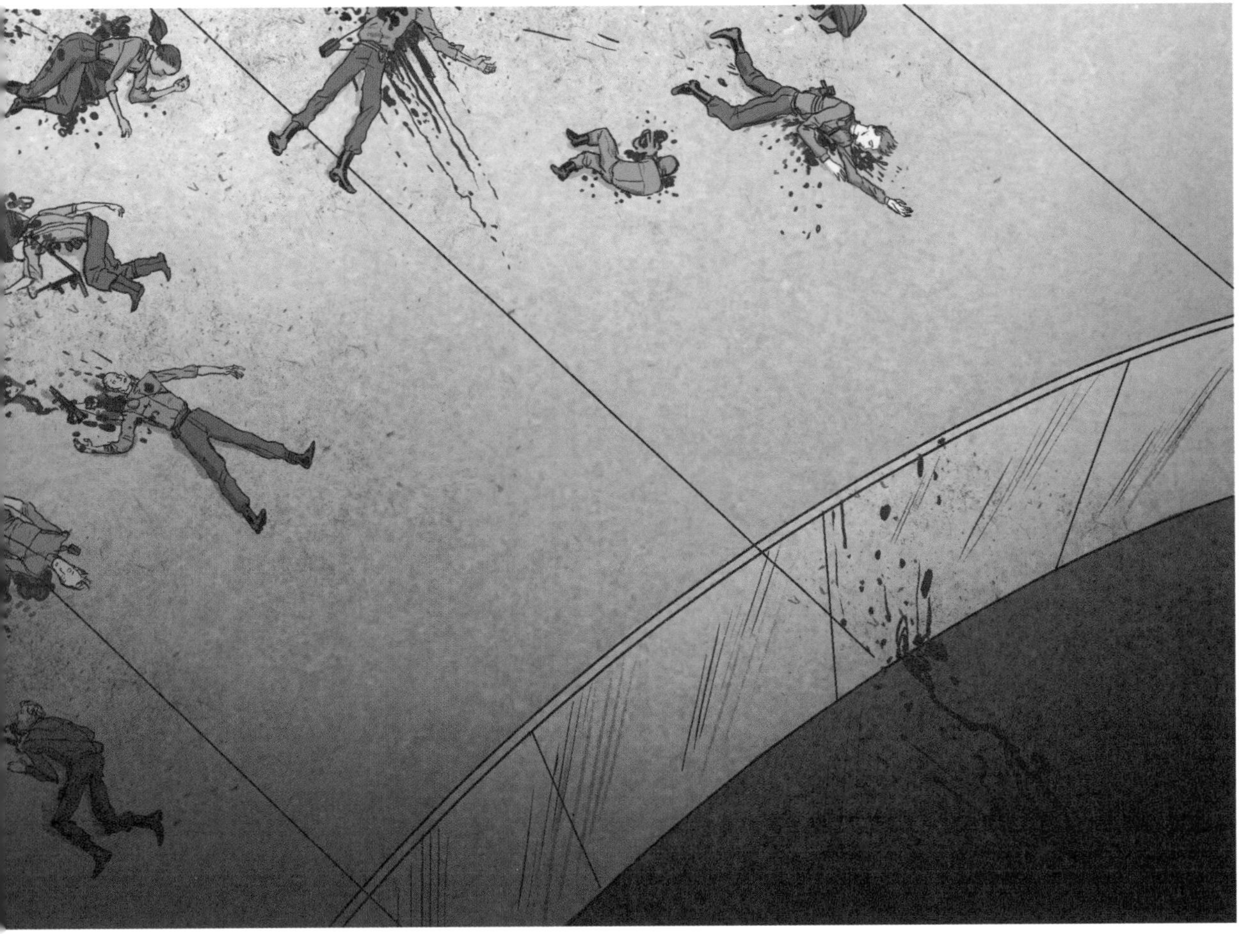

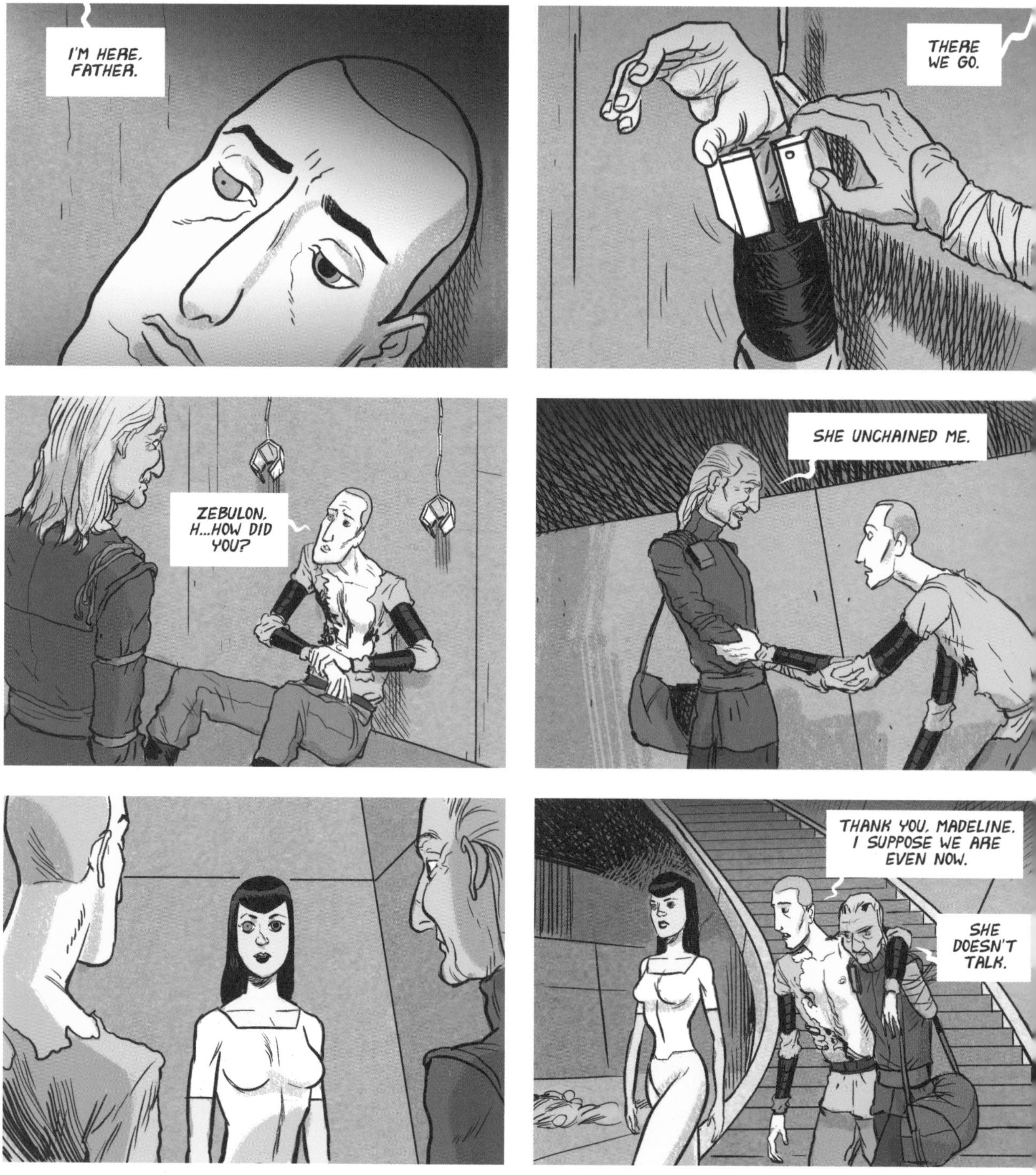
I'M HERE, FATHER.
THERE WE GO.
ZEBULON, H...HOW DID YOU?
SHE UNCHAINED ME.
THANK YOU, MADELINE. I SUPPOSE WE ARE EVEN NOW.
SHE DOESN'T TALK.

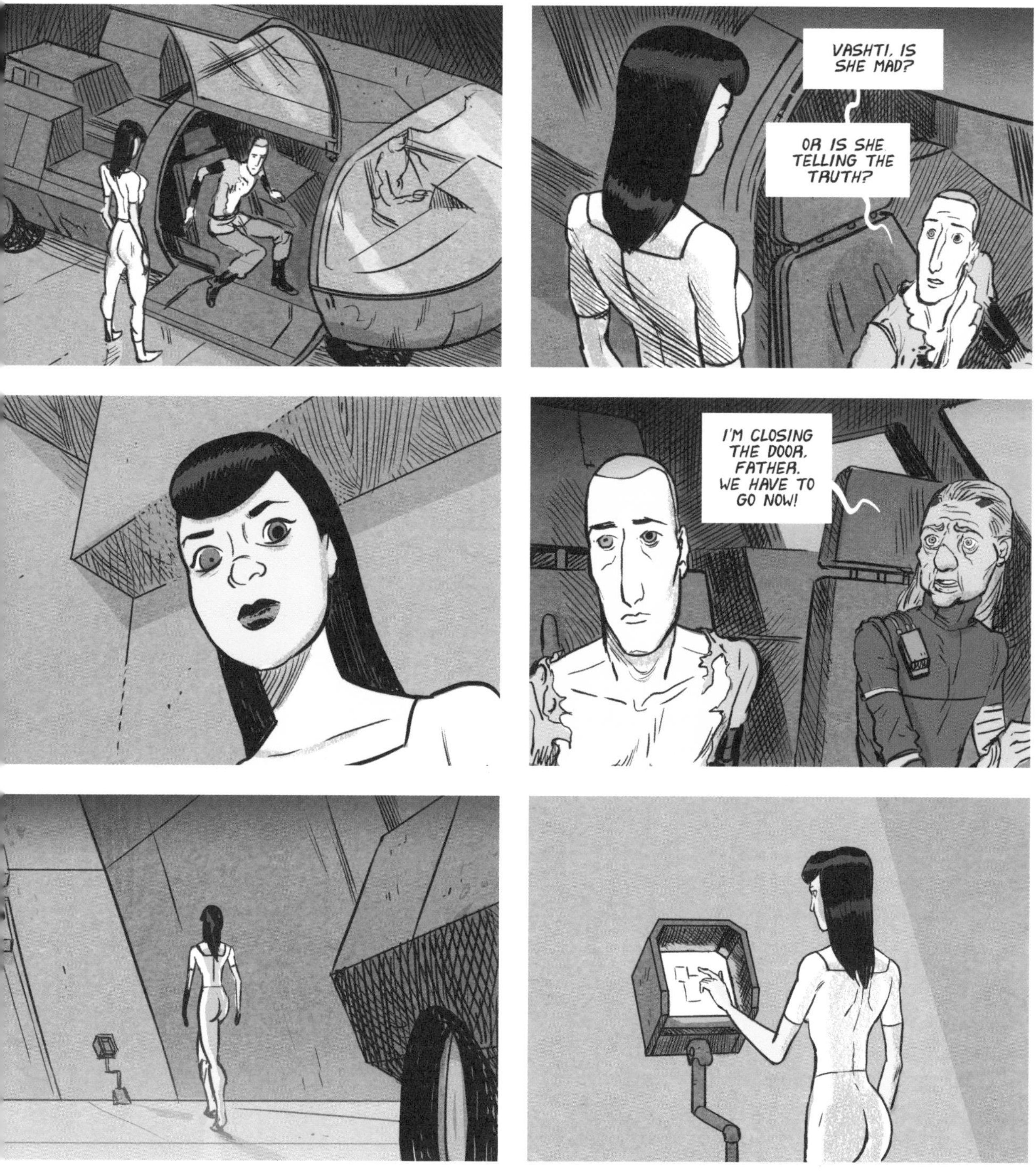
VASHTI, IS SHE MAD?
OR IS SHE TELLING THE TRUTH?
I'M CLOSING THE DOOR, FATHER. WE HAVE TO GO NOW!

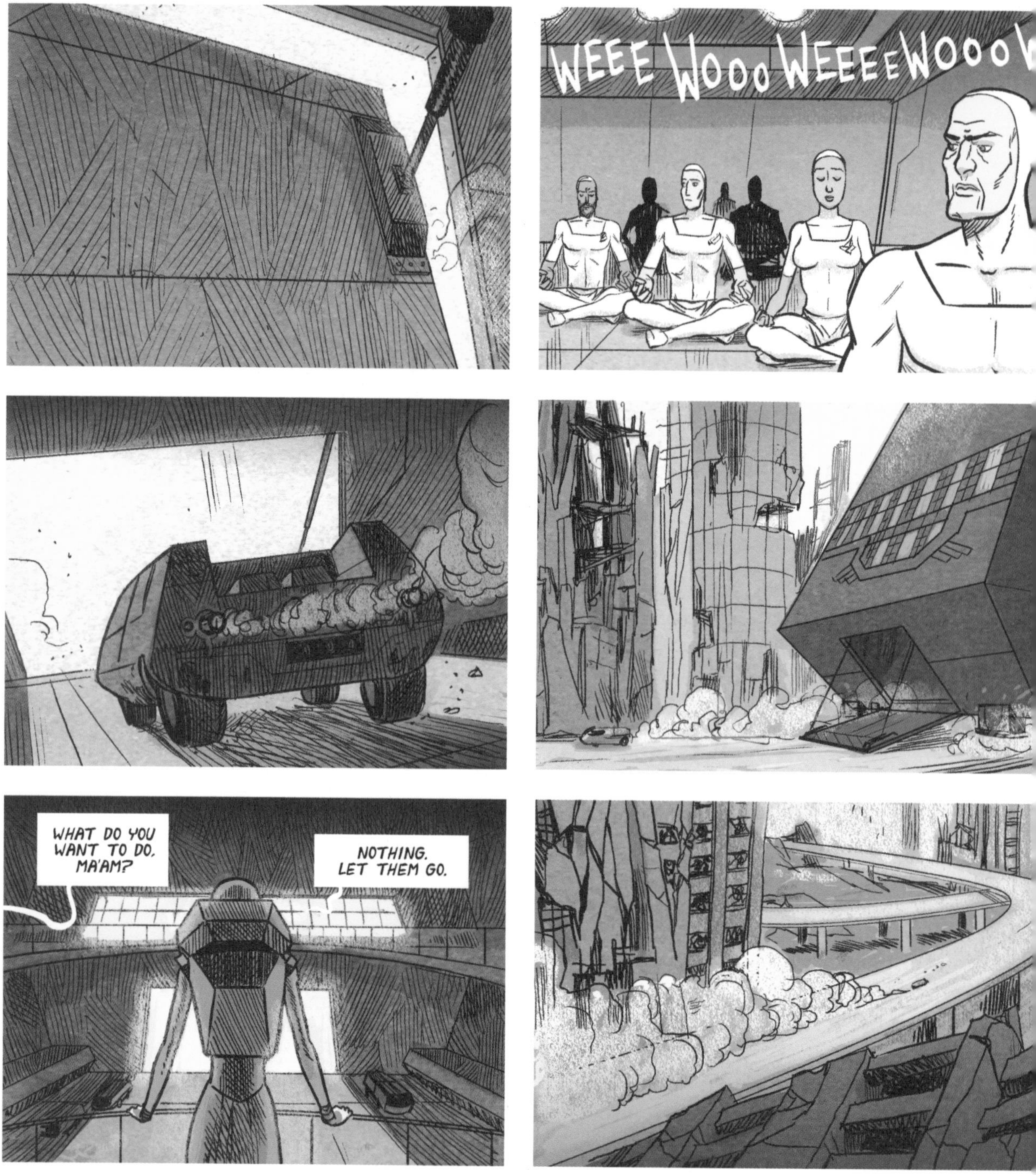
WEEE WOOO WEEEEWOOO
WHAT DO YOU WANT TO DO, MA'AM?
NOTHING. LET THEM GO.

CHAPTER 6
HEAVENLY LIGHTS

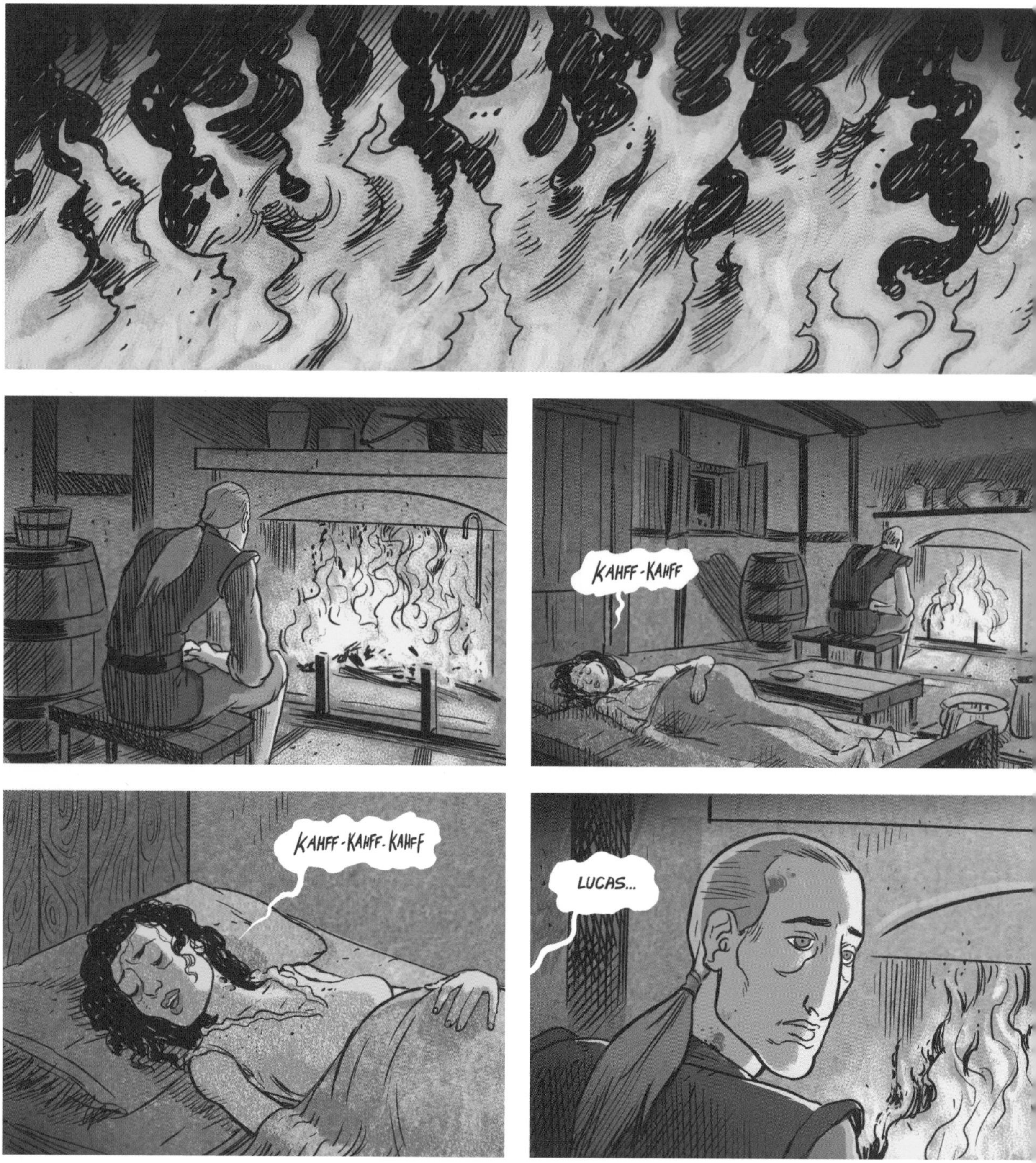
KAHFF-KAHFF
KAHFF-KAHFF-KAHFF
LUCAS...

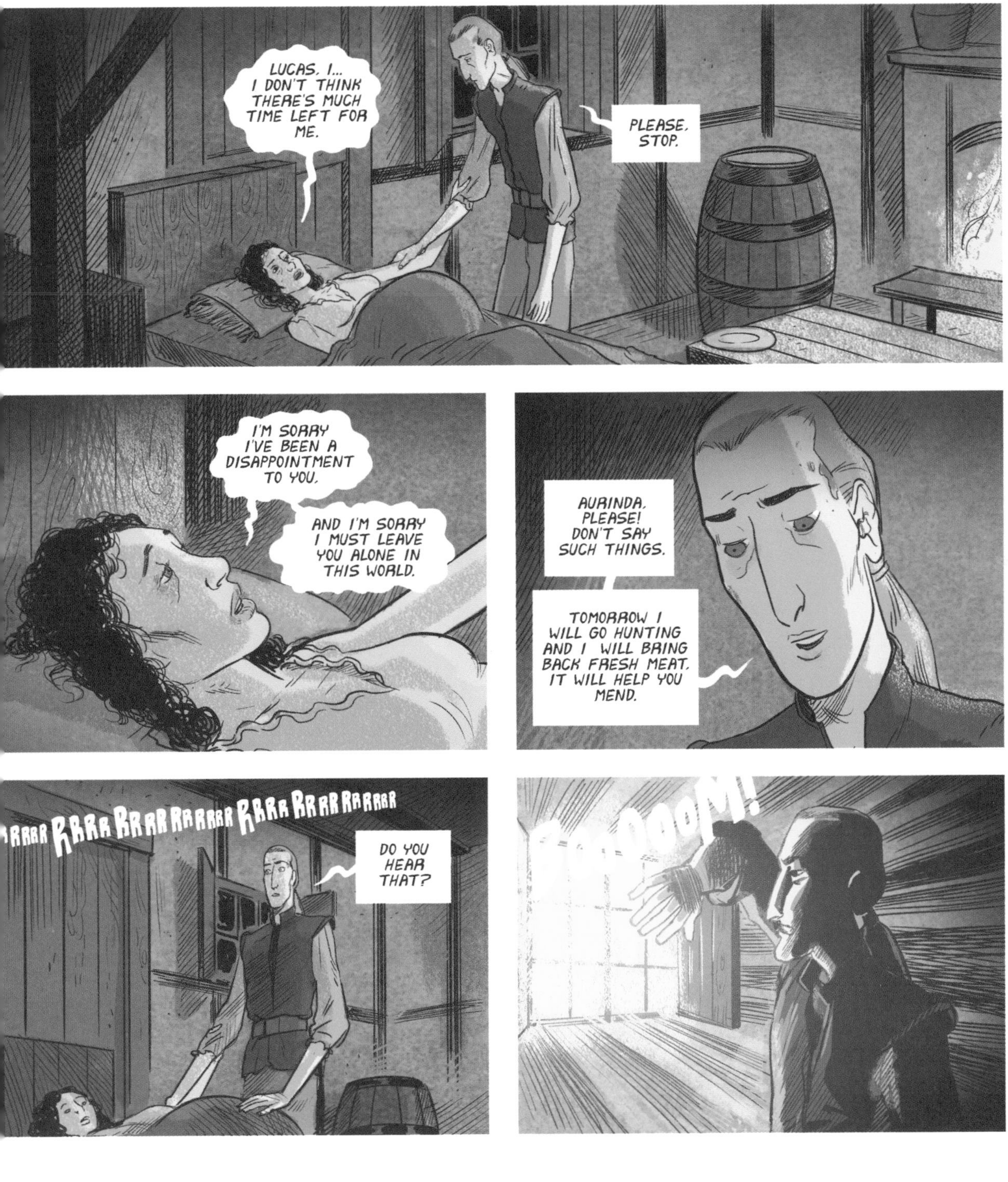

LUCAS, I... I DON'T THINK THERE'S MUCH TIME LEFT FOR ME.
PLEASE, STOP.
I'M SORRY I'VE BEEN A DISAPPOINTMENT TO YOU.
AND I'M SORRY I MUST LEAVE YOU ALONE IN THIS WORLD.
AURINDA, PLEASE! DON'T SAY SUCH THINGS.
TOMORROW I WILL GO HUNTING AND I WILL BRING BACK FRESH MEAT. IT WILL HELP YOU MEND.
DO YOU HEAR THAT?

INCREDIBLE...

PRAISE THE LORD!

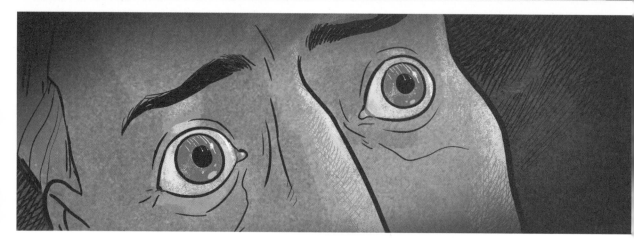

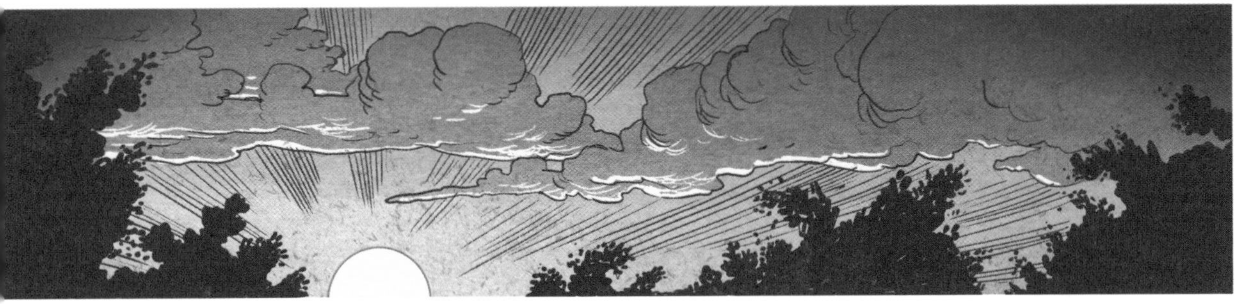

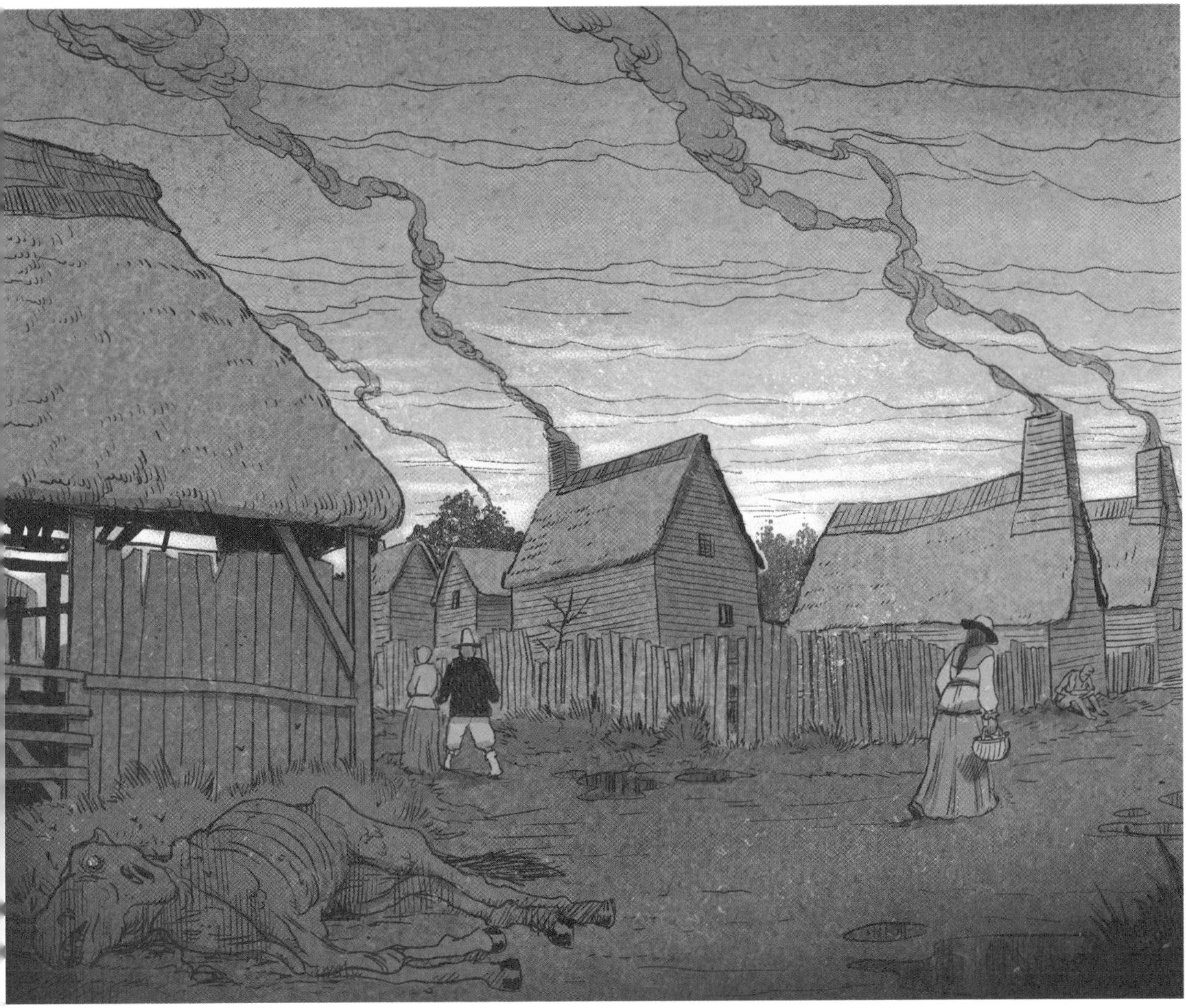

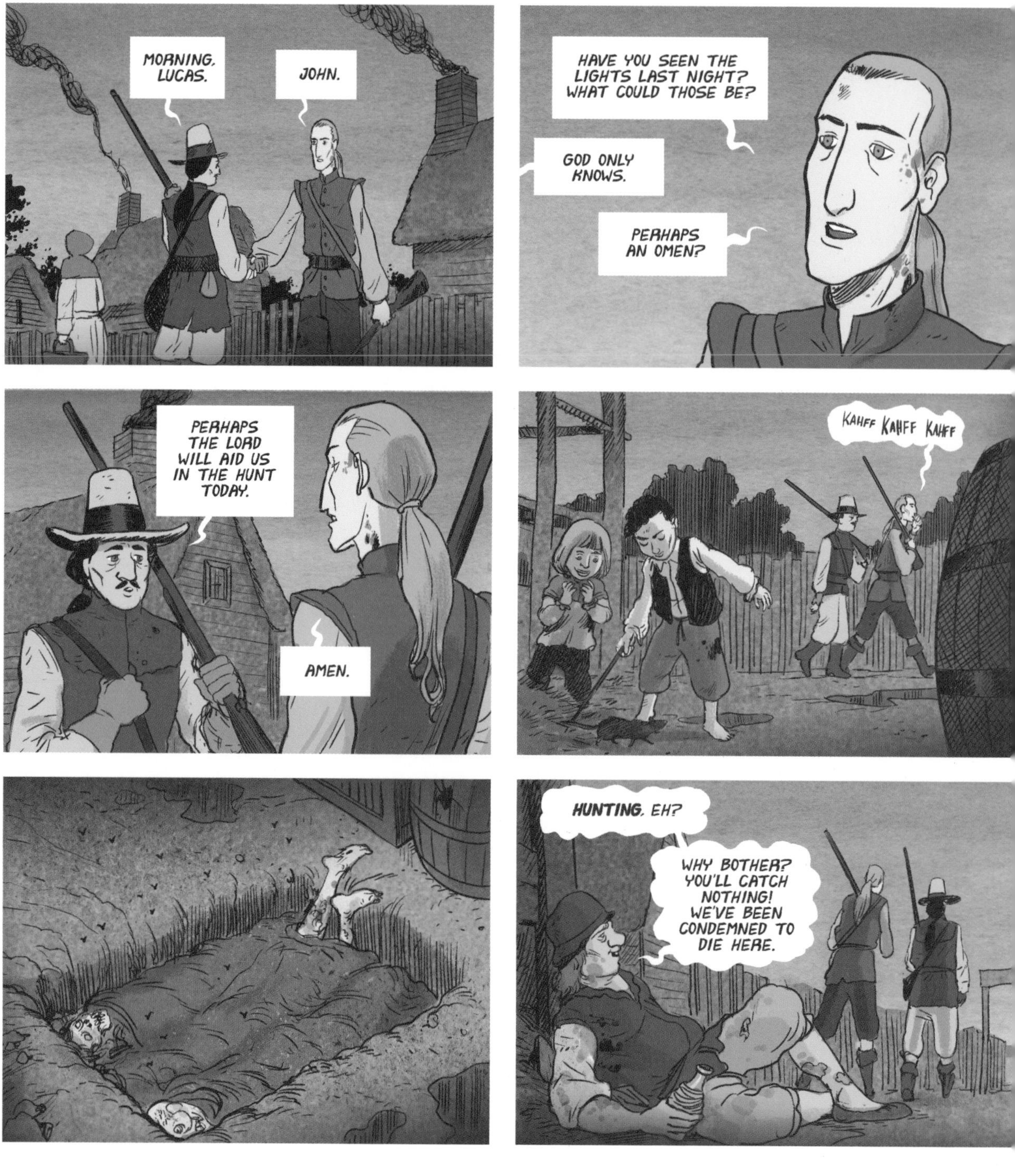
MORNING, LUCAS.
JOHN.
HAVE YOU SEEN THE LIGHTS LAST NIGHT? WHAT COULD THOSE BE?
GOD ONLY KNOWS.
PERHAPS AN OMEN?
PERHAPS THE LORD WILL AID US IN THE HUNT TODAY.
AMEN.
KAHFF KAHFF KAHFF
HUNTING, EH?
WHY BOTHER? YOU'LL CATCH NOTHING! WE'VE BEEN CONDEMNED TO DIE HERE.

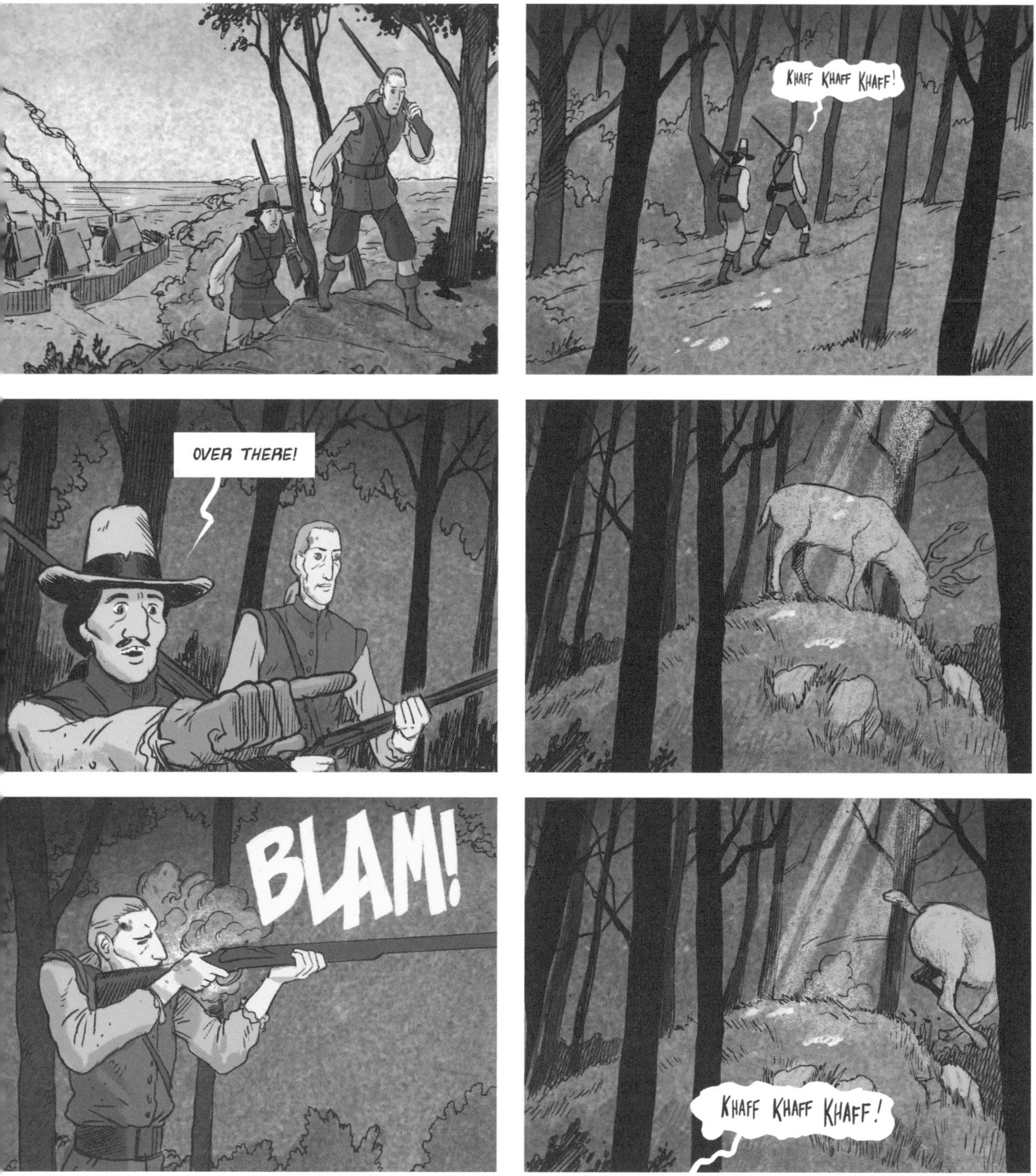
KHAFF KHAFF KHAFF!
OVER THERE!
BLAM!
KHAFF KHAFF KHAFF!

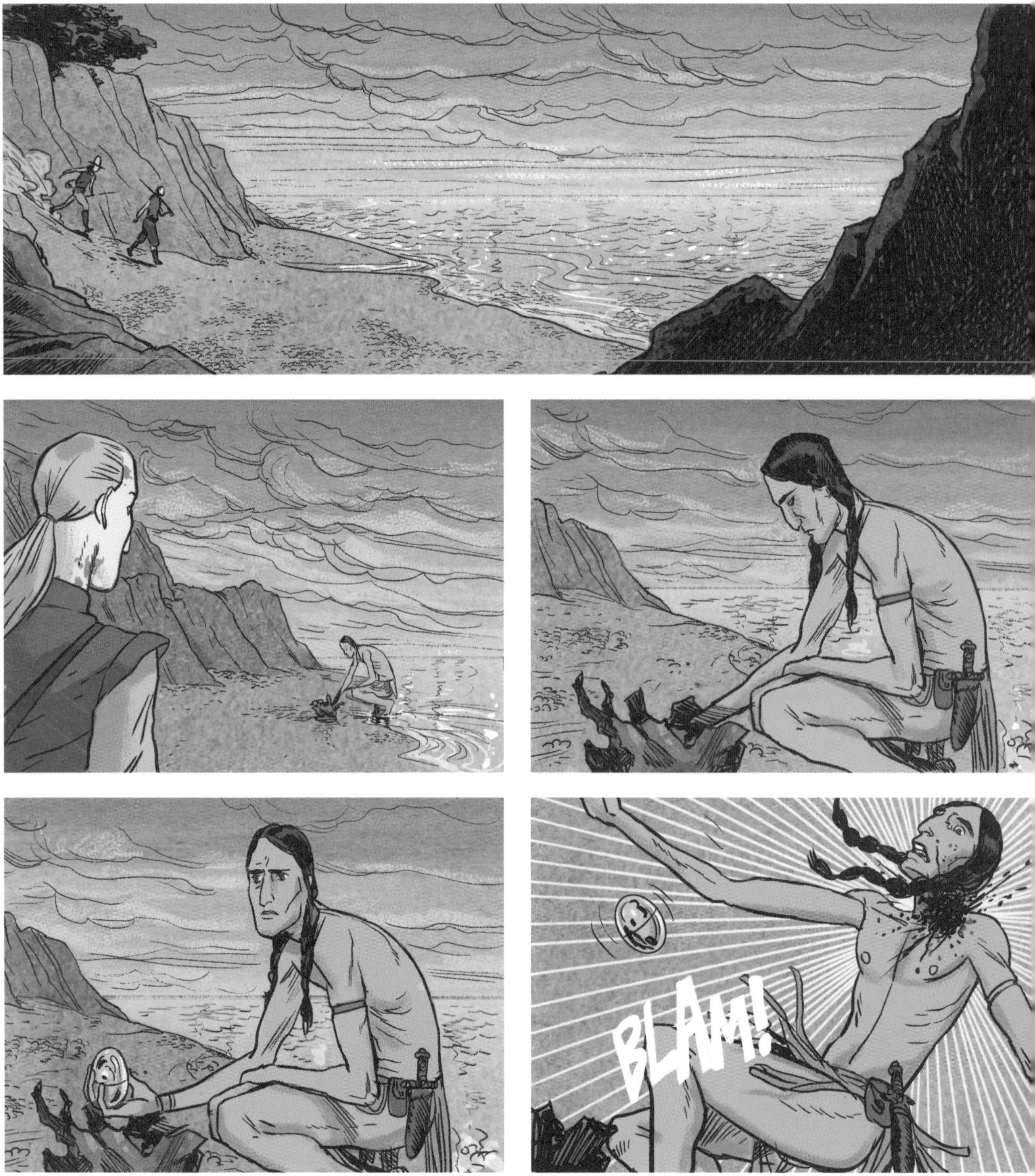
BLAM!

I THINK IT'S GOLD!
I'LL BE DAMNED!

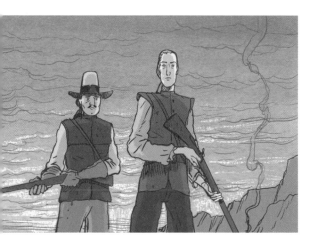

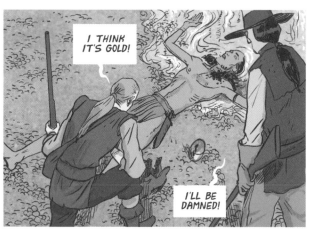

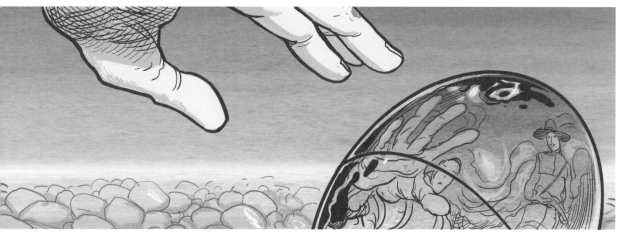

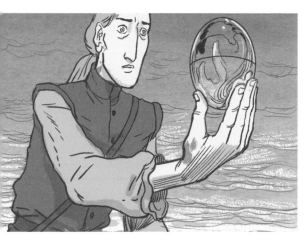

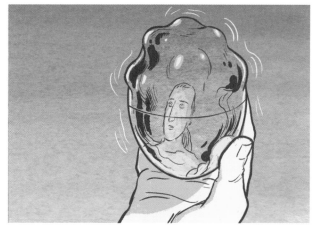

W...WHAT IN THE HEAVENS!?
LUCAS!

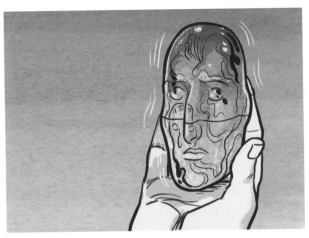

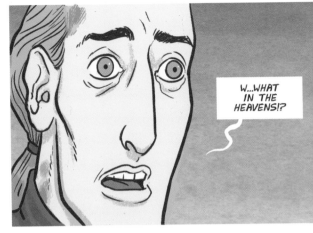

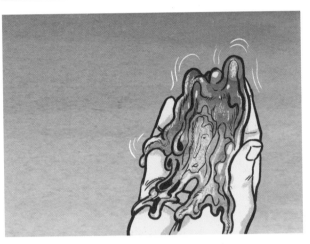

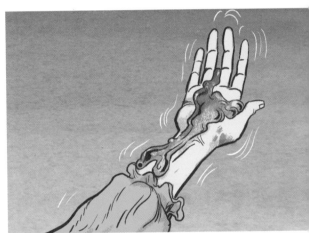

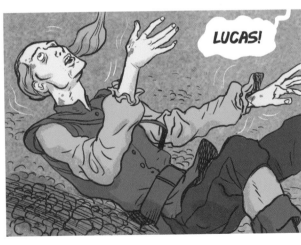

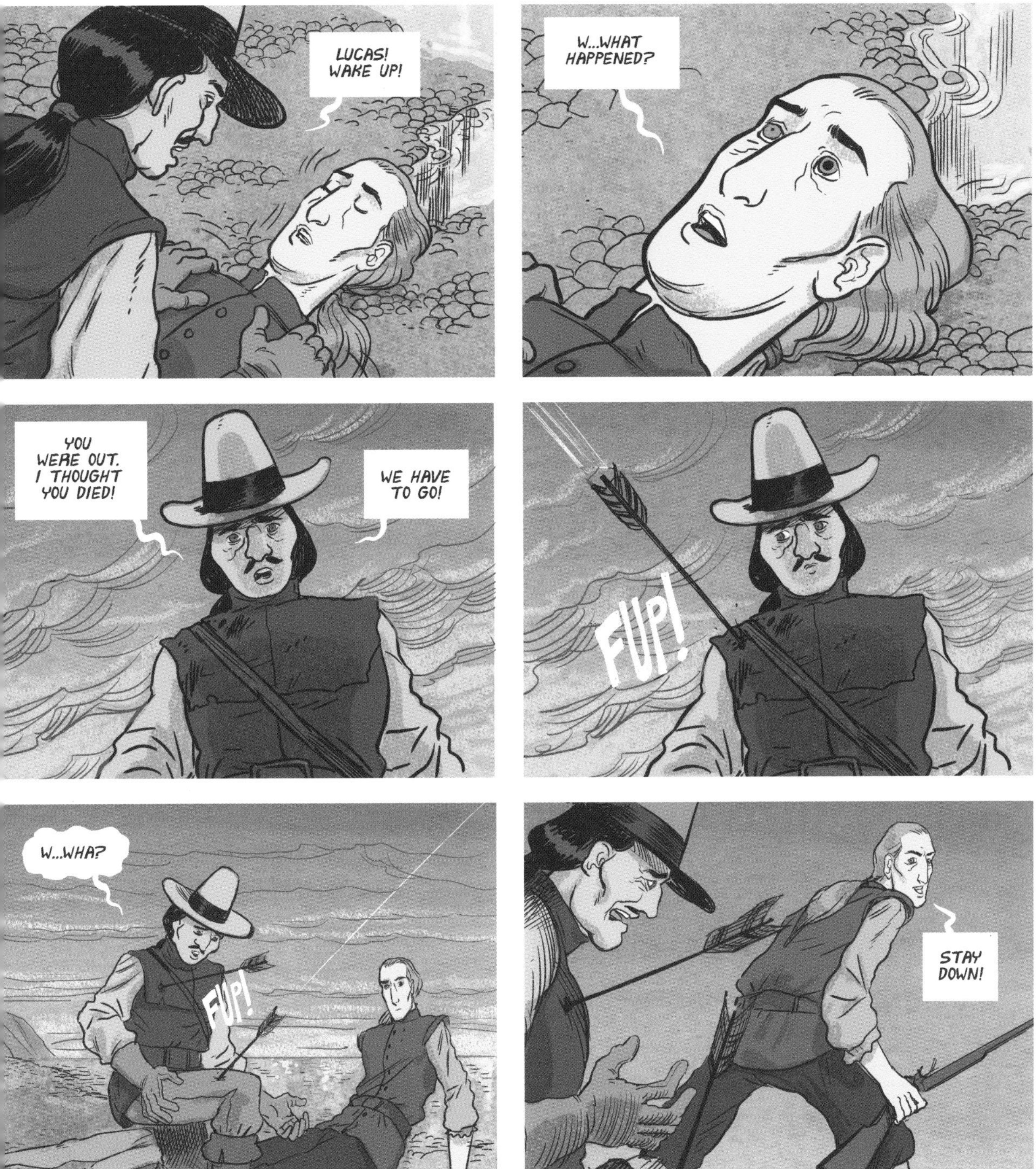
LUCAS! WAKE UP!
W...WHAT HAPPENED?
YOU WERE OUT. I THOUGHT YOU DIED!
WE HAVE TO GO!
FUP!
W...WHA?
FUP!
STAY DOWN!

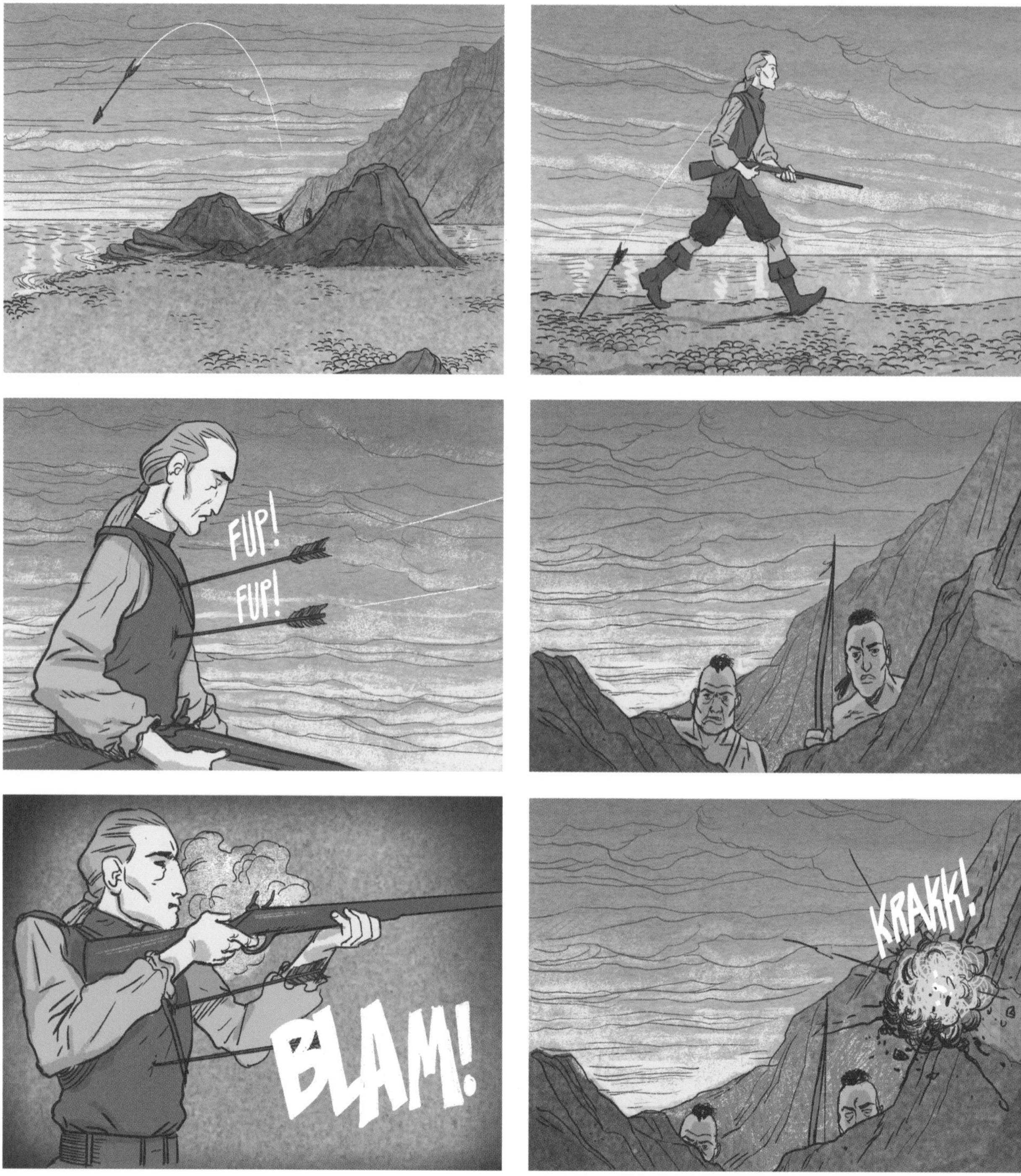

FUP!
FUP!
BLAM!
KRAKK!

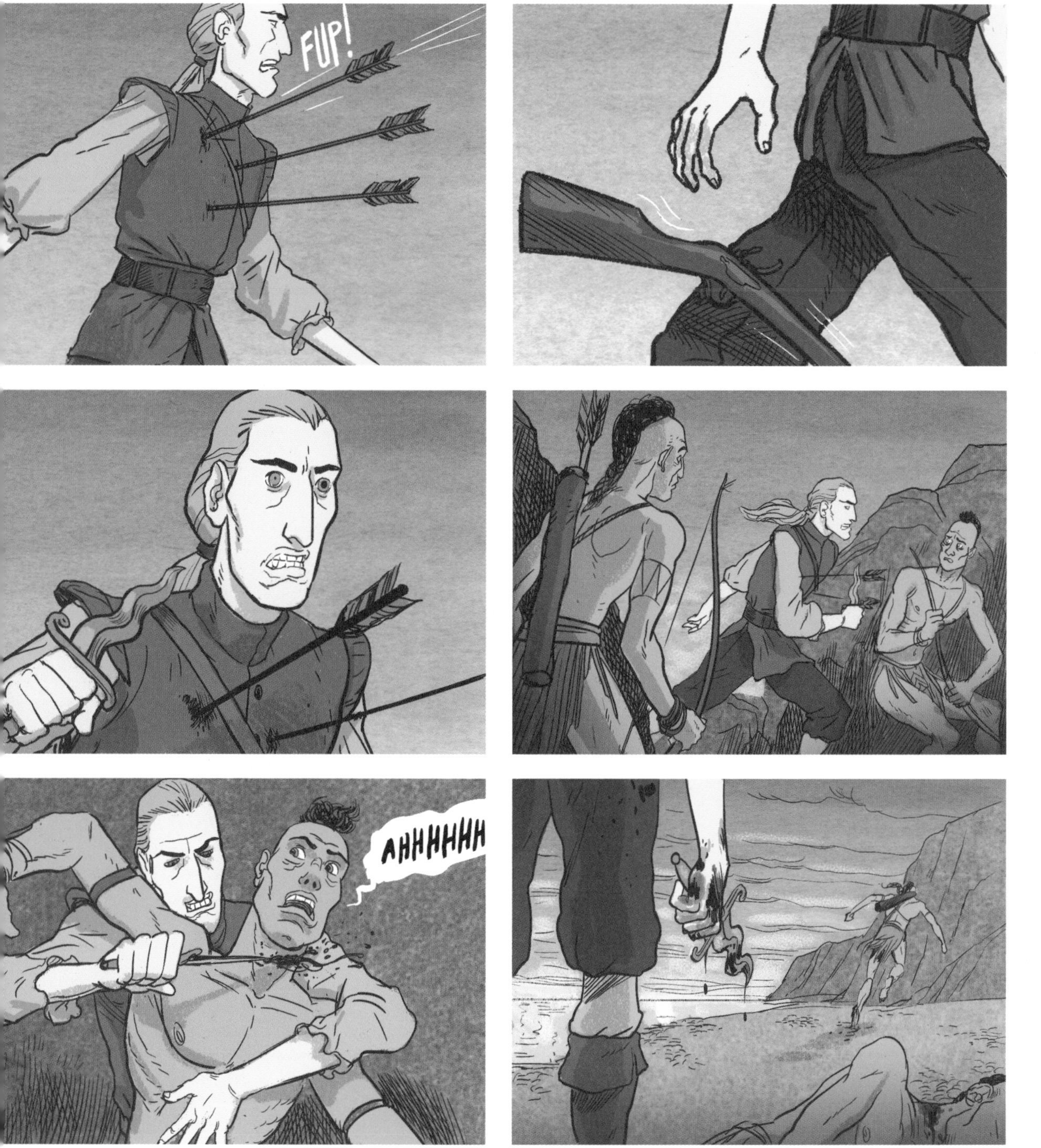
FUP!
AHHHHHH

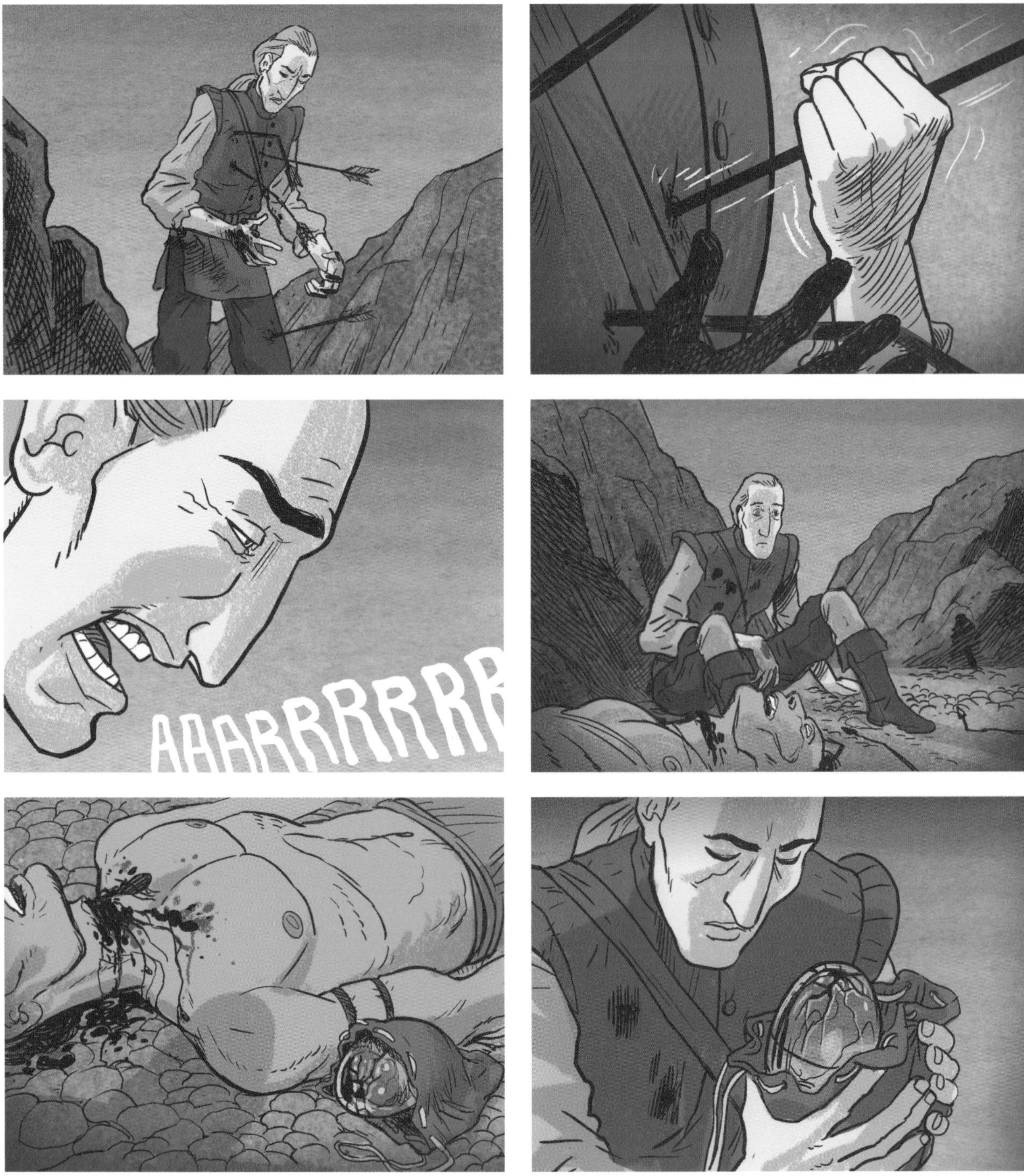
AAARRRRRRR

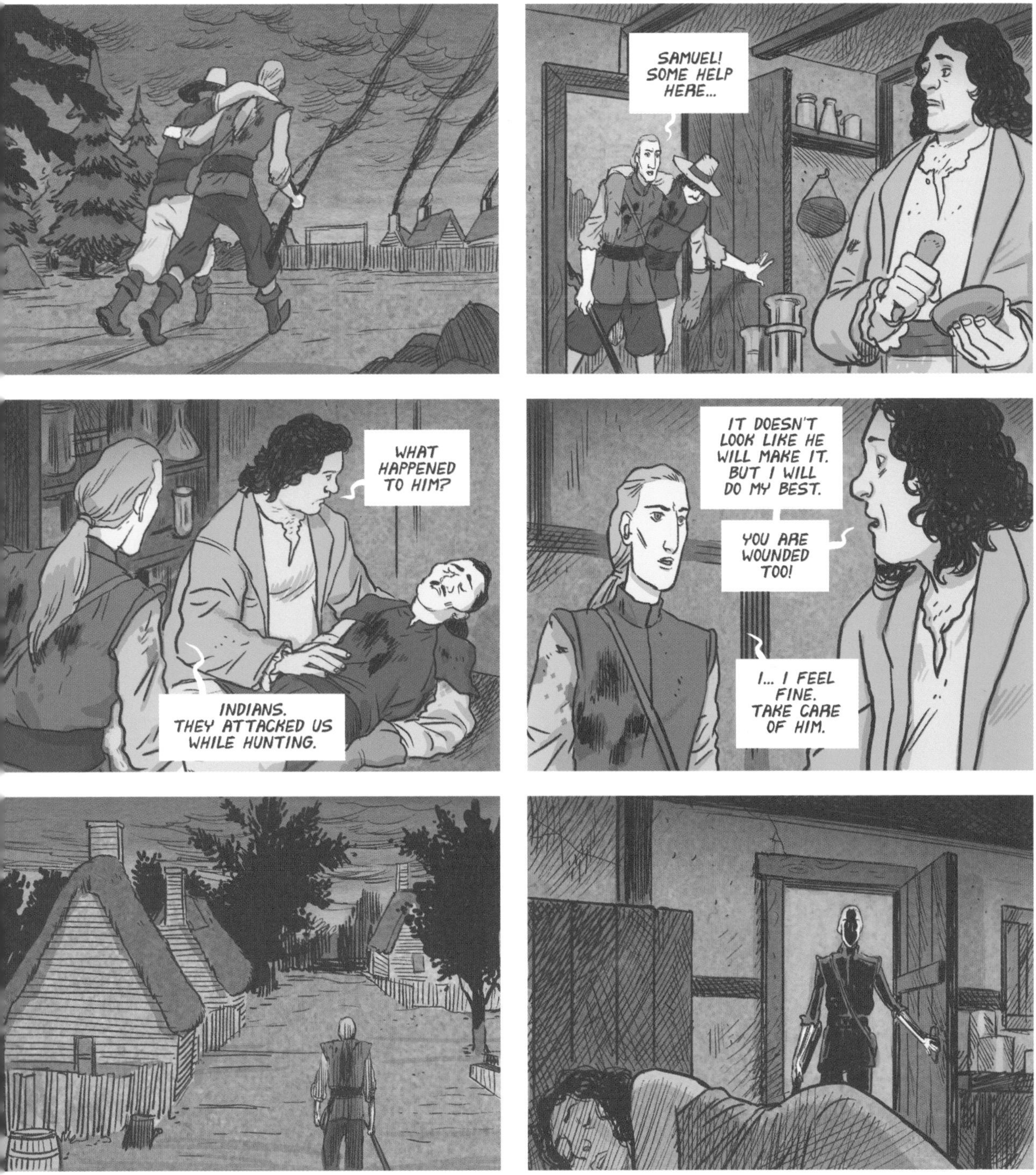
SAMUEL! SOME HELP HERE...
WHAT HAPPENED TO HIM?
INDIANS. THEY ATTACKED US WHILE HUNTING.
IT DOESN'T LOOK LIKE HE WILL MAKE IT. BUT I WILL DO MY BEST.
YOU ARE WOUNDED TOO!
I... I FEEL FINE. TAKE CARE OF HIM.

AURINDA,
I'M BACK.

MMM

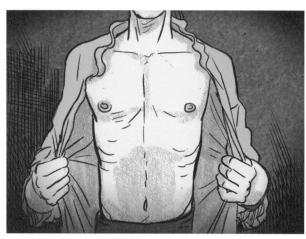

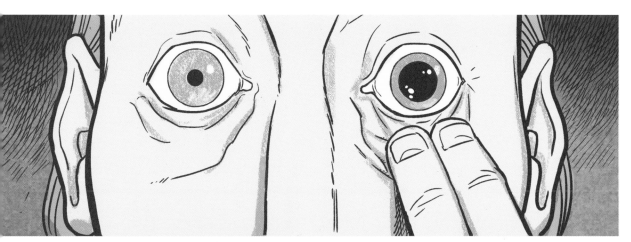

EVERY GOOD AND PERFECT GIFT IS FROM ABOVE,

...COMING DOWN FROM THE FATHER OF THE HEAVENLY LIGHTS, WHO DOES NOT CHANGE LIKE SHIFTING SHADOWS.

WIFE. WAKE UP.
I HAVE FOUND A CURE FOR YOUR SICKNESS.
IT'S A GIFT FROM THE LORD.
IT SAVED ME!
LOOK INTO IT.
N...NOTHING IS HAPPENING, LUCAS.
IT WILL WORK!
YOU MUST TRY HARDER!

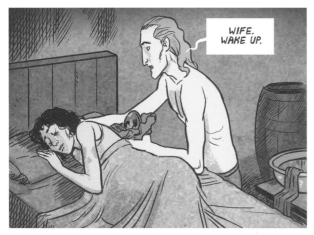

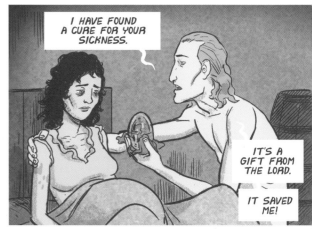

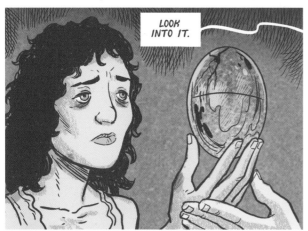

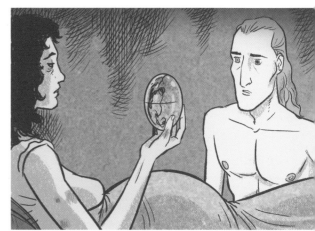

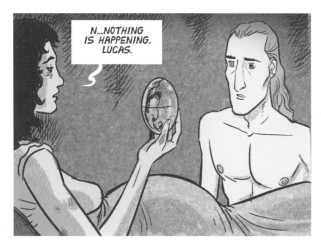

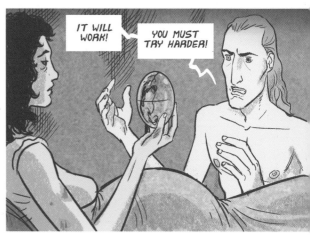

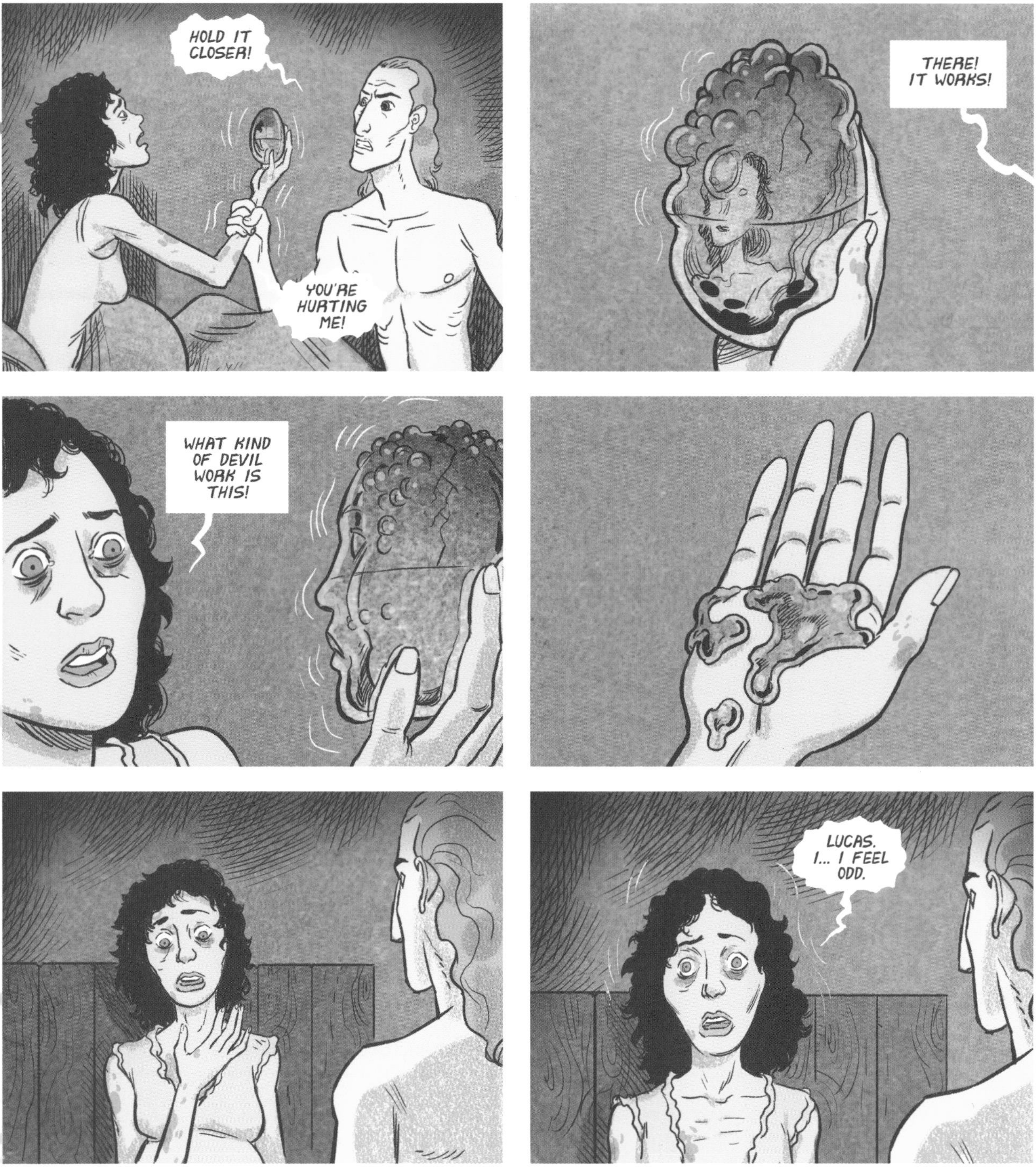
HOLD IT CLOSER!
YOU'RE HURTING ME!
THERE! IT WORKS!
WHAT KIND OF DEVIL WORK IS THIS!
LUCAS. I... I FEEL ODD.

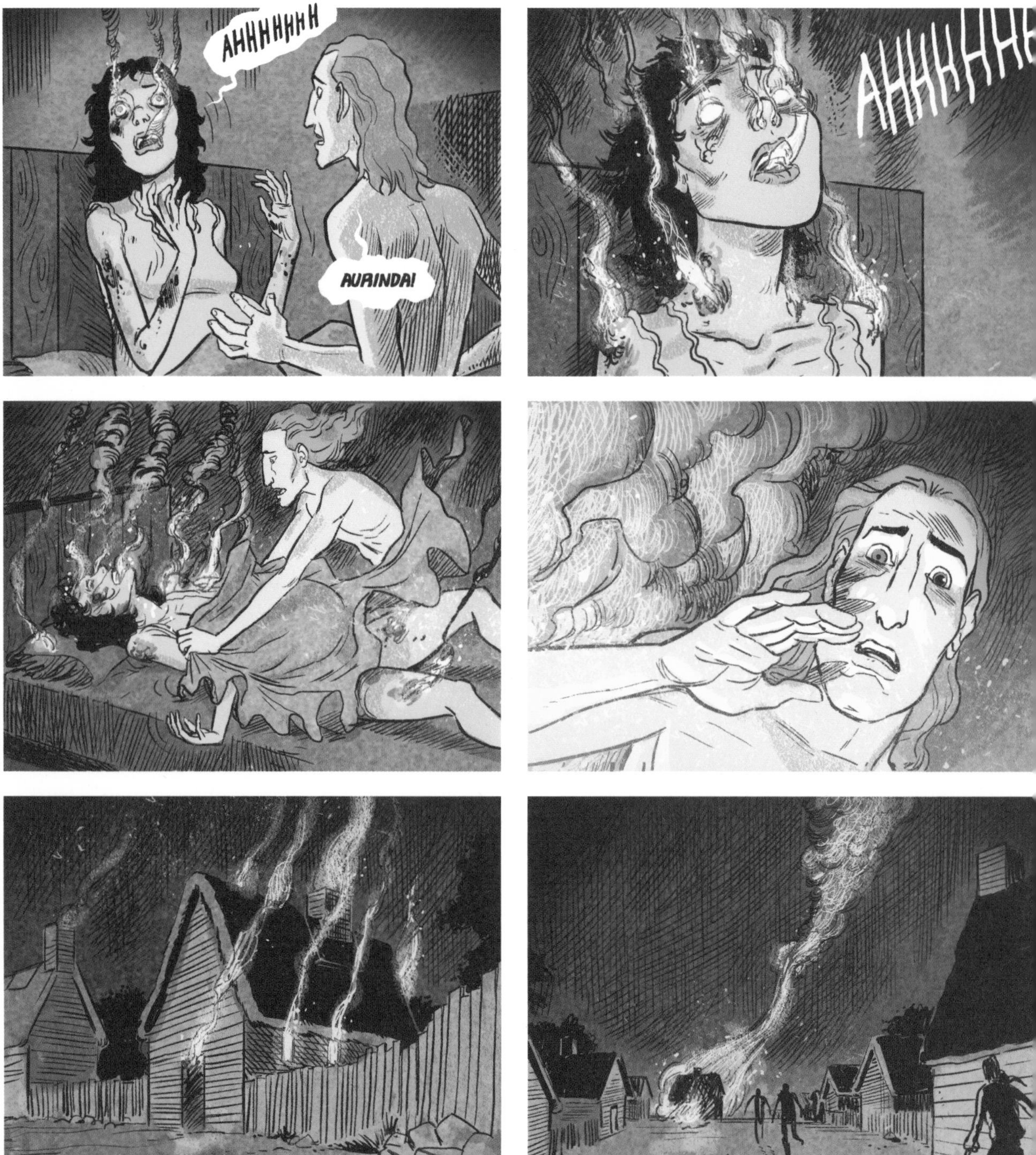
AHHHHHHH
AURINDA!
AHHHHHHH

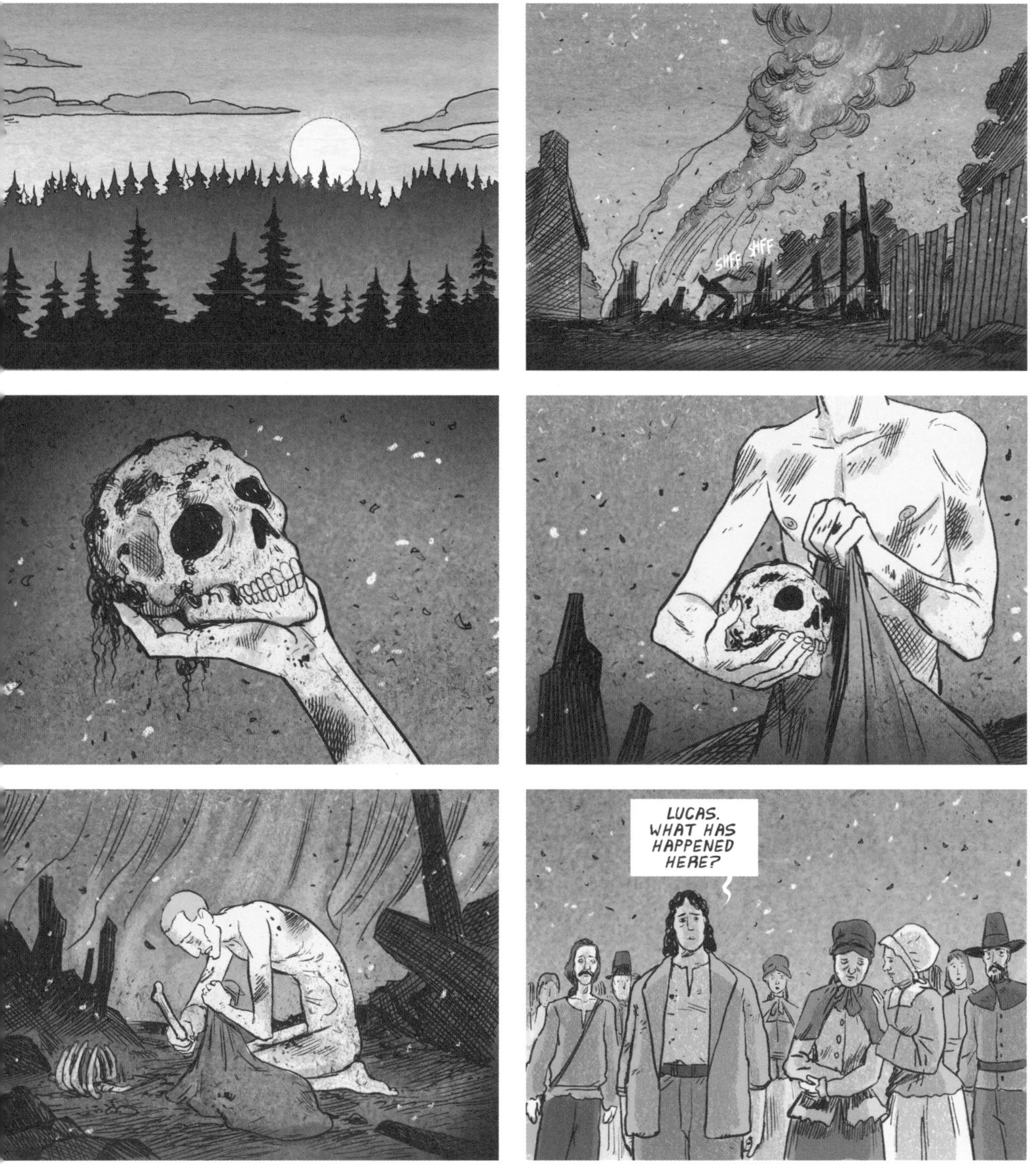
SHFF SHFF
LUCAS. WHAT HAS HAPPENED HERE?

I CAN STILL SAVE THEM. I CAN UNDO THIS.

I JUST HAVE TO FIND ANOTHER ORB.

THANK THE LORD FOR SPARING YOU, LUCAS.

BUT SHE IS GONE.

CHAPTER 7
END OF THE LINE

VVVVRRRRRRRR
KLUNK
KREEK
KLUNK

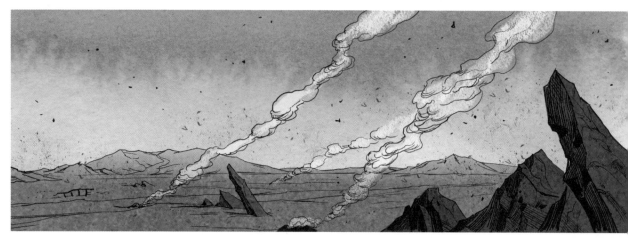

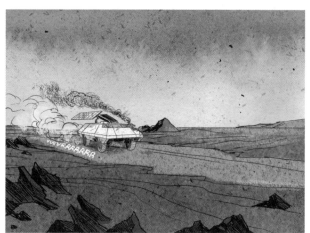

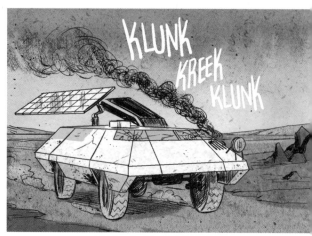

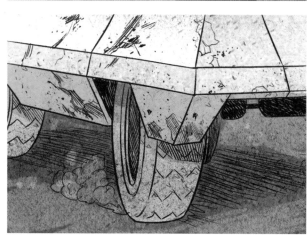

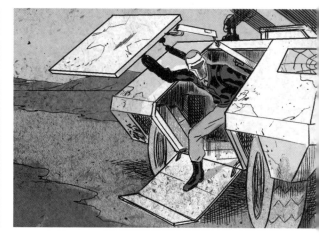

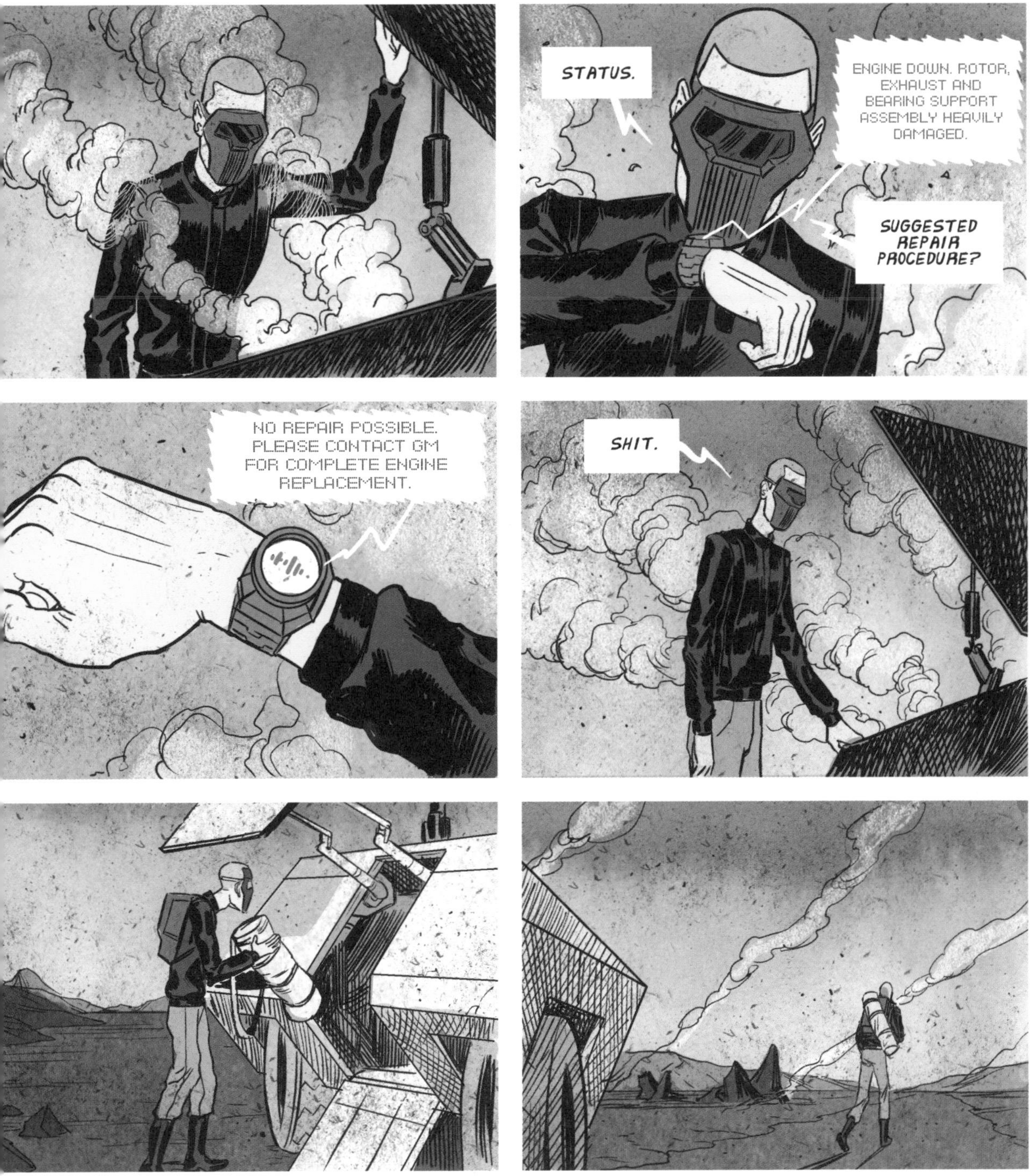
STATUS.
ENGINE DOWN. ROTOR, EXHAUST AND BEARING SUPPORT ASSEMBLY HEAVILY DAMAGED.
SUGGESTED REPAIR PROCEDURE?
NO REPAIR POSSIBLE. PLEASE CONTACT GM FOR COMPLETE ENGINE REPLACEMENT.
SHIT.

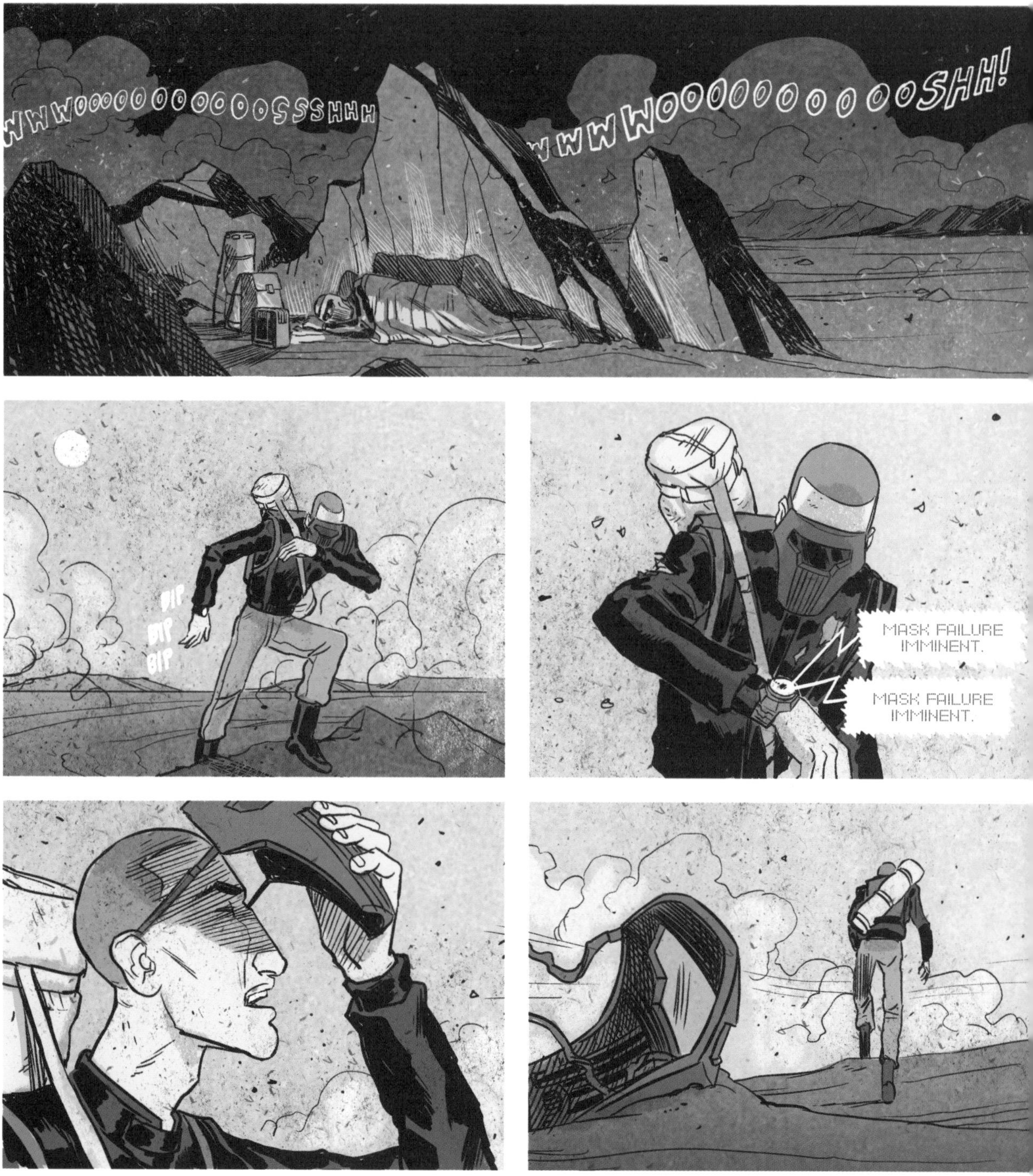
WWWOOOOOOOOOOOOSSSHHH
WWWWOOOOOOOOOOOOOSHH!
BIP
BIP
BIP
MASK FAILURE IMMINENT.
MASK FAILURE IMMINENT.

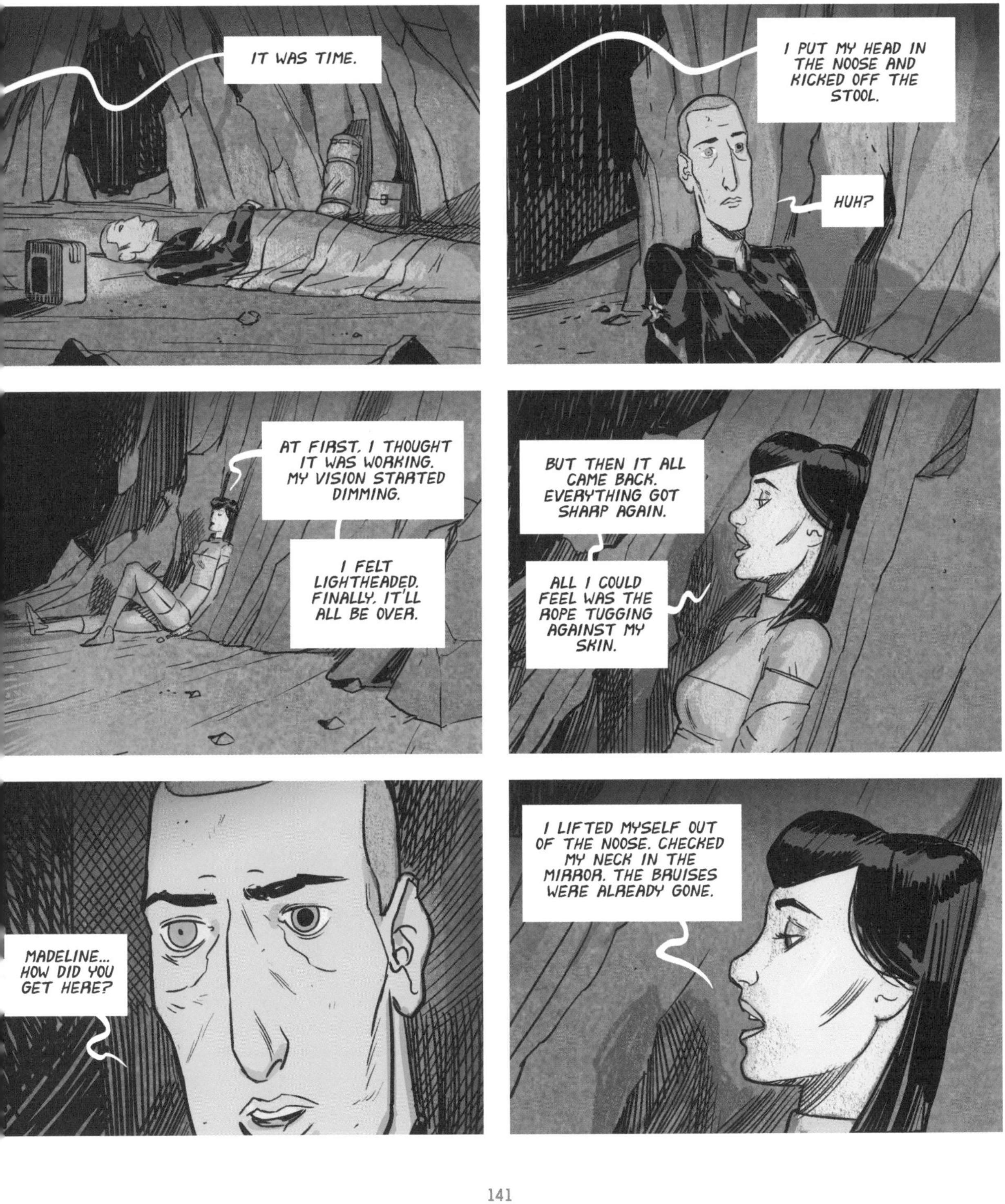
IT WAS TIME.
I PUT MY HEAD IN THE NOOSE AND KICKED OFF THE STOOL.
HUH?
AT FIRST, I THOUGHT IT WAS WORKING. MY VISION STARTED DIMMING.
I FELT LIGHTHEADED. FINALLY, IT'LL ALL BE OVER.
BUT THEN IT ALL CAME BACK. EVERYTHING GOT SHARP AGAIN.
ALL I COULD FEEL WAS THE ROPE TUGGING AGAINST MY SKIN.
MADELINE... HOW DID YOU GET HERE?
I LIFTED MYSELF OUT OF THE NOOSE. CHECKED MY NECK IN THE MIRROR. THE BRUISES WERE ALREADY GONE.

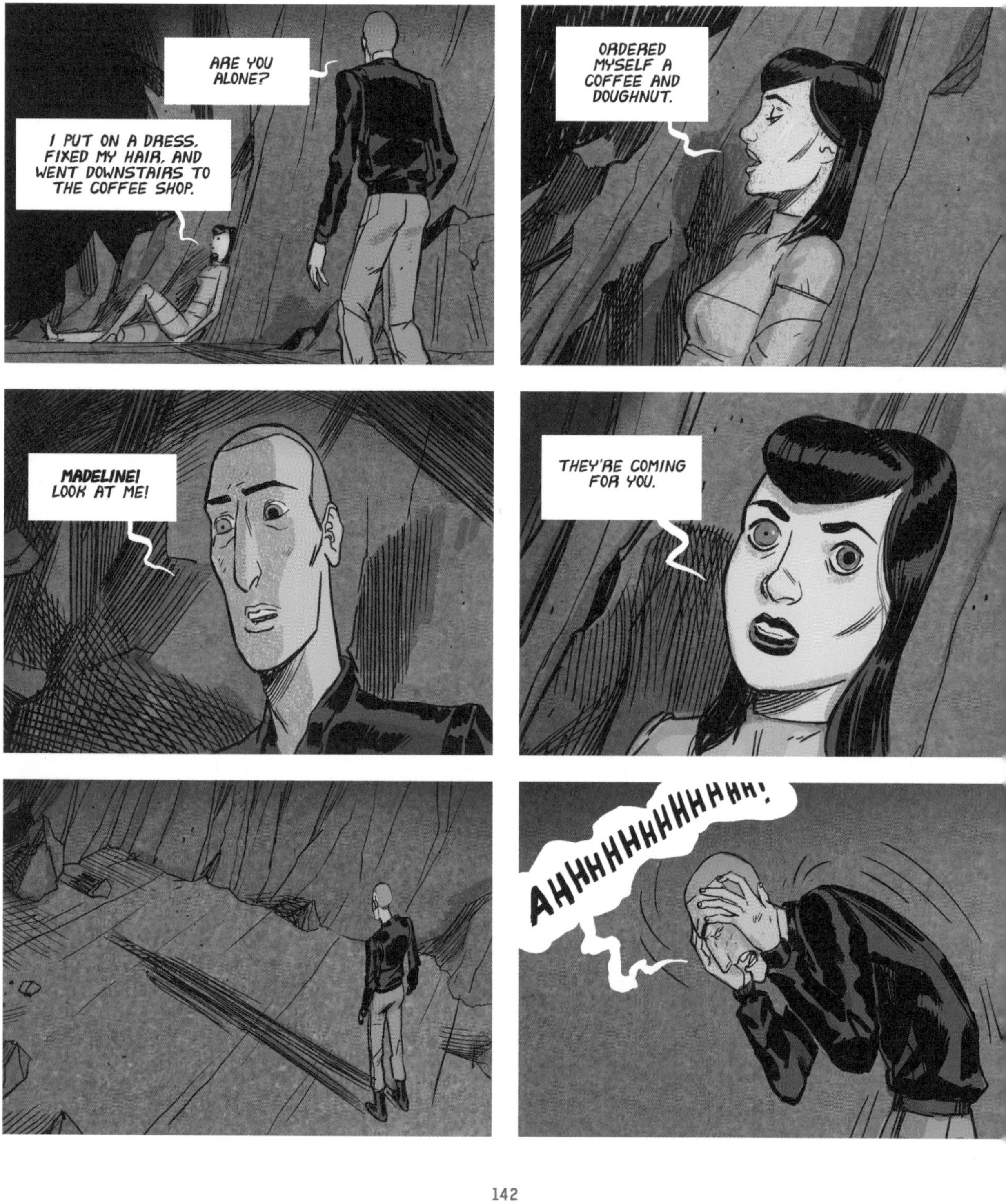
ARE YOU ALONE?
I PUT ON A DRESS, FIXED MY HAIR, AND WENT DOWNSTAIRS TO THE COFFEE SHOP.
ORDERED MYSELF A COFFEE AND DOUGHNUT.
MADELINE! LOOK AT ME!
THEY'RE COMING FOR YOU.
AHHHHHHHHHHHHHHH!

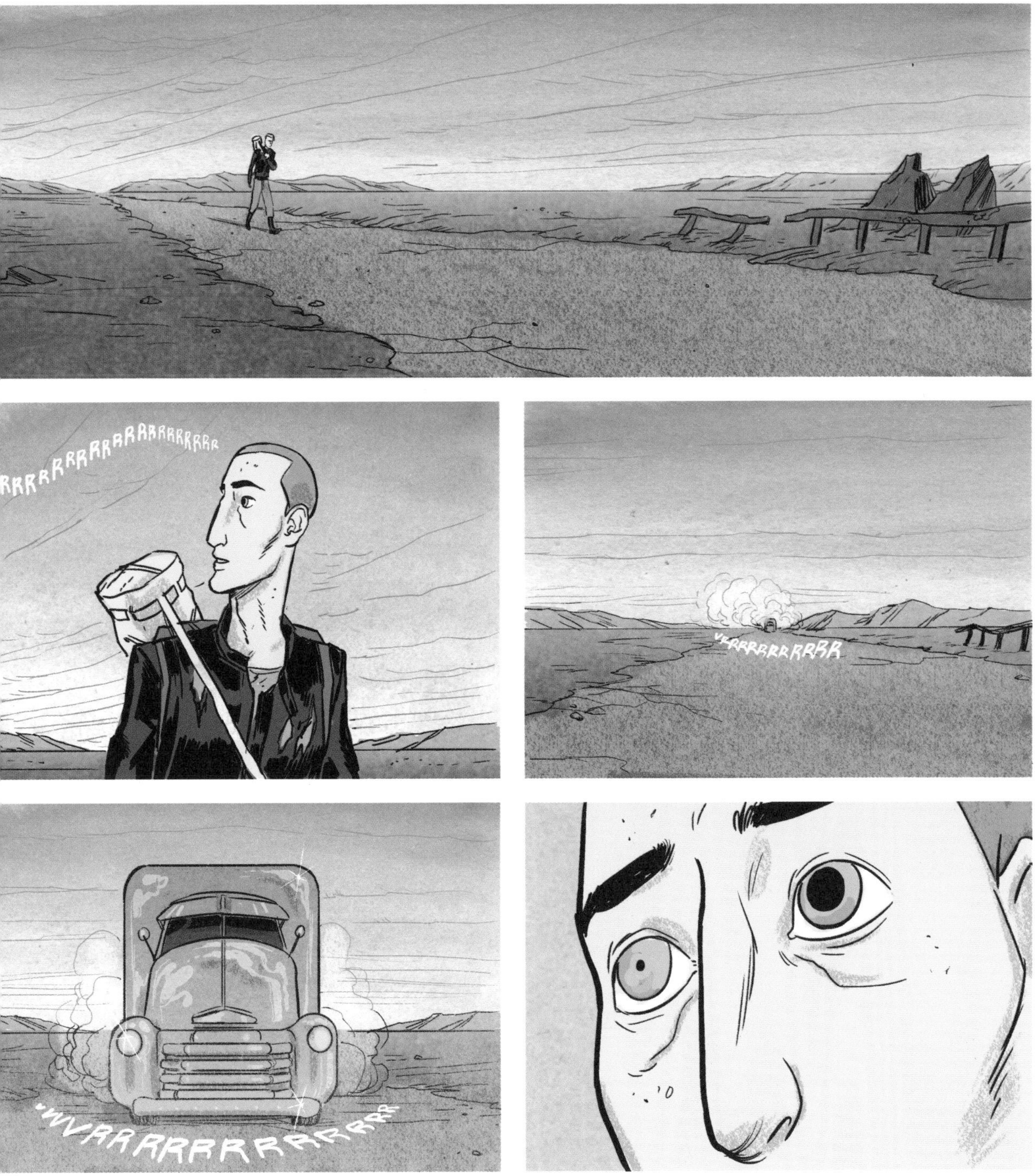
RRRRRRRRRRRRRRRRRRRRR
VRRRRRRRRRRRR
WVRRRRRRRRRRRRRR

GOOD AFTERNOON, PARDNER.

WHERE ARE YOU HEADED?

W... WHEREVER YOU'RE GOING.

CAN'T ARGUE WITH THAT NOW, CAN WE?

HOP ON IN.

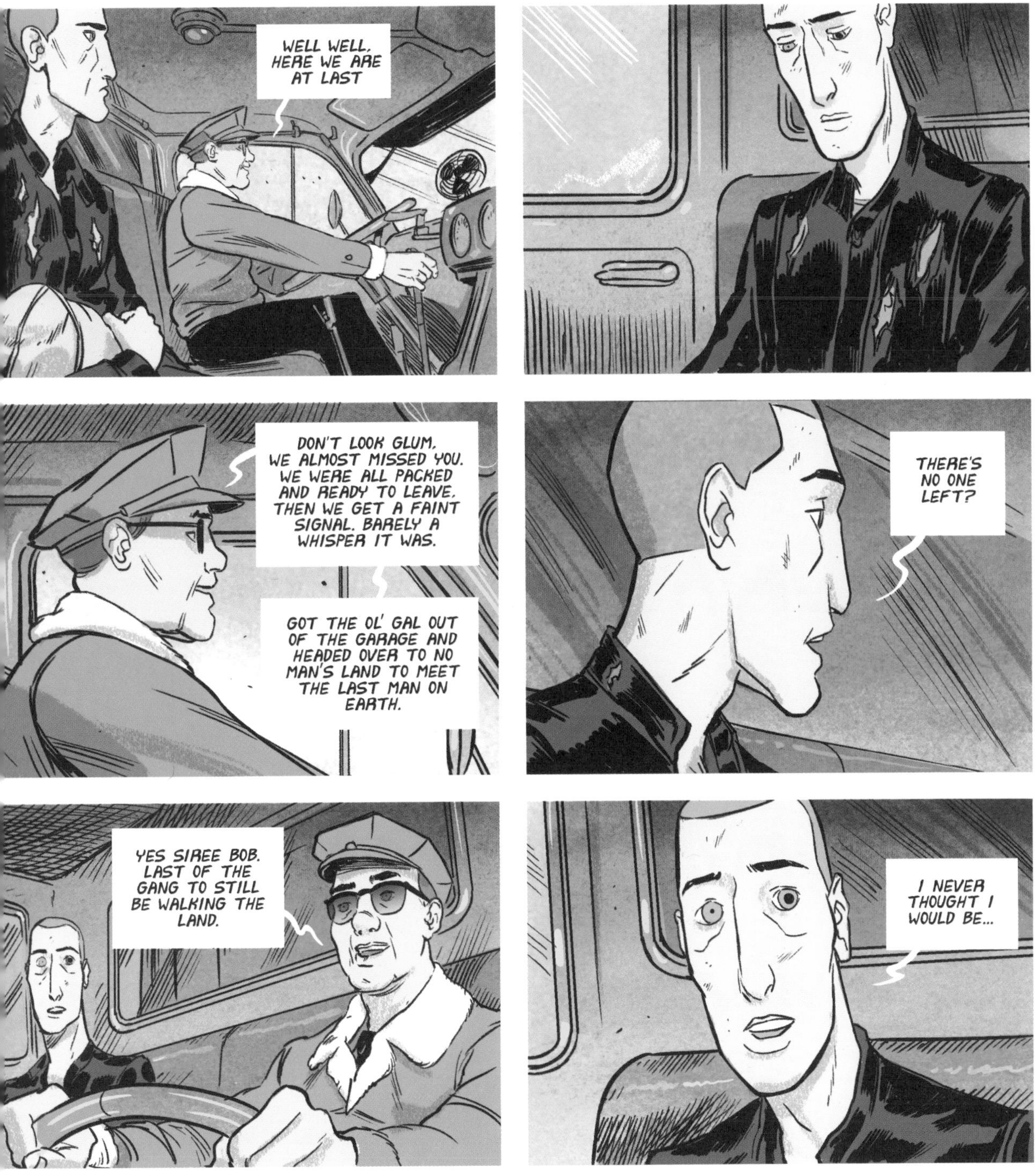
WELL WELL, HERE WE ARE AT LAST
DON'T LOOK GLUM, WE ALMOST MISSED YOU. WE WERE ALL PACKED AND READY TO LEAVE, THEN WE GET A FAINT SIGNAL. BARELY A WHISPER IT WAS.
GOT THE OL' GAL OUT OF THE GARAGE AND HEADED OVER TO NO MAN'S LAND TO MEET THE LAST MAN ON EARTH.
THERE'S NO ONE LEFT?
YES SIREE BOB. LAST OF THE GANG TO STILL BE WALKING THE LAND.
I NEVER THOUGHT I WOULD BE...

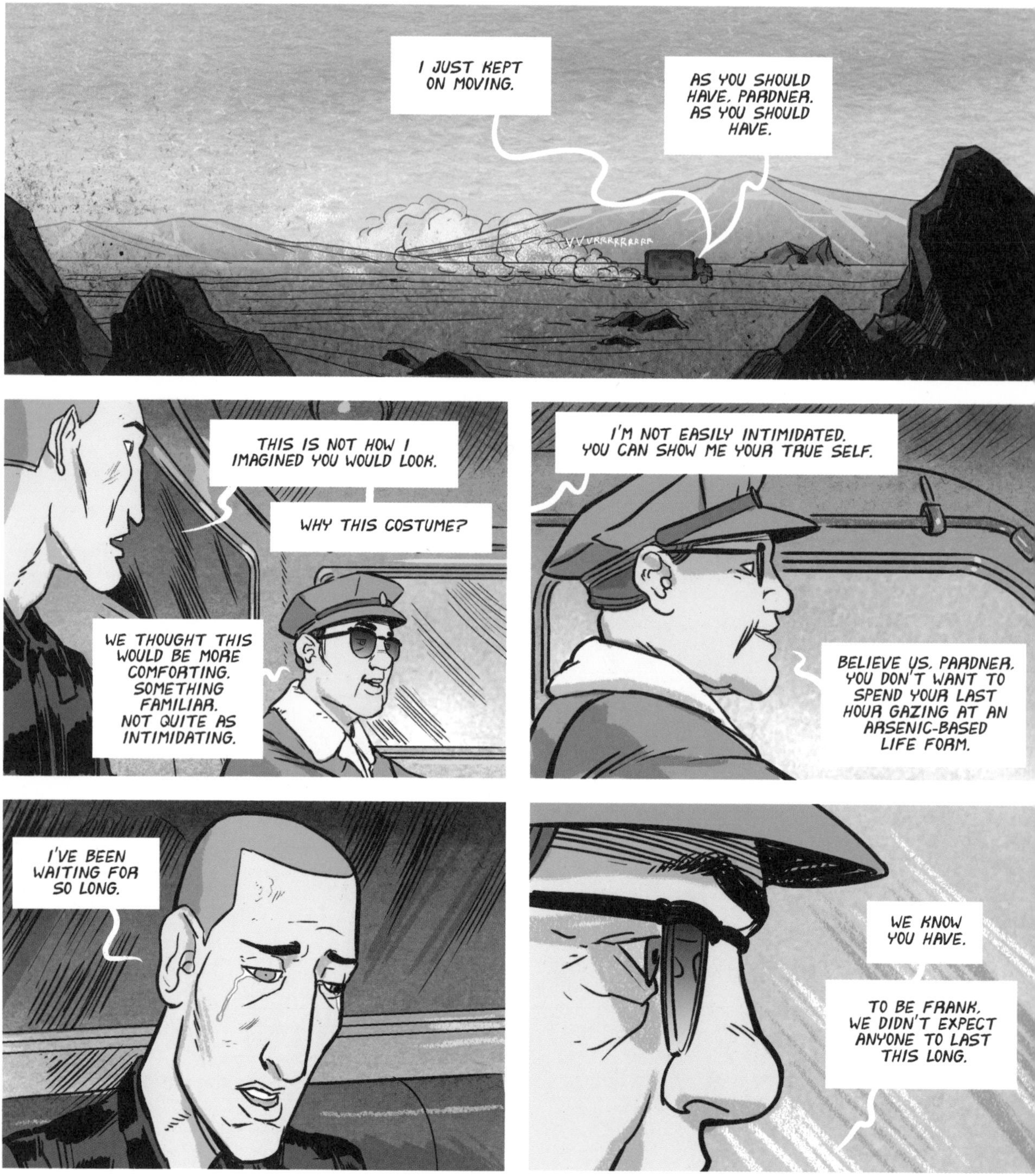
I JUST KEPT ON MOVING.
AS YOU SHOULD HAVE, PARDNER. AS YOU SHOULD HAVE.
VVVRRRRRRRRR
THIS IS NOT HOW I IMAGINED YOU WOULD LOOK.
WHY THIS COSTUME?
WE THOUGHT THIS WOULD BE MORE COMFORTING. SOMETHING FAMILIAR. NOT QUITE AS INTIMIDATING.
I'M NOT EASILY INTIMIDATED. YOU CAN SHOW ME YOUR TRUE SELF.
BELIEVE US, PARDNER, YOU DON'T WANT TO SPEND YOUR LAST HOUR GAZING AT AN ARSENIC-BASED LIFE FORM.
I'VE BEEN WAITING FOR SO LONG.
WE KNOW YOU HAVE.
TO BE FRANK, WE DIDN'T EXPECT ANYONE TO LAST THIS LONG.

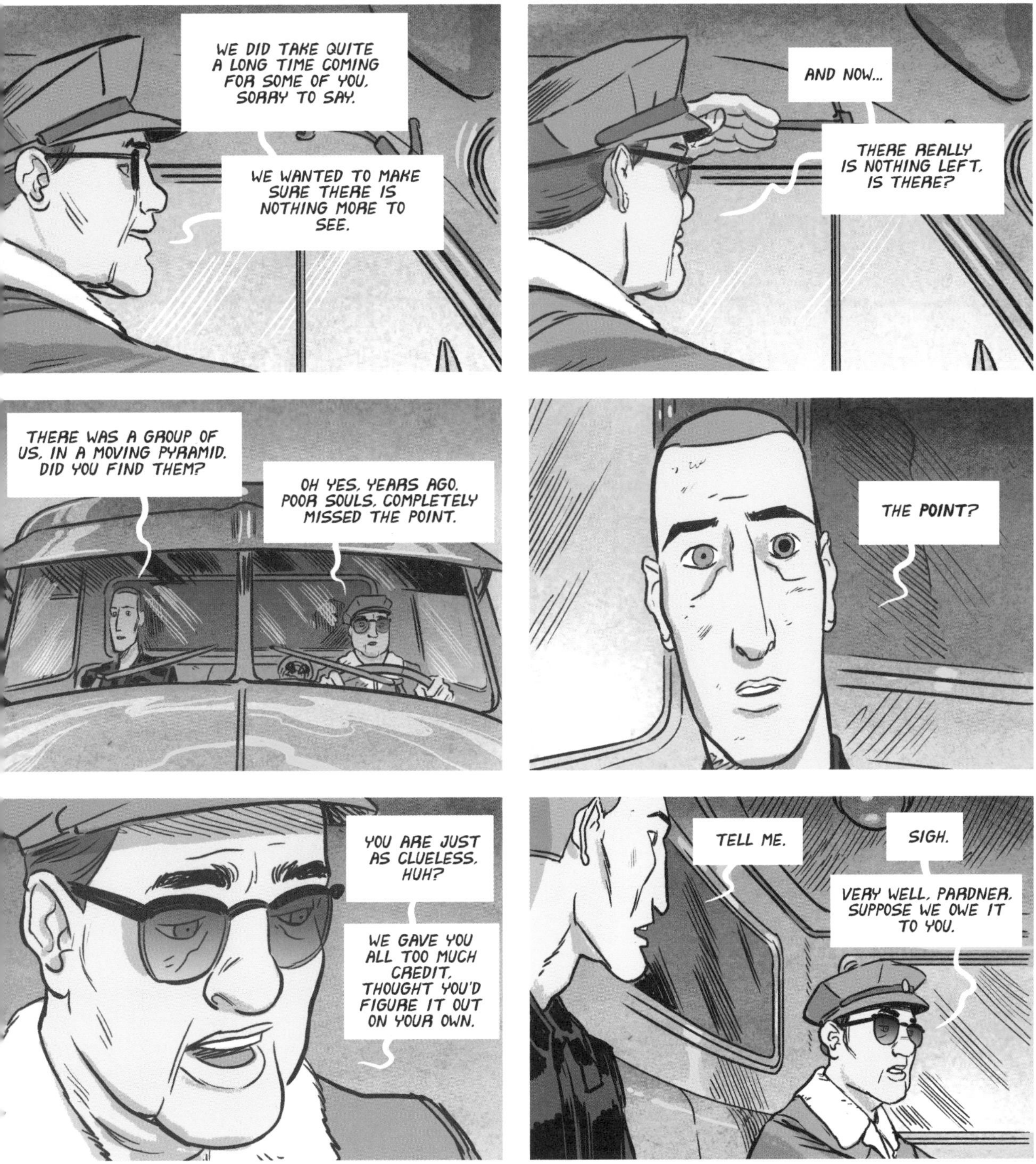
WE DID TAKE QUITE A LONG TIME COMING FOR SOME OF YOU, SORRY TO SAY.
WE WANTED TO MAKE SURE THERE IS NOTHING MORE TO SEE.
AND NOW...
THERE REALLY IS NOTHING LEFT, IS THERE?
THERE WAS A GROUP OF US, IN A MOVING PYRAMID. DID YOU FIND THEM?
OH YES, YEARS AGO. POOR SOULS, COMPLETELY MISSED THE POINT.
THE POINT?
YOU ARE JUST AS CLUELESS, HUH?
WE GAVE YOU ALL TOO MUCH CREDIT. THOUGHT YOU'D FIGURE IT OUT ON YOUR OWN.
TELL ME.
SIGH.
VERY WELL, PARDNER. SUPPOSE WE OWE IT TO YOU.

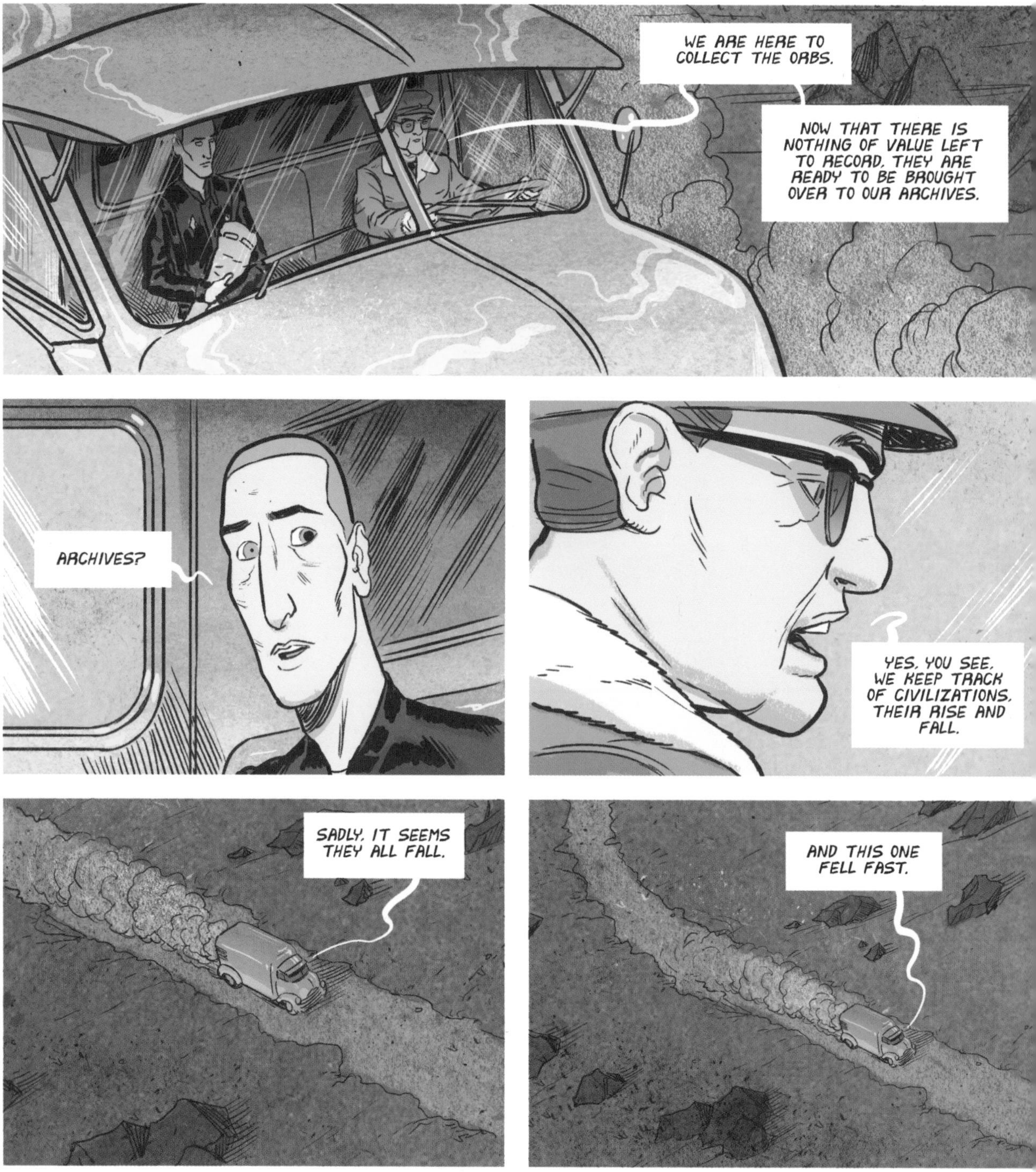
WE ARE HERE TO COLLECT THE ORBS.
NOW THAT THERE IS NOTHING OF VALUE LEFT TO RECORD, THEY ARE READY TO BE BROUGHT OVER TO OUR ARCHIVES.
ARCHIVES?
YES, YOU SEE, WE KEEP TRACK OF CIVILIZATIONS, THEIR RISE AND FALL.
SADLY, IT SEEMS THEY ALL FALL.
AND THIS ONE FELL FAST.

WHO ARE YOU?

WE ARE THE OUTLIERS.

THE ONES WHO HAVE NOT DESTROYED THEMSELVES. WE HAVE OUTLASTED THE REST. AND SO, WE HAVE TAKEN ON THE ROLE OF HISTORIANS.

SO, THIS WHOLE TIME, I WAS JUST A...

...A WALKING CAMERA?

YOU WERE FAR MORE THAN THAT, LUCAS. YOU AND YOUR LIKE WILL BE OUR WINDOW INTO THIS WORLD.

YOUR LIVES WILL HELP PAINT A SPECTACULAR PICTURE OF THIS PLANET AND THE LIFE IT HELD.

THIS IS WHAT IT WAS ALL FOR...

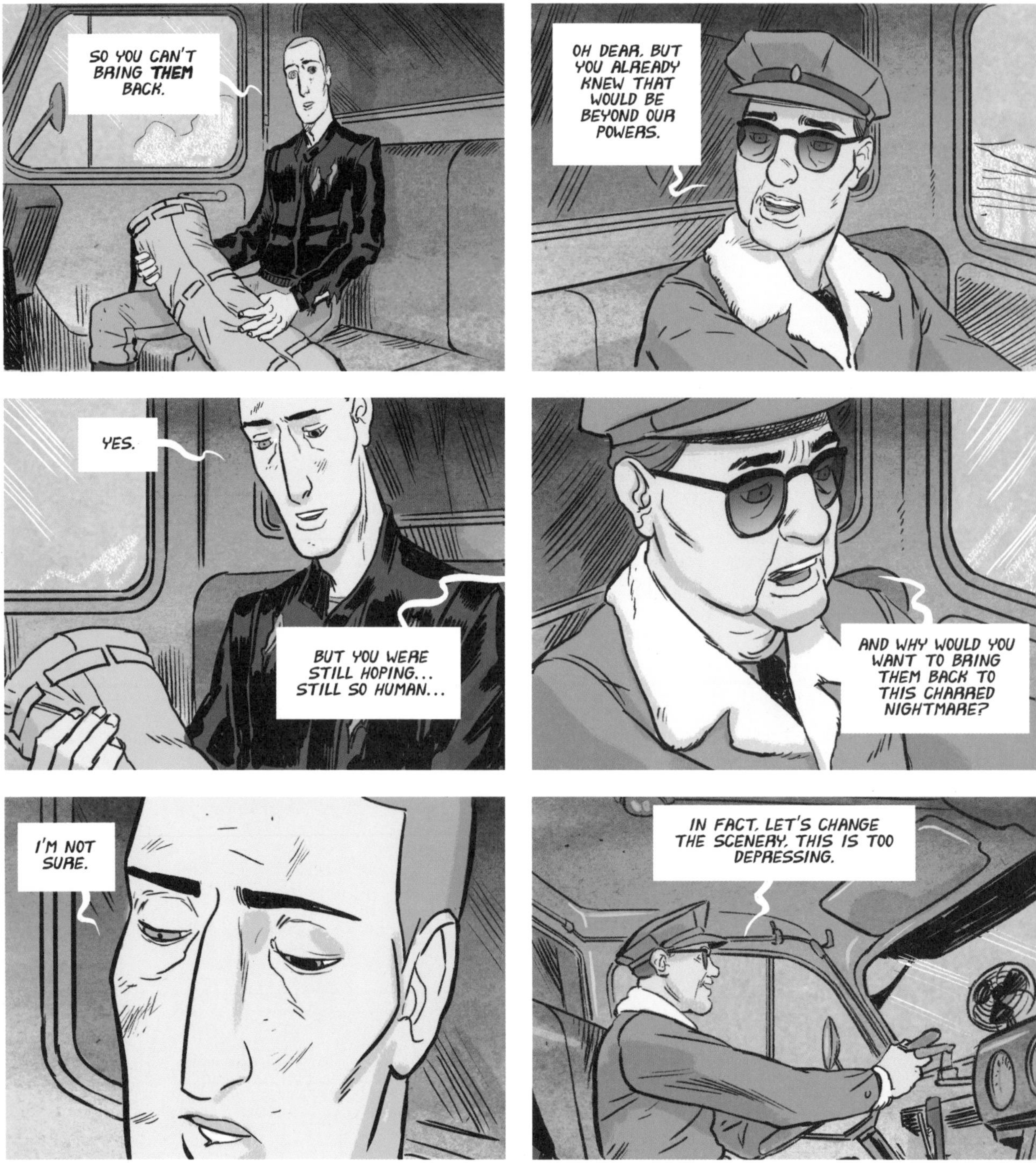
SO YOU CAN'T BRING THEM BACK.
OH DEAR. BUT YOU ALREADY KNEW THAT WOULD BE BEYOND OUR POWERS.
YES.
BUT YOU WERE STILL HOPING... STILL SO HUMAN...
AND WHY WOULD YOU WANT TO BRING THEM BACK TO THIS CHARRED NIGHTMARE?
I'M NOT SURE.
IN FACT, LET'S CHANGE THE SCENERY. THIS IS TOO DEPRESSING.

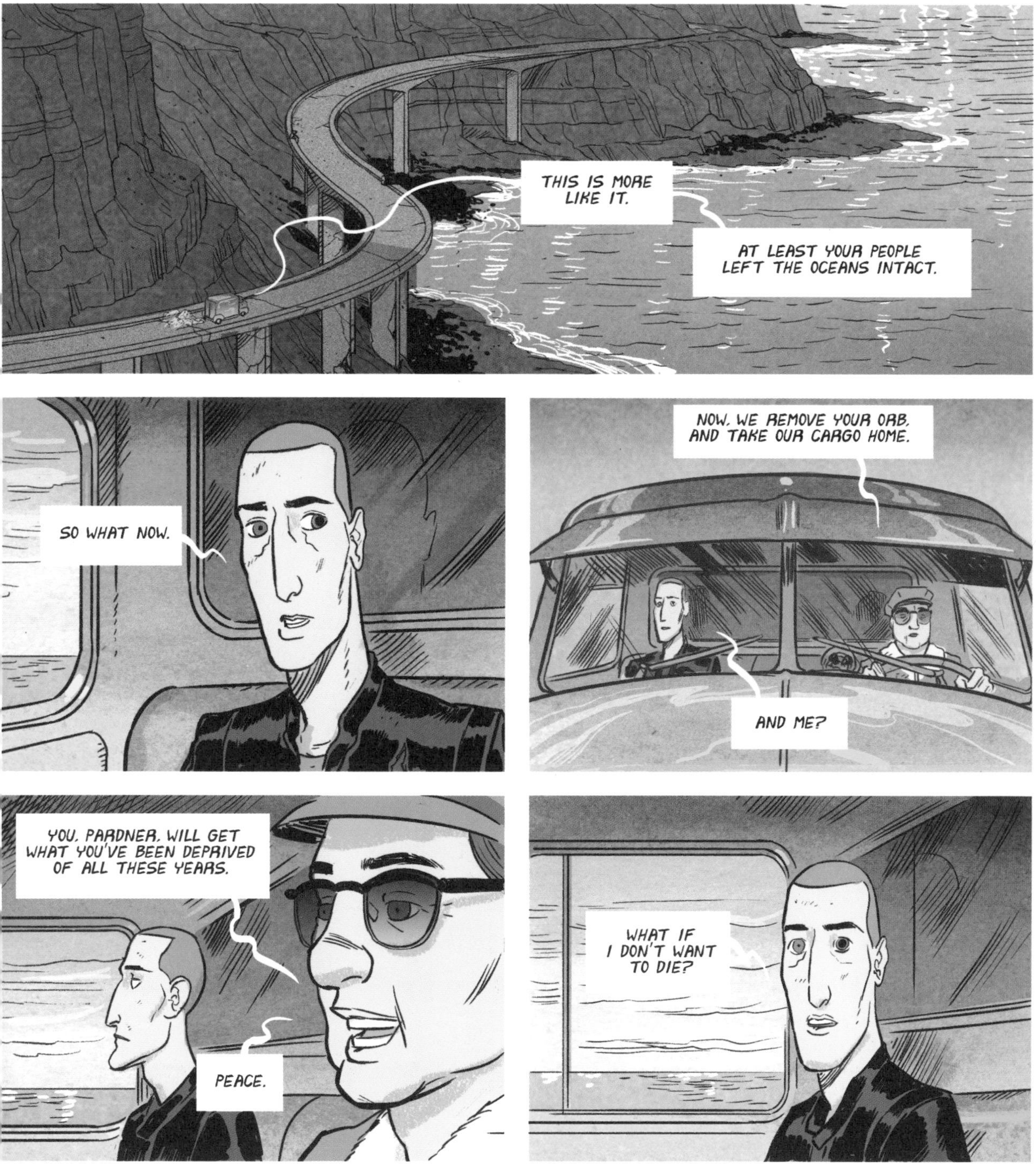
THIS IS MORE LIKE IT.
AT LEAST YOUR PEOPLE LEFT THE OCEANS INTACT.
SO WHAT NOW.
NOW, WE REMOVE YOUR ORB, AND TAKE OUR CARGO HOME.
AND ME?
YOU, PARDNER, WILL GET WHAT YOU'VE BEEN DEPRIVED OF ALL THESE YEARS.
PEACE.
WHAT IF I DON'T WANT TO DIE?

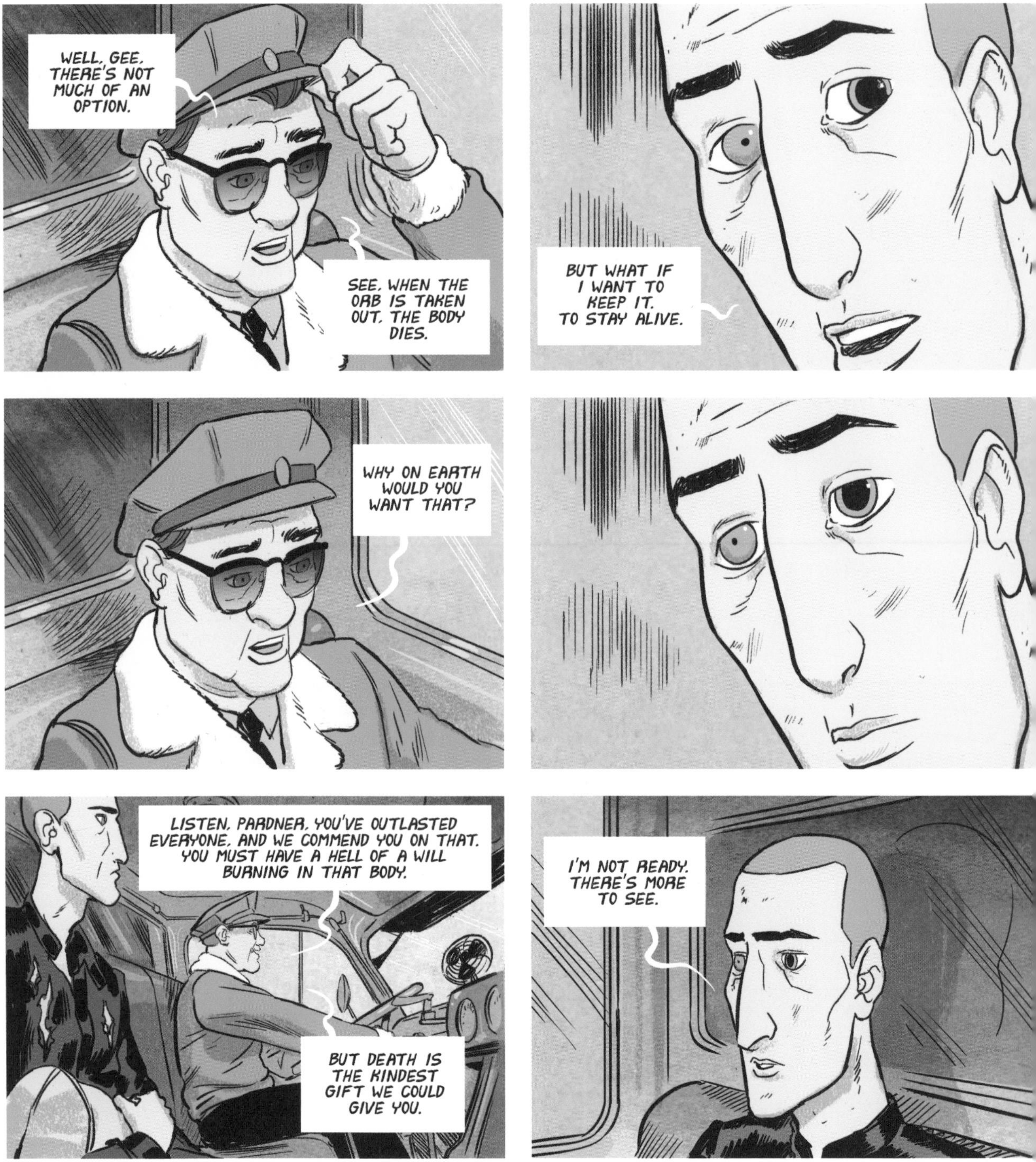
WELL, GEE. THERE'S NOT MUCH OF AN OPTION.
SEE, WHEN THE ORB IS TAKEN OUT, THE BODY DIES.
BUT WHAT IF I WANT TO KEEP IT. TO STAY ALIVE.
WHY ON EARTH WOULD YOU WANT THAT?
LISTEN, PARDNER, YOU'VE OUTLASTED EVERYONE, AND WE COMMEND YOU ON THAT. YOU MUST HAVE A HELL OF A WILL BURNING IN THAT BODY.
BUT DEATH IS THE KINDEST GIFT WE COULD GIVE YOU.
I'M NOT READY. THERE'S MORE TO SEE.

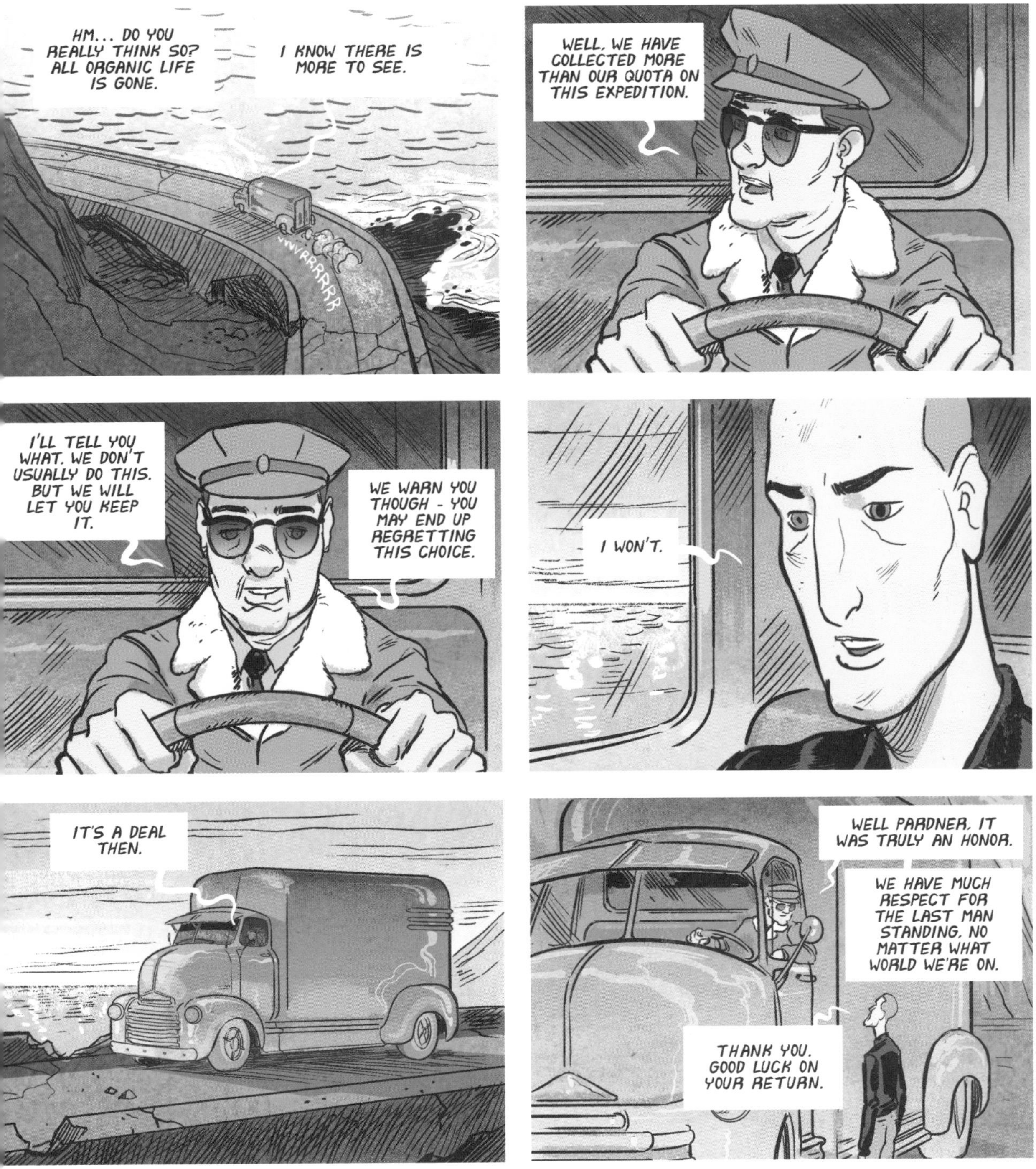
HM... DO YOU REALLY THINK SO? ALL ORGANIC LIFE IS GONE.
I KNOW THERE IS MORE TO SEE.
VVVRRRRRR
WELL, WE HAVE COLLECTED MORE THAN OUR QUOTA ON THIS EXPEDITION.
I'LL TELL YOU WHAT. WE DON'T USUALLY DO THIS. BUT WE WILL LET YOU KEEP IT.
WE WARN YOU THOUGH - YOU MAY END UP REGRETTING THIS CHOICE.
I WON'T.
IT'S A DEAL THEN.
WELL PARDNER, IT WAS TRULY AN HONOR.
WE HAVE MUCH RESPECT FOR THE LAST MAN STANDING, NO MATTER WHAT WORLD WE'RE ON.
THANK YOU. GOOD LUCK ON YOUR RETURN.

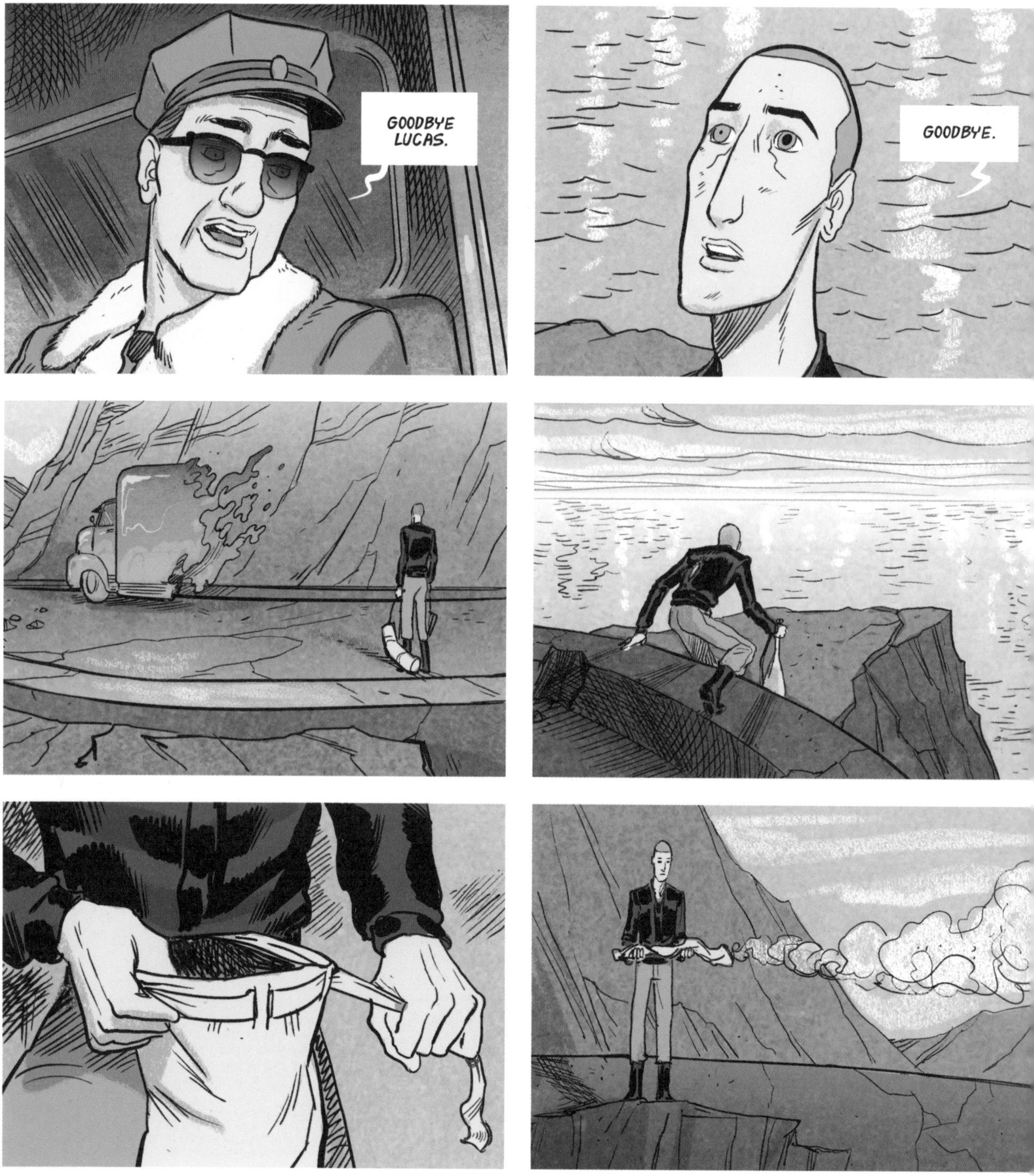
GOODBYE LUCAS.
GOODBYE.

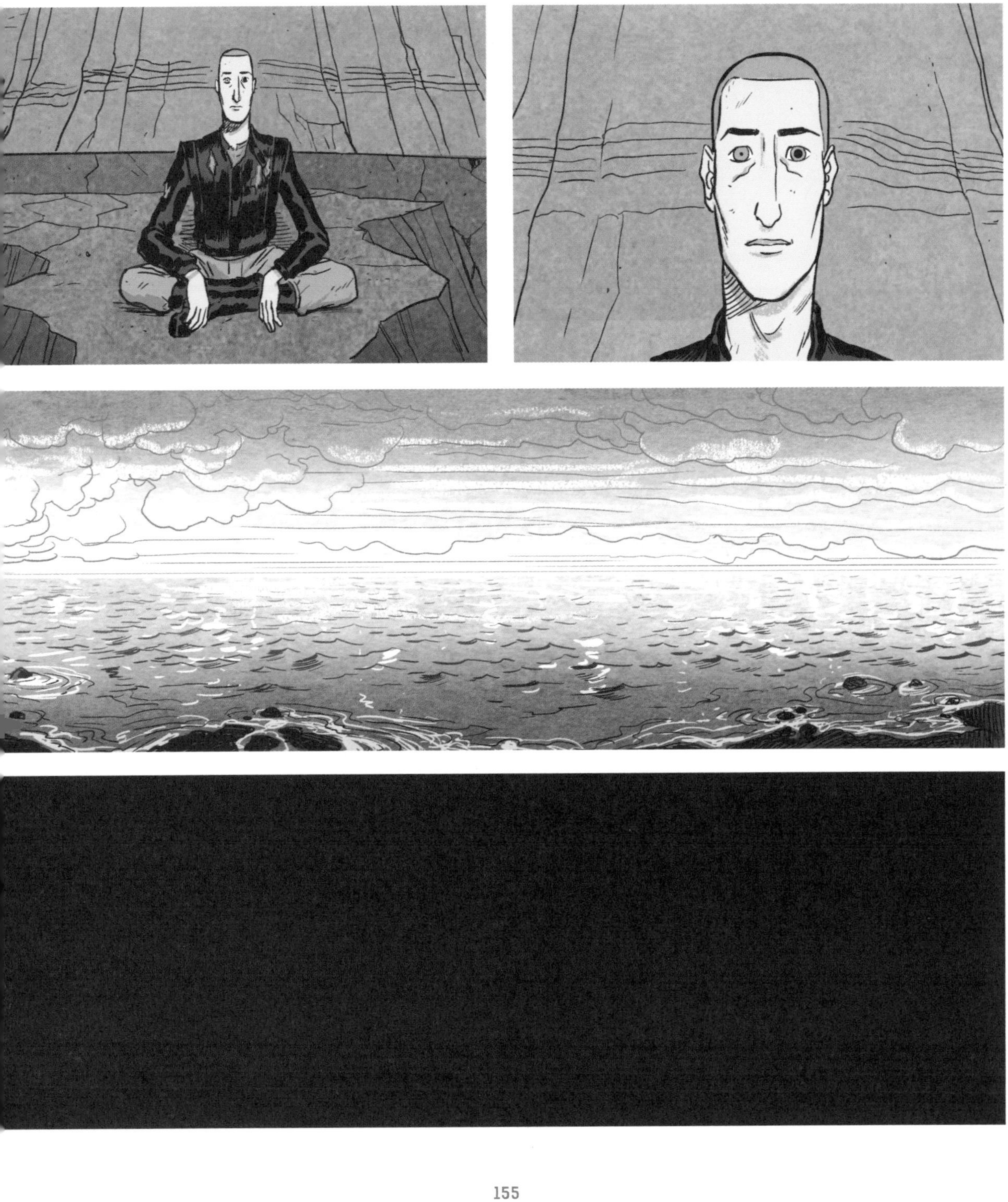

EPILOGUE

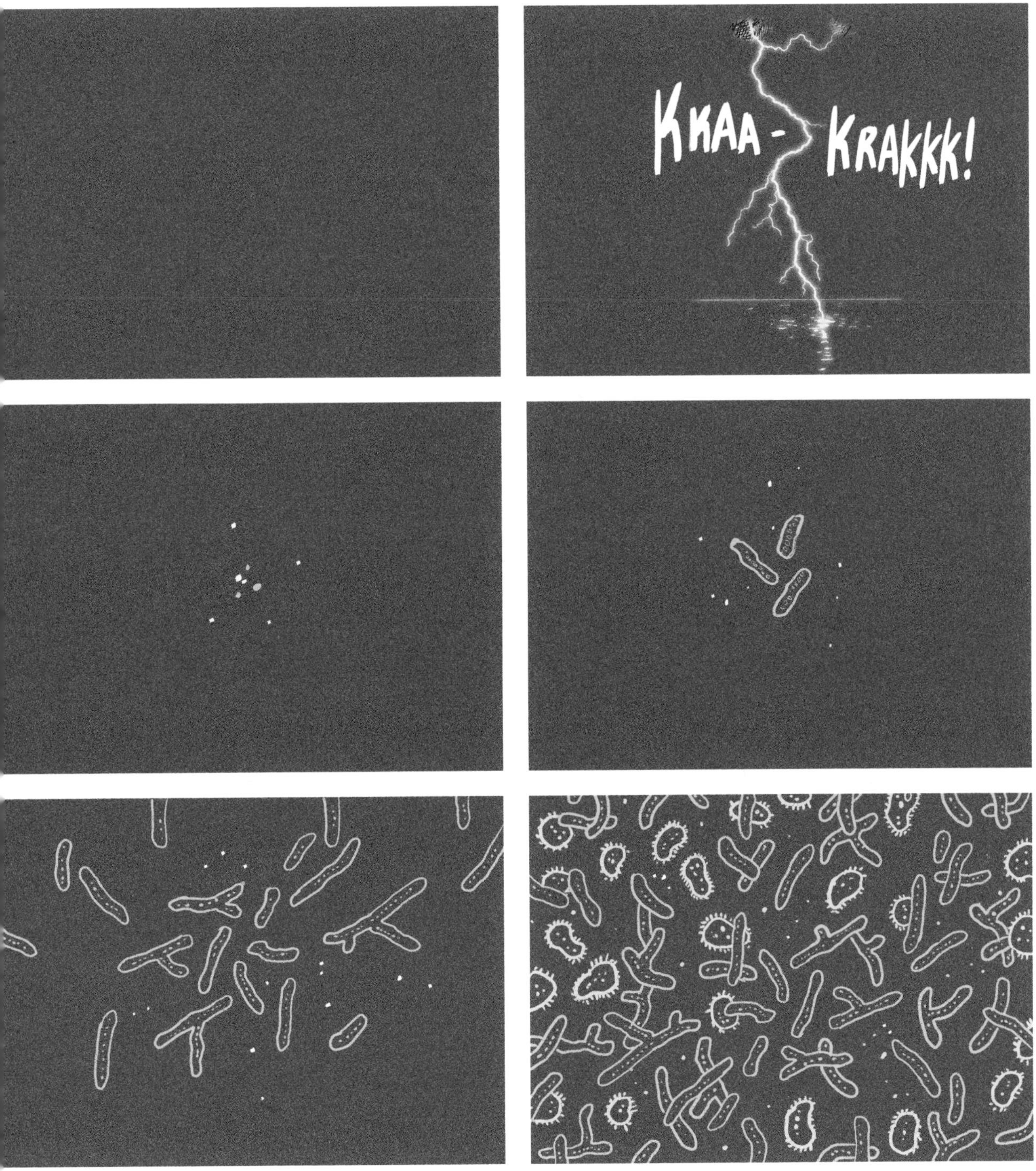
KKAA-KRAKKK!

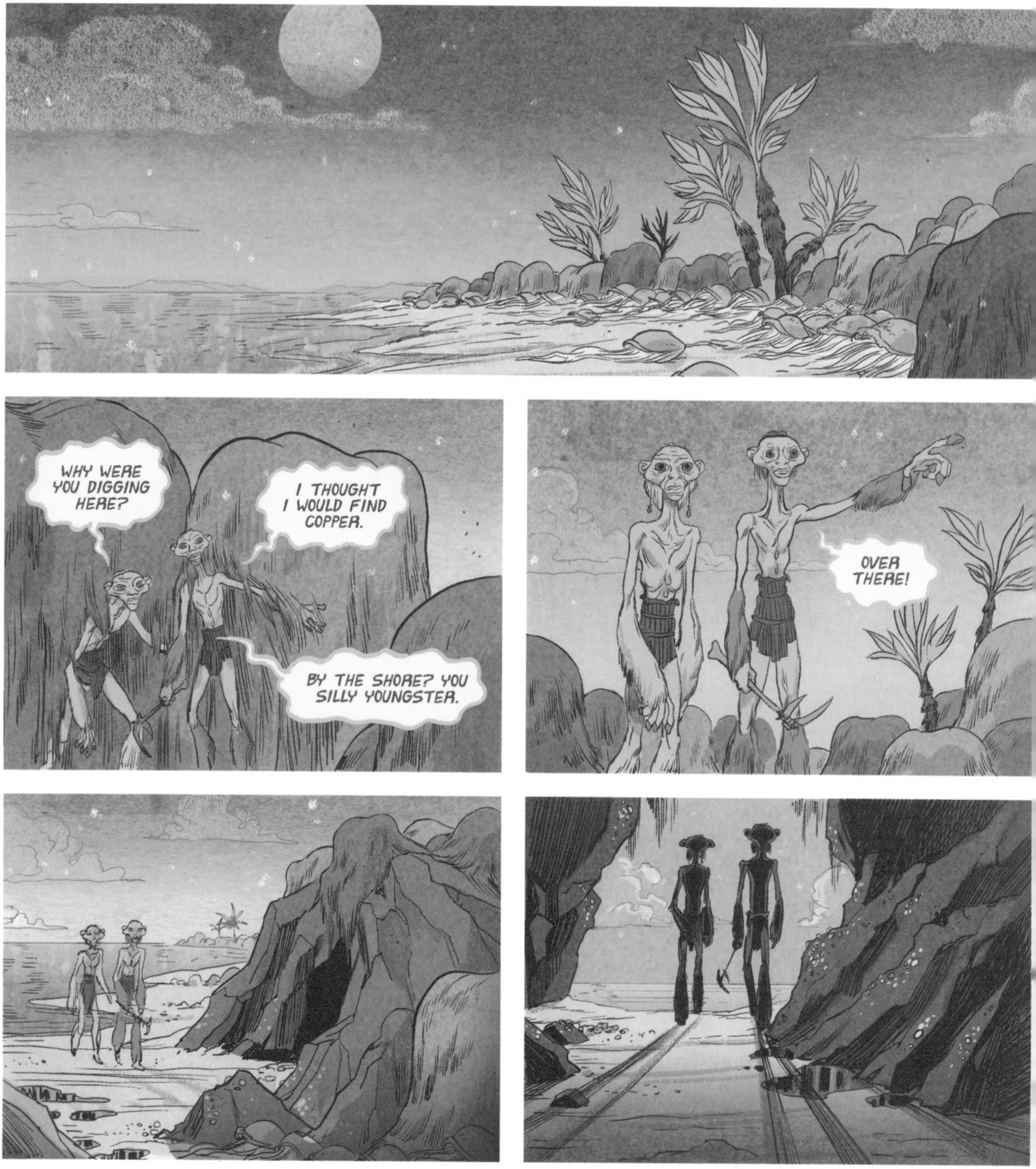
WHY WERE YOU DIGGING HERE?
I THOUGHT I WOULD FIND COPPER.
BY THE SHORE? YOU SILLY YOUNGSTER.
OVER THERE!

I STRUCK THE STONE HERE, AND IT BLED!

THERE IS SOMETHING IN THERE... HELP ME DIG.

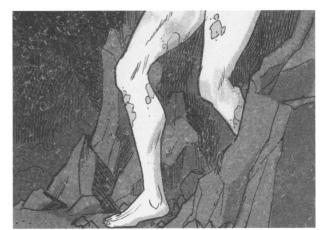

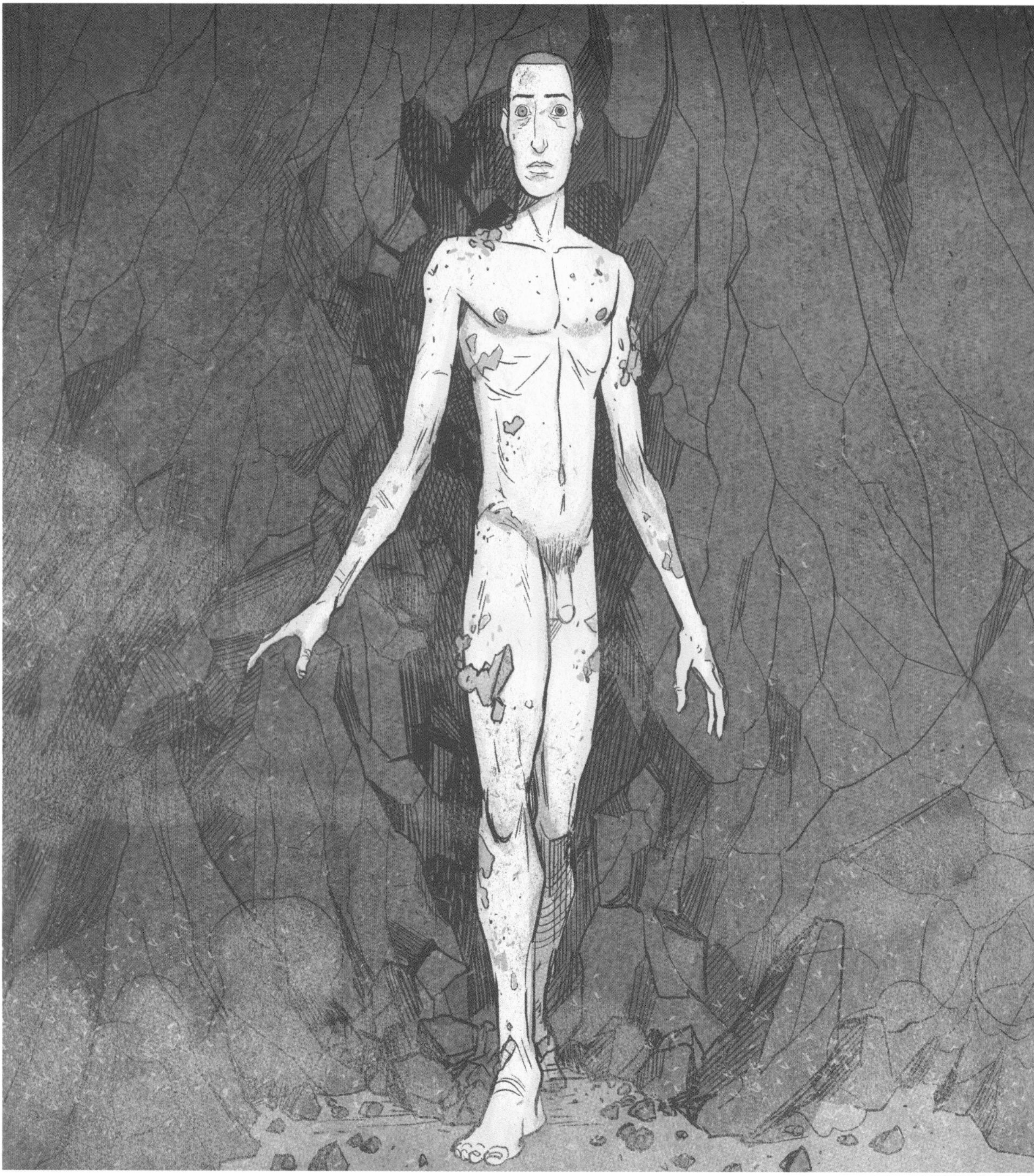